Showing Heart
The True Story of How One Boy Defied the Odds

ISBN: 978-1482746853

Cover design by Natanya Wheeler
Headshot photography by Andrew Russell

Showing Heart: The True Story of How One Boy Defied the Odds /
Leighann Marquiss – 1st ed.

This book is dedicated to my children Natalie, Ainsley, and Ryan, all of whom I think are special. To my husband, Henry, who is my best friend and confidant. And to our friends and family who took care of us in our darkest hour.

I'm twelve weeks into an unplanned pregnancy. I always silently cluck my tongue when I hear couples say, "We don't know how it happened!" Let me tell you, I know *exactly* how it happened. As a consummate planner, the last few weeks have been surreal. The first time I was truly excited about this baby was ten minutes ago as I watched it swimming contently on the murky screen.

My shirt is pulled up to my chest exposing my stomach. It's a position I've found myself in a few times over the last four years, each time getting more brazen and nonchalant. I grew up in a household where modesty was cherished, and even now, as an adult, find it hard to walk around my house half-clothed, for fear the neighbors might see me. My husband is completely the opposite—comfortable answering the door in his boxers. "They're shorts, after all," he reminds me.

The technician spreads cold, blue goo on my stomach with the bottom of her Doppler wand. The screen is fuzzy, like a TV whose antenna is out of alignment. She retraces her movements, clicking pictures and taking measurements. We silently wait for her to finish her task.

My husband, Henry, is sitting at my side switching back and forth from watching the screen and checking email on his BlackBerry. He works as a director of finance for a major government subsidized entity, so his days are filled with meetings, emails, and phone calls. There's never a moment's rest, even if you're meeting your third child for the first time.

"I'll be right back. I need to get the doctor," the sonographer says.

Having been through two other first-trimester sonograms, one where a doctor was called and one where she wasn't, I know the procedure. "Is something wrong?" I ask.

"The doctor will be in to explain everything to you," she says softly. "The only thing I can tell you is it's the heart. It doesn't look good."

My eyes follow her as she leaves the room. "Maybe it's Chiari," I say, referring to a condition that runs in Henry's family. "It affects the heart sometimes."

Ever astute, he says quietly, "Maybe. It sounds worse than that, though."

My throat tightens as blood rushes through my veins. Tears manage to find their way down my face and into the crevices of my ears. Henry moves to my side and gently strokes my hair. His large hands wipe tears gently from my cheeks. Those few small gestures are enough to grant me my sanity.

He moves into the hall. He's calling work, taking the rest of the day off. Snippets of his conversation waft through the door. "There's something wrong with the baby . . . I'm going to stay with Leighann . . . something with the heart. We don't know yet . . . we're waiting for the doctor." My husband doesn't take time off work. Ever.

The sonographer and Henry rejoin me. "There aren't any doctors in the office today. The doctor on call is across the street at the hospital OR. She's going to talk to you over the phone. I'm so sorry," she says.

A nurse leads us to the doctor's empty office. We put the phone on speaker and listen as she says, "I'm really sorry to have to tell you this over the phone. We're concerned there is something wrong with the fetus' heart. In situations like this, we send you to a specialist to confirm our sonographer's suspicions. She sees a lot, but we want you to see someone who looks at abnormalities day in and day out, to make sure she's right."

"What are we talking about here?" Henry asks. "Will this baby have a normal life?"

There is a pause on the other end of the line. "We don't expect the fetus to make it to twenty weeks. With this condition most fetuses die in the first trimester. If it does live, we'll do a c-section to avoid putting any stress on the heart."

I suddenly can't understand a single word being said. I look at Henry and see his mouth moving . . . the doctor's voice . . . it's there, too, but it's all gibberish. I try to gain some sense of understanding, but it's as if I'm standing at the mouth of a cave, straining to hear voices deep in its caverns. There are echoes and intonations, yet nothing comprehendible. Twenty weeks . . . twenty weeks. It reverberates through my brain like a mantra. Twenty weeks minus twelve. I have eight more weeks with this baby.

Eight. More. Weeks. Numb and confused, I close my eyes, shutting out the world around me. I feel Henry's hand reach out for mine. He curls his fingers around my tightly closed fists and strokes them with his thumb. All I can do is sit and weep puddles on the pretty mahogany desk.

"WE SHOULD CALL our mothers," Henry says. We're standing outside the medical building in the bright sun. I'm hiding behind my sunglasses. I don't remember leaving the doctor's office or leaving the building. Henry's staring at me, waiting for a response.

"I can't talk to anyone right now." My voice is barely a whisper.

"I'll call them," he says.

Still dazed, I look at him, trying to understand his urgency to call our families. *He needs to process . . . to analyze, to bring it into the open and out of his brain.* "You can call them, if you want. Please tell them not to call me, though. I can't handle it right now." Between us, we have eleven siblings—I have six and he has five. I need a few days of mental space to sort things out. The opposite of Henry, I process internally.

"I'll handle it all. I'll tell our moms. I'll get the girls from the sitter. You go home. I'll meet you there in a few minutes," he says. He's amazingly calm. I can't get my tears to stop.

LATER THAT NIGHT, I lie in my bed waiting for Henry. He's out with our good friend Jason to process the news of our dying child. Jason and his wife, Bridget, are some of our closest friends. They have five kids of their own. She's pregnant with their sixth. We're due two weeks apart.

We spend a lot of time together as families, our kids mixing as if they're siblings. Henry connected with Jason at a men's event at our church then introduced us wives. I remember Bridget saying, "Where have you been? How could I have not met you before?" We'd all been going to the same church for about seven years. My question was, "Is there anything you can't do?" Bridget is the most creative, patient mother I've ever met.

It doesn't surprise me that Henry seeks Jason out. I lie there, wishing we were processing together. When I told him I didn't want to talk to anyone, I didn't mean *him*. It's after midnight when he finally slips into bed beside me. "How do you feel about the baby?" I ask.

"Disappointed." He's asleep the moment his head hits the pillow.

SITTING IN THE specialist's office the next day at noon, I'm in shock. I knew I was supposed to get a second opinion, but being in a doctor's office not a full 24 hours later is mind-numbing. Luckily, my neighbor Amber was free to watch Natalie and Ainsley. At four and two, they have no idea there is a storm cloud hanging over our house. They're happy to play with friends two days in a row.

"Mrs. Marquiss?"

I follow the sonographer back to a dim-lit room and get situated on the examination table. While we're exchanging names and pleasantries, I'm wishing Henry is getting out of his meeting and able to make it before our consultation with the doctor. My brain isn't exactly firing on all cylinders. Prior to yesterday, I felt independent and in control. Today, I'm a totally different person. Relief comes instantly when he walks through the door after only a few pictures.

The doctor enters and starts working with the sonographer to see what they can find. They chatter among themselves about terms and body parts we don't understand. We're left to wait for the verdict.

"This is the fetus's heart," the doctor finally says. "See here how the chest comes in a nice curve and then this bump?"

I look at the fuzzy screen and clearly see the heart interrupting the curve of the baby's torso, like a misplaced cloud sticking through the center of a rainbow. It's unlike any of the pictures I saw of Natalie or Ainsley.

"Yes, I see it," I answer. Henry nods.

"This is called ectopia cordis. It's when the heart is not in the place it's supposed to be. In this case, it's protruding outside the chest cavity."

"What do you mean?" Henry asks.

"It's sitting outside the body," the doctor explains. "This bump right here," he points with his pen, "is above the baby's chest bone. The rest of it," again pointing with his pen and following the arch of the heart back under the chest, "is inside. It's an extremely rare condition. The heart itself is also malformed. We don't see any pulmonary arteries or all the chambers. The fetus is so small right now, though, that it's hard to get accurate pictures of everything. What we do know is this heart isn't compatible with life. It won't function properly. In fact, if you look right here," his pen moves up and down the side of the baby's body, "you can see fluid collecting along the flanks, a sign of congestive heart failure. We see this in adults near the end. The more the fetus grows, the harder the heart will have to work, and already it isn't keeping up. There really isn't anything we can do. Why don't you guys come into the other room? We'll talk about where to go from here."

I wipe blue goo from my belly for the second day in a row. We follow the doctor to a conference room and sit down at a table.

"There are three options," he says. "One: terminate the pregnancy. Two: test for chromosomal issues. Or three: go home and wait for the pregnancy to naturally terminate."

Henry and I look at one another, speaking volumes in one glance. "We'll wait for a miscarriage," I say. After twelve years of marriage, there's no need for discussion.

"Why don't I give you some time to discuss it," the doctor says. "Take a minute to figure out what's best for you guys."

"We don't need time," Henry says. It falls on deaf ears. The doctor is already excusing himself from the room. "I'll be back in a few minutes," he calls out over his shoulder.

I already know what my husband is going to say. I ask anyway. "What do you think?"

"I think you're right. We should wait. We're not going to terminate. If the baby is going to die anyway, there's no reason for testing. The only other option is waiting for the miscarriage."

Choosing the last option is a second-nature decision for me. I researched the topic of abortion during high school and fall very much in the "an embryo is a unique life" category. I won't go into the science of why I believe this. Pro-choice vs. pro-life isn't my agenda. It's just that this decision was one I made long ago never imagining I'd actually face making it. Because it's such a difficult decision for many women, it's understandable that the doctor gives us space to sort things out.

He finally pokes his head in the door to check on us. "Did you guys decide what you want to do?"

"We're going to let nature take its course," Henry says.

"Look," the doctor says as he takes his seat. "I want you to understand what's going on here. This fetus isn't going to live. There's no hope. I don't want you continuing this pregnancy, thinking we can save the fetus. We can't. There's nothing we can do. The heart is malformed, and malfunctioning as it is. It's not going to last much longer. Termination can be done later in the pregnancy, but it gets more . . . complicated. And difficult for the mother."

"Is it dangerous for Leighann to stay pregnant?" Henry asks. I bristle at the thought of having to protect my child from the doctor and my husband.

The doctor pauses. "There's always danger of high blood pressure. If something like that should happen, we'd want to terminate the pregnancy right away."

Relieved, I roll my eyes, something my parents tried unsuccessfully to break me of as a teenager. He's obviously grasping at straws. There are more complications from terminating than staying pregnant. I've never had any issues before, especially high blood pressure. "Anything else?" I ask.

"Nothing more than a normal pregnancy," the doctor concedes. "I want to make sure you're hearing me clearly. This fetus won't live. If you continue the pregnancy and go past the twenty-four–week mark, don't have the doctors stop your labor. Let your body get rid of the baby. Don't risk your life by having an emergency c-section to try saving the fetus. There's nothing that can be done."

It's as if he can't hear us, can't understand that we believe him. He's trying to convince us our baby won't live. We already believe him. There's no question in our minds. Nothing can be done. There's no hope. Hope isn't the point. It never was.

"We understand," I say. "I won't have any life-saving measures taken. We hear you loud and clear. We're going home to wait for me to miscarry, which we expect to happen in the next few weeks."

On the way out, I catch the sonographer in the hallway. "Do you have any pictures of the baby I can take with me?" I ask.

She looks surprised. "I didn't print any out. I'm sorry."

Disappointment floods over me. I've always been able to get sonogram pictures of my babies. I don't know that I'll be back.

PREGNANCY MAKES YOUR body do funny things. It pulls on muscles you think are strong, and pinches nerves you didn't know existed. The week after diagnosis, I'm hypersensitive to every stretch, pull, and cramp, wondering if today is the day I'll have a miscarriage. I can't feel the baby move yet, so there is no assurance that it's alive, other than my raging morning sickness, which is really more like all-day sickness. I spend a lot of time in the bathroom, hugging the toilet, and the rest of my time lying down as much as possible to ward off nausea.

I once asked my paternal grandmother what she did while my grandfather was serving in WWII. She said, "I was morning sick."

"Yes, I know," I replied. "But what else did you do?"

"Nothing. I was sick all the time," she said.

I didn't get it then. *Okay, so you were sick. But you just did nothing?* I thought. I *completely* get it now!

The phone rings off the hook, even though Henry swears he told everyone to give us time. I'm still not ready to talk. I need more time to process the nightmare that has become our life. I let the answering machine handle the calls.

Knowing I can't ignore them forever, I start talking to family on the third day. I find myself repeating the same phrases. "This baby won't have to know pain. There are worse things in the world. Think of all the moms in Haiti who can't feed their children tonight and are watching them die a slow death by starvation." Thoughts like these help me distance myself from the reality that *my* baby is dying and there's nothing I can do.

Henry takes on the role of informer, shielding me from having to tell most people what is going on. He answers the phone, unless I step in to do it myself. I realize I'm holding the girls tighter, cuddling with them at night and rocking my two-year-old in the middle of the day, since I'm not sure when I'll be able to rock another little body. I cry into her back, or hair, so she doesn't see. I tell everyone and myself I'll be fine. I verbalize that while I believe God can heal, I don't want to assume that's what He'll do in our case. The reality is people get sick. People die. Miracles are hard to come by.

I learned this lesson while a junior in high school. My sister, Amy, who's younger than me by twenty-one months, had a friend who was battling bone cancer. Muriel must have spent several years in the hospital, in and out with different chemo treatments. She was in remission a couple times. I remember her coming to our house wearing a wig. It looked great, but you could still tell it was a wig. Then we found out she had another tumor in her hip. The doctors suggested amputation at the waist. She'd be strapped to a chair to sit up for the rest of her life since they'd have to amputate so high. She refused the surgery. She was fourteen. She'd seen too many of her friends (they were her friends now that she'd been in the hospital so long) get body parts amputated, trying to cheat death, only to have another and then another part removed. She didn't want that life.

I prayed for her healing every night. I begged God, literally crying for her life. She died.

I don't know that I got mad at God for letting her die. However, I did question why He let her die. I never got an answer. Oswald Chambers, an early twentieth-century Christian teacher and writer, once said, "God doesn't reveal to us what He is doing, but who He is." God is good. That doesn't mean He doesn't allow bad. I've experienced both. There's nothing easy about realizing God isn't Santa Claus.

I once again find myself on my face, before the Almighty. This time, my tears are not watering a garden of hope, but one of grief. My heartfelt pleas are not for healing. They are for a quick end. The days are so tedious and heavy; I'm not sure how many of them I can live through. They stack up like bricks on my back and I'm afraid that one day, they will literally crush me. I pray for the load to be lifted, to be taken away.

It's incredibly selfish, I know. I want it all to be over for my sake, for the sake of getting on with things. The longer I'm held up by this child who won't live, the longer it'll be before I can begin again.

It's here where the Creator of the universe tells me He won't take my load. He refuses to do things my way. He doesn't tell me in an audible Burning Bush sort of way, but it's just as effective. And, just like Moses, I'm not sure I'm the right one for the job.

I'm doing a Bible study on The Fruit of the Spirit (love, joy, peace, patience). It turns out the focus of this week is faith. In the text, the author asks, "What are you *not* trusting God will do because you are afraid of disappointment?"

Seriously? Hoping for healing and not getting it is the biggest disappointment I can think of. *Why don't you believe I will heal your baby?* The thought flitters across my mind, out-of-place, like a butterfly through a burned-out forest. It's so the opposite of everything I've believed the last few days, that I sob uncontrollably. My brain pulsates with the thought, like it has sprouted its own heart, and has a sinus rhythm all its own. Is it possible that God will heal this child?

I decide I'll no longer walk around on pins and needles waiting for this baby to die, no longer pray for a quick ending to the pregnancy. I'll trust that healing will take place. What that healing looks like, I don't know. But what I do believe is that we'll meet this baby; we'll hold it in our arms. I'll celebrate my baby's life until it's taken from me. Instead of living with the fear of death, I'll live every day nurturing this life inside me.

There's a slight breeze rustling the leaves, and children's voices fill the air. Natalie and Ainsley are off playing somewhere with their cousins. Henry's grandfather passed away several years ago. His grandmother, the matriarch of this tribe, resides at her post inside making sure the desserts are handled with care and everyone gets the nourishment they need. She's been feeding mouths and souls for over eighty years. She's not about to stop now.

I sit in the living room, relaxing in the comfortable environment of family with Henry's mom, Willa, and her sisters. We haven't told anyone here about the baby—that it's inside me or that it's dying, although word travels faster than a cat with its tail on fire in this family. I was so early in my pregnancy at diagnosis that we hadn't told very many people. Now, it's hard to know what to say. There's a lull in the conversation. Henry's Aunt Lillie turns to me with a sly smile, "Is it true what I heard about you?" Out of the corner of my eye I see my mother-in-law stiffen, as if she's been sucker-punched. I say vaguely, "It depends on what you heard."

"Lillie, don't," Willa warns.

"It's okay," I say. Lillie looks completely confused. Apparently, the singed cat hasn't made it this far. "The baby isn't supposed to live," I say gently.

"What?" Lillie says trying to wrap her mind around what I just said.

"The baby's heart is outside of its chest. The doctors are saying it won't live," I say.

"I'm so sorry," Lillie murmurs. "I didn't know."

I wait quietly, while the women process the announcement that I'm a walking coffin. They're professionals. They quickly recover and share their own stories of miscarriages or words of comfort. Later, after all the others are gone, Henry and I are helping Lillie clean the kitchen, "How are you doing with the news?" she asks.

"Okay. I have good days and bad days."

"She's not okay," Henry interjects.

"He's saying that because he sees me cry. I'm trying to convince him that crying is normal. It doesn't mean I'm not okay. It means I'm processing and grieving."

Conversations become awkward with friends, too. We shared the news with our innermost circle, but there are those we don't see as often. It's hard because people are naturally excited to hear you're expecting. They go from excitement to devastation in the same breath. You're basically telling them that someone they know is dying. And you repeat this scenario over and over. It's exhausting. You become the comforter as, many times, people tear up with emotion, not sure what to do with the news. You find yourself patting their shoulder or putting your hand on their arm and saying things like, "It's okay," when it's really not.

Catching people off guard is unfair. Most people offer, "I'm sorry" or "This must be really hard." Others say things like, "You're such a strong person, so I know you can handle this," or suggest contacting others who have babies with minor non-life threatening defects for support.

The problem is, there's no great response. I find myself responding to the empathetic with words of encouragement and denial and being offended by those who think this is just another thing to deal with on my To-Do list. There's nothing anyone can say to make it better. At least there isn't for me.

The *best* is in the grocery store. Standing in line with my four-year-old and two-year-old daughters and starting to sport a joey pouch (it happens so fast with the third, seriously, so fast) is bound to warrant conversation. People love kids. They talk to them a lot. Add a pregnant lady to the mix, and it becomes a free-for-all.

"What beautiful little girls! Do you have another one on the way?" the lady gushes.

"I do," I say, pasting a runner-up-Miss-America smile on my face.

"Do you know if it's a boy or a girl?" more gushing . . .

"Not yet, but we hope to find out soon." I can't help wonder if the fact that my smile doesn't reach my eyes is a dead giveaway that I'm acting.

"Well, my goodness. You must be so excited. You'll have your hands full!"

It's about now that I start to ask forgiveness for lying. "Yes, we're very excited."

The reality is I want to sit down in the middle of the store and weep. There's nowhere I can go to get away from the reality that my child's dying. I can hardly handle talking about it with the people I know and love. I'm certainly not about to ruin this dear old lady's day. Maybe I could start shopping for groceries online.

"HOW ARE YOU this morning?" Bridget asks. We talk several times a day, not necessarily because we have a lot to say, more so because we have enough kids between us that inevitably our conversations are never really finished, just put on hold.

"Tired . . . tired of being sick. I decided this morning being bed-ridden is overrated. After spending almost the entire month of August in bed, I refuse to lose my September, too. The girls are running wild and my house is a wreck. Today's the day to be done."

"Oh, yeah?" she laughs. "How's that going for you?"

"Having vomited twice already this morning, I'm lying down again. My body isn't exactly in agreement with my brain on this one. I'm depressed. Not over the baby, but over how dirty the house is. I hustle to feed the kids and make the household function with the little time I'm up. You know how I can't stand clutter."

"Yes, I love that about you." Bridget chuckles.

"Henry suggested we get our old house cleaner to come and give it the once-over."

"Nice," Bridget says.

"I'm stoked. I thought about waiting to have her come when I can keep up with it. After today, I'm not sure when that'll be."

"Oh! Hold on. I've got a crier. I'll call you back," she says.

NAUSEA STILL PLAGUES me at my eighteen-week appointment. I've been coming every other week to listen for the baby's heartbeat. My OBs don't want to put me through any more stress than necessary so the prescribed sonograms with the specialist every third week were called off. These OB visits simply confirm what the incessant vomiting tells me. I reverently listen as the Doppler emits the familiar sound of a tornado rushing through my stomach, and then a strong *thu-thump, thu-thump, thu-thump*, as it locates the heartbeat in the lower quadrant.

"How are you feeling?" my doctor asks.

"Sick. Other than that okay," I say.

"I know this is hard on you. Not many people make this decision . . . to follow through with the pregnancy. If you need anything, you know we're only a phone call away."

"I do have one request. I'd like to find out what sex the baby is," I say. "Is it possible to order a twenty-week sonogram?"

"You're certain you want to find out?" she asks.

"I've been thinking about it a lot. I called a few other women who lost babies in the second trimester, and all of them were glad they knew."

"Not a problem," she says. "You'll need to go back to the specialist to have it done. Why don't you get dressed and I'll meet you up front?"

We're back in the same office, with the same sonographer, taking the same pictures. She swipes the Doppler wand in one direction, then back using her other hand to record the pictures via a keyboard attached to the monitor. Wax on. Wax off.

The second hand on the white industrial clock ticks by in steady time. . . . I know, because I've been watching it for ten minutes. That, and looking at a magnet stuck to the metal crossbar along the top of Brenda's desk. The miniature steer skull, complete with antlers, reminds me of Georgia O'Keefe's paintings, which leads me to conclude three things. One: Brenda likes Georgia O'Keefe. Or two: Brenda is Native American. Or three: Someone who likes Georgia O'Keefe and is Native American gave Brenda a steer skull magnet. "I like your magnet. Where'd you get it?" I venture at conversation. "A co-worker got it for me from New Mexico," she says. I was way off. There is more pointing and clicking. "My grandmother's from New Mexico," I say.

My grandmother *is* from New Mexico. She met my grandfather when she was sixteen at a dance. Grandpa was training as a fighter pilot for the Second Great War. There were no Tom Cruise back then. No Kelly McGillis. . . . There was, however, a stream of girls, waiting to meet the brave soldiers at the local five-and-dime and dance halls. Grandma was one of them. She came with one soldier and left out the back door with another. The *other* was to become her husband. Sixty-three years later they have four grown daughters to be proud of (and two adopted sons). The grown daughters have fourteen girls, and two boys. Between them, they have seven girls and four boys. That's one reason I think I'm having a girl. They run strong in our family tree.

Brenda exhales laying the Doppler in its cradle. The pictures are over for now. "Do you want to know what you're having?" she says.

We nod.

"A boy. You're having a boy," she announces.

I'm flat on the concrete looking at the sky, wondering if I'm breathing my last breath. It must've been a bus that flattened me. Something smaller wouldn't hurt so much. Air fills my lungs, assuring me that, no, I'm still here. Still here, and now facing an even greater nightmare. *A boy*. I'm losing the only baby boy I have.

"I thought I saw something on the monitor a few minutes ago," Henry says.

"You saw it on the monitor?" I say incredulous that my husband saw boy parts on the screen, and I was oblivious. I was distracted by that darn skull, I tell you.

"I was pretty sure," he says smiling.

He's proud of his sperm. I can tell. He made a boy. Henry has dreamed of having a boy since he was a boy. It was practically in our vows. Tears prick my eyes. We finally made a boy and he is slipping through our fingers.

The doctor arrives to view the pictures and go over our case. It's a different doctor than our first visit. This time, it's a youngish woman with a much better bedside manner. "I'm sorry to tell you that the fetus' heart is still outside the chest cavity. It looks like the body absorbed some of the fluid along the flanks. Overall, the prognosis is the same. Is this pregnancy something you still want to go forward with?" Dr. Soo asks.

"Absolutely," I say.

"What are the percentages of survival?" Henry asks.

"We don't see these babies living. This condition is extremely rare. We have a handful per year nationwide, and there are only a couple hundred documented in modern medicine. Nothing we can really base statistics on. What we do know is that these babies don't make it."

I turn my head away from her to cry privately. You'd think after eight weeks of grieving I'd be more calloused. Time has a way of dulling the shock, allowing us to feel more acutely. I understand every word of the diagnosis today. There are no caves to run to. The world doesn't go away just because I shut my eyes.

"I'm so sorry," she says quietly. She waits for me to turn back to her before saying, "Because you reached the twenty-week mark, I can refer you to a pediatric cardiologist, who might be able to give you more answers on this condition. We are dealing with more than one problem here: the physical defect and the heart defect. The heart we see is incompatible with life. We can't find pulmonary arteries, which are essential for oxygenating blood. You can't live without them."

"Where would you send us?" Henry asks.

"We send our patients to Children's Hospital in D.C.," she says. "We have a good working relationship with them."

"Is that the best place to go?" I ask. "We can travel, if you think there's a better option."

"D.C. is excellent. There's also CHOP and Boston, but there's something to be said for staying local. You have older children, right?" We nod. "There'll be multiple appointments and traveling to Philly or Boston would be hard on your family. You may have an extended stay. Considering your older children, I recommend D.C."

"And D.C. is good?" I ask because I need to hear things more than once.

"D.C. is great," she says patiently. "They'll set you up with a geneticist, as well, so you can look at family history. I suggest getting amniocentesis to give the geneticist more information to go on. They won't recommend treatment if there are life-threatening chromosome issues. We can perform that here before you go downtown."

"What are the chances of miscarriage with the amniocentesis?" I ask. "Isn't this pregnancy compromised enough?"

"There's such a small chance of miscarriage, and Children's will want to know about any other defects. It's best to go ahead with the test. You can schedule everything with the girls at the front desk. I'll meet you there with a referral and contact information for Children's," she says, quietly leaving the room.

WE MAKE OUR way to the car. "Will you name the baby Henry?" I ask.

"I'm not sure," Henry says.

Ever since I've known my husband, he has wanted a son named after him, and his father, and his father's father, and his father's father's father. He wants a Fifth. I uttered the words, "Stop the insanity" more than once, but know it's something really important to him. "All the Henrys were such great men. I'm proud to be named after them," he's told me on multiple occasions. "I want my son to be proud of his name, too." The question becomes, do you name a child who's dying the family name?

"I'll support whatever you decide," I say. "We can talk about it once we know more."

I SPEND THE weekend processing the fact that I'm losing a son. It's like I'm beginning the grieving process all over again. My mother went through something similar when my brother was born. After bearing six girls, she didn't stop to consider she could have a boy. She had a hard time bonding with him. She confided to my grandmother, "It's not my baby. I was supposed to have a girl, Suzanna Rae." My grandmother very wisely said, "Suzanna Rae's dead. Now stop crying about a baby that doesn't exist and go take care of your son."

The words came flooding back to my mind as I put away the thoughts of burying a little girl and moved on to bonding with my son. I wrote to family and friends in an email:

"We had our twenty-week sonogram on Friday, and we're having a boy! I was shocked beyond shocked . . . and quite honestly, it threw me for a loop as my immediate reaction was 'please God, don't take my only son.' Funny, huh, since He sent His only Son for us. I was pretty emotional over the weekend, reprocessing and grieving for my son, not my daughter, but God impressed on me the story of Abraham and how he waited so long (much longer than me) for a son, how God fulfilled that promise and then asked him to give that son back to God. Abraham's faith was so strong in God's original promise of making a great nation, using Isaac, that he was able to let go of the only visible sign of that promise and believe that God would work it out. God sent the ram as a replacement. It hit home for me this weekend that this baby, boy or girl, is God's and while He hasn't promised me a son, He has made me many promises, and I need to trust in His promises, and let go of my earthly desires. It remains to be seen if God will give us this son on earth, but I'm in a better place today, for sure. "

THE TISSUE-PAPER sheet crinkles under my weight as I get situated on the exam table. I thought my referral to Children's would take forever to schedule, but it turns out it only takes two weeks, so fitting the amniocentesis in the dead center seemed like a good plan. I'm with the other sonographer today, Kerry. She sat in on my last sonogram, so we aren't strangers. My shirt is up once again as she preps my stomach for the procedure. I go back and forth between needing to pee and needing to vomit, both signs of pregnancy, but also personal signs of anxiety. I can't stand needles: the sight of them, the thought of them, and especially the use of them. I would love to know who thought it'd be a great idea to stick a long needle into a womb and pull out some fluid. And who in the world volunteered the first time? Sadists. They were probably sadists.

There's a soft knock on the door. A doctor, who's new to me, makes his entrance. He's the third doctor I've seen in three visits. "Hi, I'm Dr. Jones, I'm performing your amniocentesis today. Are you ready?"

"As ready as I'll ever be," I say.

"Does that mean you don't want the procedure, because this isn't to be taken lightly. If you're not sure, now's the time to tell me," he says sternly.

"I'm nervous, but I think it's important to get the most information we can for the geneticist at Children's," I say a little taken aback.

"This isn't going to give them any information," he says curtly, almost as if he's angry with me. Since I've never met him, I'm sure I've done nothing to offend him.

"What do you mean?" I ask. "I was told they want to know if there are any chromosome issues. Won't this tell them that much?"

"What I mean is that this fetus has a fatal diagnosis. The defect we're dealing with is incompatible with life. I need to know if you really want this procedure or not. In my opinion, there's no reason for you to have it."

I wasn't expecting a lecture from the doctor. Thoughts race through my head and I desperately try to grab one that's coherent. One doctor told me to get this, Dr. Jones is actually angry I'm here, my OB thinks it's a good idea, but what about my blood work?

"My blood work. It indicated a high probability for Down's Syndrome," I manage to say.

"Well, that might be one reason to get it," Dr. Jones mumbles under his breath, while fumbling with my chart. The warbled thoughts scurry away like roaches caught in the beam of a flashlight. My head is completely clear as I realize Dr. Jones hasn't reviewed my entire chart.

"Dr. Soo suggested I get the amniocentesis and so did my OB," I add. I'm on fire now, the girl whose father said she was born giving a closing argument.

"This fetus isn't going to live. Its heart's outside of its chest. This is a fatal defect we're looking at. Besides, even if it does make it to birth, it needs a heart transplant to survive. Hearts are hard to come by, especially infant hearts. They're nearly impossible to find. They won't be able to keep the baby stable enough to get a transplant."

He may as well have finished his thought with, "Stop wasting everyone's time." All of us in the room knew that's what he was saying.

I recognize that Dr. Jones is angry with me. He has a personal vendetta against me doing anything to continue this pregnancy. He keeps using terms like fatal and incompatible as if we're on a children's program and they are the words for the day. He's acting like I don't realize my child has a very slim chance at life. I say a silent prayer of thanks that Dr. Price, my OB, called me yesterday to explain that because infant hearts are virtually inaccessible, doctors would use an orangutan heart. She didn't want me to be blind-sided by this information when I got down to Children's. Dr. Jones doesn't know any of this.

Dr. Jones also doesn't know I believe God is telling me this baby is going to live, or that I'm not giving up until it breathes its last breath. I'll do everything unbiased doctors tell me to do to give my son the best possible chances, even if it means having amniocentesis. "You know what? Dr. Soo, Dr. Price, my husband, and I are all in agreement that I should have this procedure. I'd like to start now."

"That's all I need to hear," he says flatly. Kerry leaves to get the procedure kit, while Dr. Jones rubs my stomach with a sterilizing agent. When Kerry returns, Dr. Jones opens it up and I accidentally glimpse the long, long, very long, skinny needle. I turn my head away quickly wishing I hadn't seen it. I ignore the screen, too. Everyone knows seeing only makes it hurt worse.

"I'm going to penetrate the abdomen now," Dr. Jones says. I feel a prick and then the weirdest pressure in my stomach. It's almost like lying on a bubble trapped inside you (except it's on the topside of me and not the bottom). The bubble doesn't roll or move at all. It's just a mass of pressure and you're squashing it. I felt this once before when I tried lying on my stomach to sunbathe when I was five months pregnant with Natalie. Needless to say I didn't get sun on my back that day and right now I'm wishing the procedure were over. Dr. Jones interrupts my thoughts by letting out a huge sigh. I'm finding him to be a bit over-dramatic.

"What's wrong?" I ask.

"The fetus moved over to the area where the needle is. I can't draw out fluid until it moves away," he says. He stands there for a few seconds and then starts pressing his fist on my stomach to "encourage movement." He does this for five minutes. The white industrial clock tells me all of this with not so much as a smile. All the while, I'm experiencing the intense pressure accompanied by pain from the additional pressure of Dr. Jones' hand. And lucky me, I'm now feeling nauseated. *Great.*

Never one to let grass grow under my feet I ask, "What do we do if the baby doesn't move?"

"We can make another puncture site," he sighs, "I was hoping it'd move by now."

"Does another puncture site increase the odds of miscarriage?" I ask.

"Not at all." He continues kneading my stomach firmly with his fist while looking at the screen.

"Do you think we can try that then, because I think my morning sickness is kicking in," I say.

He carefully removes the needle, preps another spot on my stomach and inserts the needle again. In a matter of ten seconds (and I'm not exaggerating. I have nowhere else to look but at my friend, the clock) the needle's out. "Okay, that should do it," he says. That should do it? That's it? He just made me suffer for five minutes for something he could get in ten seconds? This guy's a piece of work.

THE NERVES ARE bouncing around inside of me so violently that I start shaking while walking to my car. I somehow manage to unlock my car and get in through the blur of tears making their hasty escape. I lean over my steering wheel, gripping it as if it were a lifesaver. Even amid my uncontrollable sobbing, the rational part of me is confused at this sudden outburst. Am I crying because of my confrontation with Dr. Jones? Am I relieved the procedure is over? I finally decide it's because I'm a woman and I'm pregnant!

Kerry instructed me to lie low for several hours to allow my womb to heal. I'm nervous the holes will leak or make my belly pop like a balloon pricked by a pin. I try everything in my power not to cough or sneeze.

Bridget drops the girls off at 3 P.M. and sets them up with a movie. "You doing okay?" she asks. I'm lying on the couch in my living room.

"Yeah, just nervous," I answer.

"Do you want me to take the girls back to my house? It's not a big deal. They fit right in with my gang and practically disappear," she says sitting down beside me.

"I'm good," I assure her. "Henry should be home in a few hours. He'll help me."

Two hours later the movie is over and the girls are jumping on the couch around me. "Girls! Mommy has a boo-boo on her tummy. Please stop jumping. Why don't you go find another movie?" Excited at the idea of two movies in one day, my television-deprived children scream like the little girls that they are, and run to the TV room. By the time Henry gets home, my nerves are shot and I'm regretting not taking Bridget up on her offer. "Hey, how was the test?" he says giving me a peck on the cheek.

"Crazy. Nerve-wracking. Emotional. I'll tell you about it once the girls are in bed. Do you mind putting them down? I'm supposed to take it easy for twenty-four hours."

"Sure, not a problem. Girls!"

As Henry puts the girls to bed, I do some research online. I'm learning that the internet is a dangerous place. I have yet to find a live case of ectopia cordis. A friend sent me the blog of a woman whose son is due to arrive in less than a week—only one day after we have our consultation at Children's. Although, it isn't the same defect, he has a bad heart and the thought processes are the same. Will this child live? How long? Will I see it? All the things I've been thinking about the past ten weeks. She has me thinking and I'm unable to settle my mind.

Will I have to pick out a casket? What will I bury him in? Do I really want to plan that far in advance? If I plan for these things, does this mean I'm not trusting God to heal this baby?

THAT FRIDAY, I head to an event at church. Laughter rings out, as ladies mingle, enjoying time with others in their same life-stage. I've come to these mom's outings several times and I always have a good time.

My phone buzzes in my diaper bag. Seeing the number of the maternal fetal specialist's office pop up on my screen is enough to turn the blood in my veins to ice. I walk quickly down the hall to find an empty room. "Hello?" It's Friday, October 23, several days after my amniocentesis and less than a week before we're due at Children's.

"Mrs. Marquiss?"

"This is she," I answer, barely above a whisper.

"This is Mary Anne from the specialist's office. I have the preliminary results from your amniocentesis." I break down into sobs. I don't mean a quiet tear here and there. I mean heavy, ugly crying, the kind where your face is contorted and mascara is running down your cheeks so thick the members of KISS are jealous. "Honey, don't cry. I haven't even told you anything yet," Mary Anne says sweetly.

"I know. I'm sorry. It's just that I have yet to receive any good news from your practice," I choke out in a high, squeaky voice.

"Well, today it's not bad news," she says brightly. "The preliminary results show no chromosomal issues. The final results will be back in ten to fourteen business days."

"Does this mean everything's okay?" I ask.

"It means the preliminary results show nothing for Down Syndrome. The final results may test positive for another issue," she explains.

Downs was all I was worried about, since my blood work showed a higher than normal odds for it. It seems now we're in the clear. This *is* good news. Good news, indeed. I dry the tears from my eyes by doing the only thing a sophisticated woman in my position can do . . . I lick my finger and wipe under my lower lashes to remove any black that may have pooled there during the downpour. I'm obviously very classy. It would be poor form returning to the party looking like I've just been to a raccoon family reunion. I take a deep cleansing breath, whip my hair over my shoulder, and return as if nothing happened, only to be peed on by my potty-training two-year-old. Sophistication is over-rated anyway.

I'm standing in line at Children's National Medical Center in Washington, D.C. You'd think we were at a ride at Disney by the length of the line. Apparently, unbeknownst to me, you have to stop at a security desk, hand over your license, have it scanned, and then receive a badge for the exact department you're visiting, to get into the hospital. You also have to promise to give them your firstborn.

A few people have tried sneaking past only to be called back by one of the two receptionists. This is a major medical facility treating hundreds of children. It's obvious they want them all to be safe. It's also obvious we'll be late for our appointment. I didn't figure in a twenty-minute wait in the security line.

Henry emerges from the elevator bay to my left. He dropped me at the entrance and then parked the car, hoping I'd be able to run upstairs and check in on time. Now I realize any running on my part could result in a full-on tackle by the security guard standing to the right of the receptionist desk. Henry falls in line beside me, giving me a "how long is this going to take?" look. "You should've seen it when I got here," I say in response.

We're finally cleared through security. After another twenty minutes sitting in the cardiology waiting room, we're ushered into a darkened room and introduced to our sonographer, Amanda. The tissue paper on the bed crackles like Rice Krispies as I settle in. Amanda squeezes the cold, gooey gel over my stomach and moves her probe across it. The gray, fuzzy pictures start to move. My baby!

A man knocks and enters the room. "This is Lowell," Amanda says. "Lowell is a fellow working with Dr. Donofrio, and will be in with us today." We exchange pleasantries. They begin going over the pictures Amanda's getting on the screen. I gaze around the room, which is decorated with a jungle motif on the wall and a TV hanging above the exam table. It's clearly decorated with children in mind. Henry's sitting in a chair near the foot of my bed. The sonogram and combined echocardiogram last a long time . . . almost two hours. The room is dark and warm, making it hard to stay alert. I doze during some of it and notice at one point Henry's asleep, too. I suddenly hear the word "pulmonary." My ears perk up. Just two weeks ago I was told our baby doesn't have any pulmonary arteries. My heart does a little flip-flop at the thought they might've seen some. I'm also guarded. I don't know many medical terms and who knows how many may start with pulmonary.

"We're done here," Lowell says. "We're going to let Dr. Donofrio look at the pictures, and then she'll meet with you to go over what she sees."

A few minutes later Lowell, Amanda, and a dark-haired woman wearing a white lab coat, step into the room. "I'm Dr. Donofrio," she says extending her hand. "If you don't mind I'd like to take one more look to make sure we have what we need."

I uncover my stomach once again, and strain my ears so hard to eavesdrop on the conversation that my head hurts. "What about right here," Dr. Donofrio is saying, "Is that the PA?"

"It's not in the right place. It should be up here," Lowell says, pointing at the screen. "It's not normal."

Dr. Donofrio gives him a quizzical looks and says, "Yes, that's why they're here." I laugh along with them. "I really think that's it," she continues. "See how it's long and skinny?" she draws her finger across the screen like she's finger-painting. "I think because it's lower than it should be it's stretched out thin. That's why we're having a hard time seeing it . . . Okay, let's meet in the consultation room," she says to Henry and me.

If wiping blue goo off your stomach were an Olympic sport, I'd highly consider becoming a contender. I'm getting super efficient at not only getting it off in record time, but only using one paper towel to do it. I show off my new skills to Henry before meeting everyone in the room down the hall. Dr. Donofrio takes out a pad of paper and starts educating us on the human heart. "The heart has four chambers," she says, and starts to draw an anatomical heart on a piece of paper upside down from her vantage point. It reminds me of the waitresses at the steakhouse, except that we're talking about the person responsible for fixing my child's heart, as opposed to fixing my steak.

Dr. Donofrio points with her pen—"The right atrium, the left atrium, the right ventricle, and the left ventricle." She goes on to explain that while they can't get a clear picture of our son's right ventricle because his sternal defect is in the way, they know it's not the proper size, based on proportions between the different valves connecting the chambers. Additionally, the pulmonary arteries, instead of coming straight down and being open are pulled to the side and squished. She draws in the details on the paper heart while talking to us. "We think there's a right ventricle there," she says, "because we see blood flow, but we're not sure how big it is. And that's a big question for this baby. One that won't be answered until he's born and we can actually see what's going on. The other big question is his sternal defect.

"Ectopia cordis is extremely rare. It happens when the baby is forming in the beginning weeks. The skin starts on one side and wraps around the body meeting itself in the middle like an envelope. For whatever reason, in cases like this, the skin doesn't meet, and the heart ends up outside the chest wall. The sternum is typically missing or short as well.

"We know there's a sternal defect, but we weren't able to see the sternum on the sonogram today. This type of test doesn't show the details of bone very well. I'd like to send you to have a fetal MRI, so they can take images of the sternum to find out what we're dealing with. We'll plan to ventilate him immediately after birth, anyway. The sternum is important to breathing. It creates a vacuum, enabling the diaphragm to contract and pull air into the lungs. Without a proper sternum, this may be impossible.

"The other things the MRI will clear up for us are if the chest wall can be repaired, and how much room is inside the chest cavity for the heart. This will determine how soon we can close up the chest. We may have to postpone the repair, until his body is big enough to handle the heart. This can be anywhere from two months to a year. We won't know until we get more information. Best-case scenario: this baby is born, it's lungs work properly, the right ventricle is able to support blood flow, and we're able to repair the chest wall within a few months of birth. Worst-case scenario: this baby has a major defect, as well as ectopia cordis. One of our colleagues has seen ten ectopia cordis babies, pretty much making him an expert. In his experience, if there is a major heart defect that needs open-heart surgery as an infant combined with ectopia cordis, it's fatal. However, if it's just ectopia cordis, the babies seem to fare pretty well.

"I think what we have is something in the middle. If we can get oxygen saturations at eighty or higher, we won't have to do open-heart surgery as an infant. That would be the best thing."

By the time we leave, Dr. Donofrio and her team have given us a Cardiology 101 course and gone over every option they can think of for when our son is born. There are unanswered questions; however, we're at least talking about treatment options instead of termination options. The best news of the day is that he has pulmonary arteries and an aorta. A transplant won't be necessary.

We drag ourselves to the car a little after four o'clock. I lay my head on the seat and close my eyes. Six hours of getting a crash course on our son's condition and meeting with a geneticist is enough to make any pregnant woman want a nap. The thought that our baby has a chance at surviving keeps me awake. As much as I hated talking about the surgeries, synthetic skin and hearts that don't work, I love that we talked about *our baby*. Dr. Donofrio is the first doctor to give our baby a future.

"What'd you think?" Henry asks, exiting the parking garage and making a right onto Michigan Avenue.

"Is it weird to say I'm excited that a doctor just gave our baby a slim chance at life?" I answer.

"It's better than no chance, huh?" his eyes sparkle, as he grins my way.

I gaze at the man I've known since tenth grade. I hardly ever think of that time, mostly living in the present. I easily remember what made me love him: his strong character, his sense of humor, and his even personality. He still makes my skin tingle and my heart beat faster.

I remember the exact moment I first saw him. He was standing in the hallway outside homeroom. He was the new boy: tall, blond, with a skater haircut. I've always been attracted to tall boys. They make me feel safe.

It took until the end of our sophomore year for us to start "hanging out." That's what you do before you can drive. Walk each other to class, sit together at lunch. Heavy stuff!

We started talking about getting married "someday" our senior year. I remember thinking I'd get my college degree, then walk down the aisle. I was a headstrong, independent girl in so many ways.

When Henry told me during Christmas break of our freshmen year of college he didn't want to go the next three years apart, I decided he was worth changing my dreams for. This hunk of a boy was turning into a man before my eyes. I knew his beliefs, knew his strengths and weaknesses, and had seen him handle his five younger siblings. I wasn't sure I'd find anyone more qualified. My heart told me I didn't want to try. We married that summer. I finished my degree part-time while working full-time. He finished his schooling on an athletic scholarship that made our marriage affordable.

Neither of us talks much about our feelings. We have a strong aversion to vulnerability and a healthy sense of independence. It's a wonder we've been married twelve years. It isn't a fairy-tale marriage, but it's a good one. Solid, loving, committed. We haven't really done much processing together about this baby. Now as we drive home, I feel a renewed sense of hope that we might just see him alive.

November 2008

I spent the last two days with one of my very best friends and former coworker Melissa, strolling around a food show in downtown D.C. and going maternity clothes shopping. It's Sunday evening and I'm excited to reconnect with Henry. The kids are already in bed when I walk into a spotless house. *Nice*, I think. *He even cleaned the house.* "You wanna come up and see the clothes I bought?" I yell down the basement stairs. I can see he's on the computer. "Sure. Be there in a minute," he says.

He sits on the couch telling me about his weekend with the girls. "Saturday was the best day of my life. The girls are just . . . awesome."

"The best day of your life? I wasn't even there!" I joke, pulling on a cute denim skirt.

"We've had some good days, too, but Saturday was the best," he says again. I realize he's a little loopy. I look him straight in the face. He doesn't seem completely drunk. Of course, I've never seen him drunk. He has a drink every now and then, but we've never been heavy drinkers.

As we continue the conversation, I realize he's getting worse. He starts being silly and repeating himself. I'm annoyed. "This isn't exactly what I wanted to come home to," I say. "I hope you're not drunk, because I really want to *connect.*" It's a lost cause. We head upstairs to the bathroom to get ready for bed. I catch a glimpse of myself in the mirror. The first time I was pregnant I enjoyed my growing belly. I felt alive and sexy. The second and now third time I feel about as sexy as a snake that swallowed a mouse. At the halfway point with Natalie, I was just starting to wear maternity clothes. Now at twenty-three weeks, there's no way I could get my jeans up past my thighs. Believe me, I've tried.

"I'm getting fat," I say nonchalantly.

"You're not fat. You're just pregnant . . . with my son."

I look over, startled. Henry hasn't talked much of "his son." Now his eyes threaten their own impression of the Great Flood. He mumbles something unintelligible. "What?" I say.

"I hope this baby lives," he repeats through clenched teeth, tears streaming down his face. It's the first emotion I've seen him have since we heard the news twelve weeks ago. I go to him and throw my arms around him. He buries his head in his hands.

"I'm so sorry," he says. "I'm so sorry to be such a disappointment. It's my fault. I can't fix this."

"It's not your fault. You're not a disappointment. This isn't something we can fix," I say softly. My words do nothing for him. He's drunk, irrational. We hug and he continues crying for some time. I take his contacts out, wash them, and put them safely in their case and begin to wonder if I can get him to bed. He's been saying the same things now for the last ten minutes and I see this going nowhere. How do you get a man twice your size where you need him to be when you're not supposed to lift heavy objects? At 6'9", 280 pounds, I think he qualifies as a heavy object.

He leans on me, as I walk him to bed. We fall in a heap. Wrapping his arms around me, he starts groping my body. He wants to *connect,* too, and I'm not sure he's capable of not crushing me under his weight. Plus, aren't you supposed to *not* sleep with drunk people—don't they regret it in the morning? Oh, okay, that's probably if you aren't married to them, but I'm not in the mood to have sex anymore.

I grab his hands and hold them around me. "I'm not having sex with a drunk man," I say firmly. He responds with more groping. I finally get him settled down. "Give me a second, I'll be right back."

"LEIGHANN? LEIGHANN? WHAT are you doing?" His feet pound heavily on the steps. I'm surprised the kids are sleeping through the noise. He sits down beside me on the couch. "Aren't you coming upstairs? I thought we were having sex."

"No. I told you I would tomorrow. I'm checking my email. I was hoping you'd fall asleep. I think you'll feel better."

"What time is it? I need to call my brother," he changes the subject.

"Midnight. You can wait until tomorrow."

"He's a night owl. He'll be up. Besides, we were having an important conversation about Rob. Rob was buried in his bike uniform. Did I tell you that?" he says, crying again.

Henry's cousin, Rob, died suddenly last week in his sleep. We still don't know why. He was two years older than us. Henry has said nothing about the death or the funeral other than to ask the cause and to tell me the funeral was "nice" and his aunt's eulogy of her only son was "very thought out." When I asked him how he was feeling, he wasn't interested in sharing. Talk of Rob turns to more talk about the baby and our financial losses in the recent economic downturn.

"This is the worst year of my life," Henry sobs.

"Honey, you really need to go to sleep," I say.

"Can you take my contacts out?" He asks.

"I already took them out and I already told you that three times," I say wearily.

"When?" he says, astonished.

I can only laugh. Getting to bed is harder this time. Henry's feet refuse to move the way they should, and we shuffle on the stairs, with me trying to hold him up. Falling together into our bed, he wraps his arms around me tightly and is asleep within seconds. We rarely fall asleep cuddling. *We should do this more often*, I think as I drift off to sleep myself.

IT'S DARK WHEN the alarm goes off. I'm headed downtown today for an MRI. I move quietly through the darkness trying not to wake my sleeping family. My mother-in-law, Willa, will arrive to watch the girls in time for Henry to leave for work. Her help is invaluable as, once again, we call on her to babysit. She never complains about the hour and a half drive. Many times, it's her calling me to see if I need help. With the number of doctor appointments mounting as we near the third trimester, her availability is a necessity. Between Willa, and my friends Bridget and Katie, I'm able to go to most appointments child-free.

Leaving the house before the crack of dawn isn't my idea of fun. Whoever thought of starting a procedure before the sun is awake needs to have their eyelashes plucked out one at a time. By the time my MRI starts at 7 A.M., I'm nauseated from being on the move so early in the morning. Like with my prior pregnancies, if I don't eat every hour and a half to two hours, everything in my stomach makes a grand comeback. I know to avoid tomatoes, orange juice, and chunky things. Cereal and cocktail sauce, of all things, taste just about the same at their encore. Good times, good times.

My mother warned me an MRI is not fun for the claustrophobic. I keep this in mind as I take my place on the table. The conveyor-belt like table moves into the dreaded tunnel of doom. When it stops, my eyes are perpendicular to the beginning of the tunnel, with the top of my head sticking out. *This isn't that bad*, I think. *Any further and I'd flip out.* Before I can finish the thought, the conveyor belt starts up again and rolls completely inside the tunnel.

Oh, my freaking gosh! One, two, three, one, two, three. Long, cleansing breath. Counting in my head has always been a great way to fight off panic, not that I've needed it too many times in my life. There was the time I went parasailing, and the wind was whipping so hard I thought I was going to flip. But, overall, I've really had a pretty calm life. About the time I'm on the third round of counting, a large whirring sound, much like that of a jet engine starts, followed by rhythmic beating similar to that of an agitating washing machine. Suddenly, a jackhammer gyrates somewhere inside the machine, as if little construction men are physically chiseling out a minute picture of the contents of my womb. I take myself to a happy place, singing songs and counting in the recesses of my mind. Through my zenlike meditation, I notice the click of a camera—seriously, it really sounds like a camera—accompanied by clicking noises and various fire-alarm–like buzzers every few minutes. This goes on for forty-five minutes. "How are you doing?" the tech asks through a speaker in the tunnel.

"I'm . . . okay. How much longer, do you think?"

"I finished the first set of pictures, but my machine just froze on the second set. I'm going to have to start them over . . . probably twenty to thirty more minutes. I'm really sorry."

The next thing I remember is the tech's voice through the speaker saying, "We're all done." I managed to sleep through the last half of the test. I'm a superstar!

I eat an apple on the way to the ultrasound rooms. They're located on the same floor down a series of hallways. Today's high-risk ultrasound will be much like the ones I get on a regular basis at the maternal fetal specialist's, just a little more in-depth. I recline on the examination table, and lift my shirt for the ever-present blue goo. I'm beginning to think I should buy stock. The radiologist, responsible for reading baby boy's MRI and ultrasound, pokes her head in the room. After a brief scan of the pictures the sonographer is taking, the doctor turns to me, "I read the MRI. The good news is that the baby has a sternum. It's short, but it's there. It also seems that the ribs are all fully formed and meet with the cartilage in the center, as they should. There *is* cartilage damage where the heart and chest wall protrude through. The rest of the sternum looks beautiful."

I smile at her words. "This is the first time anyone has said this baby looks beautiful."

She smiles back. "As far as chest reconstruction, this is an easy fix and doesn't pose a problem at all."

I head upstairs to the cardiology clinic for an echocardiogram. Amanda greets me like an old friend. I ask about her girls and she asks about mine. I learned of her daughters on my first visit. They're a few years older than Natalie and Ainsley. Dr. Donofrio and I meet to go over the findings of all the tests I've had done today. Even though I knew there'd be a consult, I came alone. It seemed silly having Henry sitting around in the various rooms while every specialty took their own set of pictures.

Henry's job entails meeting with other key executives throughout the day, making decisions, and streamlining policies and processes. He also has a team of accountants that report to him and crunch the numbers for all the non-performing loans (those already in, or headed toward, default) in the organization's portfolio. We're living through the worst economic downfall since the Great Depression and Henry's employer owns over 30 percent of all the mortgages in the United States. Let's just say that his portfolio is in the trillions, so there are lots of numbers to crunch. Because his day basically consists of meetings, his schedule remains rigid. To compound the problem, with the recent economic crisis, the government stepped in and increased oversight. Everyone is on edge, feeling like Big Brother is looking for a reason to haul them in front of a Senate hearing. Instead of having him in the flesh, we decided to conference him in once I'm with Dr. Donofrio. He picks up on the second ring.

"Hey, hon, Can you talk?" I say.

"Go ahead," he says on speakerphone.

"So, we have good news today, Henry," Dr. Donofrio says. "There is a sternum, even though it's short. And there is enough room in the chest cavity for closure. Both great. I also was able to talk with Dr. Jonas, our surgeon. He's world-renowned. People travel from all over to see him. He agrees it's reasonable to move forward. It's really all going to depend on the right ventricle. I'm still seeing blood flow going into the right-sided chamber today, which means there's something there. We won't know how much until birth. If we could get enough function to last us a year before having to do heart surgery, it'd be fantastic. That gives the baby time to grow and get strong. Even though it's risky in the first few weeks to have surgery, we can do it, if necessary.

"We'll continue to watch the function of the heart by echo. I don't see any signs of stress today. If we start seeing decreasing heart function, we'll consider taking the baby early. Right now, I'd like to do a c-section somewhere between thirty-seven and thirty-eight weeks."

I immediately think of my nephew, who was in the NICU at birth due to RSV, a life-threatening respiratory virus. For some reason, white male babies who are taken early by c-section, have a higher rate of lung problems. The nurses have a name for it: "Wimpy-White-Male Syndrome."

"Can we push it to thirty-eight?" I ask. "I'd like to wait as long as possible. In fact, I'd love to do thirty-nine weeks, if you'll let me."

"We can do thirty-eight, but no more than that. I don't want to take the chance you'll go into labor. This needs to be a highly controlled process from start to finish. We routinely have planned births over at Washington Hospital Center. We'll send a pediatric cardiac team who'll stand by during delivery. I see no reason why we won't be able to stabilize the baby, then transport him through the tunnel to the cardiac ICU here. The plastic surgeon, Dr. Boyajian, and his team will put a Gortex cover over the heart to decrease the chance of infection. Heart infection is likely to be a huge risk."

"Will they do surgery right away?" Henry interjects.

"For the Gortex cover, yes. For the heart, we'll wait as long as we can to do anything. The important thing is taking things as slowly as possible. The heart tells us how fast to go," Dr. Donofrio says.

"Will the surgeons put the heart flush with the chest?" Henry asks.

"They won't move the heart at all," Dr. Donofrio explains. "In the past, doctors tried moving the heart back into the chest by compressing it, but the heart doesn't respond well. In fact, it's fatal. The heart is," she pauses looking for the right word, ". . . claustrophobic. It doesn't like being smashed. When they've done these surgeries, they've found that the big vessels coming to the heart may get kinked off, causing the heart to stop. The plan is to leave the heart where it is, and close the chest around it. Dr. Boyajian's working to come up with a plan on how to do that. He's really fantastic. He's worked on a ton of cases, none exactly like this, but lots of burns, co-joined twins, and really difficult cases. If anyone can do this, he can. You really have the best minds working on this case."

My brain is on overload. I feel like a printer with a paper jam that cannot take one more thing in and process it. We wrap up the session, and agree to see each again in a month. Meanwhile, I'll continue seeing my OB every other week and the fetal specialist every three, which basically means a doctor appointment every week. Although it's a lot, having a plan is way better than staring at the walls, waiting for the unknown.

On the way home, I run into Target to grab diapers for Ainsley. It's so much easier without lugging a toddler and preschooler and baby on the way. I whisk through the aisles, a mom on a mission. I pass the Christmas ornaments, awaiting holiday shoppers. It's a week before Thanksgiving, and they're already getting picked over. I quickly scan them to see if there is anything that'll work for the girls' collection. My eyes land on one that reads, "Baby's First Christmas." Time stands still. The list in my head disappears. Will this baby have a first Christmas? I blink back tears on the brink of overflowing. It's useless. I feel like the little Dutch boy holding his finger in the hole of the dike. I back slowly away from the Christmas display. There is nothing here for the girls, and I'm not buying anything for the baby just yet. I make my way to the diapers, forced to walk through rows of baby clothes, socks and fuzzy blankets. Crying in the middle of Target isn't exactly what I had in mind.

Things like this happen more often than I care to admit. One minute I'm perfectly fine, only to be sucker-punched by a reminder that my child's on death row. The truth is, even if he survives birth, I have no guarantee how long he'll live. I just read on a blog yesterday (yes the internet again!), of a woman who lost a heart child at six years old. Six! Up until now, I'd only been thinking in terms of getting my son safely through birth, and the projected year of procedures and surgeries. Now, I'm left wondering if he'll make it through childhood. The only way to get through moments like these is to focus on the present. What do I need to do today? Not what does tomorrow hold? Today has enough worries of its own. I focus on the plan we've been given, and hope I heard God right when He challenged me to trust Him that this baby would live.

Strong. It's a word I hear often these days. "You're so strong." What does that really mean? They say it because I didn't terminate the pregnancy. They say it because I talk about God's goodness. They say it because they don't see the tears streaming down my face unexpectedly in the middle of the night, in the middle of the day, or driving in the car. They can't sense my waves of panic at the sight of newborn babies.

I don't feel strong. In the beginning, my doctor told me I was strong for allowing nature to take its course and not determining the timetable for my baby's death. Strong . . . for going through with a pregnancy we didn't expect to last. Honestly, looking back, I was probably in shock and denial. Denial of what really could happen. What they were all talking about, but afraid to say. They knew this baby might survive to twenty weeks; that it had happened before, if the mother chose not to terminate.

I'm not in denial any longer. I knew terminating would only raise more questions, and not give me closure. Questions like: What would've happened if I'd left well enough alone? How many weeks would the baby have survived, if I hadn't chosen for him? Was a miracle waiting in the wings, only to be eclipsed by my wanting to feel less pain?

No, I'm not strong. Only now, am I figuring it all out. Research and waiting have given me more answers. To know if this baby has a chance, I had to wait past the "point of no return," the point where legally the doctor must take life-saving action for the baby, if I go into pre-term labor. That's what the specialist meant when he said, "it gets complicated." Not for me, of course. It would be the same for me. I'd still go home empty-handed; carrying only baby weight around my middle.

They knew this baby might survive to forty weeks, and then what? Most likely death. They knew what they weren't telling me, and what I couldn't see. My expectation was exactly what they *were* telling me. The baby would pass within a few weeks or a month. I knew that miscarrying would be hard. I'd grieve like never before. It'd change my life, my marriage, and my thinking. Yet they knew better than me. They knew it would take unbelievable willpower and strength to take this baby to full-term just to watch him die.

Now, I understand. They knew allowing the pregnancy to continue to full-term would be an emotional roller coaster for my family and me. I read it on blogs of other mothers who've lost their babies. I see their pain and know it will be my own—barring a miracle—in ten short weeks. The reality of this discovery rips through my soul, leaving a gaping wound.

If he lives? If God, in fact, did speak to me and give me not just something to hold on to while I live through this storm, but actually a real, true, promise? We're galloping into the unknown at full speed. Will his little heart do its job? Dr. Donofrio says maybe. The experts—if there's such a thing with this condition—say a heart with this many problems, is fatal for babies with ectopia cordis. My baby's heart has problems. As much as I want to hope his right ventricle is working, I somehow know that we're dealing with a somewhat malfunctioning heart. Dr. Donofrio's pretty certain of this, and my gut's following her experience.

We prepare the only way we can. We have several plans that'll be revised as the doctors monitor his condition. They'll make judgment calls, and take action with little time for discussion or research on our part. Our research must happen now.

If he survives the first few days, his car seat will remain empty for the foreseeable future. How many trips will I make to visit him in the CICU? How many nights will I wake to phantom cries? How many days before I bring him home, if at all? The roller coaster ticks up the track.

This baby boy isn't my only concern. I have two other children to take care of, to nurture, to guide into little beings. The weight of responsibility for my daughters is debilitating. How will they react? How will I be able to visit the baby and make him feel loved and protected, while attending to the needs of my first and second born? Will they resent their brother? Will they get bored with visiting him? How will I be able to cope at home, knowing my baby is lying in an ICU, fighting for his life? How long will this take? Weeks, months? This is probably where strong comes in. I can't see, through my haze of despair, to know what strong looks like, or if I can be it. I'm not sure there's enough of me to stretch that far.

This is, dare I say, the easy part. The hard part is a blip further up on the horizon. Talk to me then about strong. Talk to me about how well I'm holding up, and how impressed you are with my outlook. About how well I'm handling things and processing things and not losing it all over your shoulder in public. 'Cause I'm not sure the word you'll use is strong. I'm having a hard enough time getting through my doctor appointments. Speaking of which, it's time for another one.

I head to the Children's Hospital clinic in Fairfax, Virginia, for a routine echo. Fairfax is located nineteen miles outside of the city and a mere twenty minutes from my house instead of the fifty-minute drive to the main hospital on the other side of D.C.

Pulling into the parking garage, my stomach gives a quick lurch, then flutters like butterflies escaping from a baby boy with a net. Five minutes ago, I was chowing down on a Wendy's cheeseburger, and slurping root beer, while watching the clock and the traffic in front of me. Entering the garage was like going through the Stargate into another world, where my tasks aren't things to be checked off, but things that can mean the difference between life and death.

I'm not anxious about the echo. We know what it'll say. I'm not expecting life-altering news. Believe me, our life has been altered enough already. It's more that reality is settling down deeper inside me, getting comfortable putting it's feet up on the table and helping itself to a glass of water. The idea that our son is critically ill can no longer be a clinical theory. As someone who craves planning and organization, adjusting to new things is difficult. Pulling up to a pediatric cardiologist's office was never in my plan. Having a baby diagnosed with a fatal defect never made the list. Shocker, I know. Never once in all the years I sat around with friends, making lists of baby names did I chose a name for a baby who might not live. Never once, did I wonder what a name would look like on a gravestone, marking a casket fit for a doll. No one *plans* for these things.

I did plan other things, lots of other things. I planned how many kids I wanted and how far I wanted them spaced out. I planned it down to the detail for specific reasons, and now it's all messed up (strike up the violins). I'll never have four kids spaced two years apart. I may not even have three kids spaced two years apart.

It's not that important, but it was a darn good plan. I chose four, based on very concrete and logical reasons. When I was in second grade, my family went to Circus World. Johanna, my older sister, and I rode the roller coasters together. Amy was five at the time, and really wanted to ride, however, she needed someone to go with her. Mom couldn't go because she was pregnant with Christine—the fifth in line. Katie wasn't eligible because she was just one at the time. Dad didn't want to go, because he gets motion sick and hates roller coasters. Amy begged and Dad caved. He always was a softie. Now that I have children of my own, I understand why.

He told her he'd go, at the same time threatening if she didn't like it, he'd never ride on another roller coaster with her again. As you can imagine, she hated it. It scared the life out of her. On the outside, though, her little face was smiling and she was screaming—the good kind—for all she was worth.

There's a point to this. Everyone should have a roller coaster partner. No one should feel like the odd-man out. And you can't just have two. Two? There's no detective work in figuring out who hit the kid crying or who grabbed the toy from the toddler. It's obvious—your only other child! No, I need a challenge. I want to put good use to my deductive reasoning, interrogative and problem-solving skills. There's a reason I went to college.

I'm getting ahead of myself. Right now, I'm carrying a child that has a very small chance of living. It killed my plan. Honestly, I'm more worked up about what life will be like if this baby does live. How long will he live? It's a reoccurring question. One I can't get out of my mind, because there's no way anyone can answer it.

Will he have a normal life? Will he be sick all the time or tired all the time? Will he live past adolescence? Will there ever be a day when I won't be thinking about this baby's heart? Does the parent of a heart baby ever feel at peace?

If you think about it too long, it drives you mad. So, for now, I push the questions out of my mind (knowing they'll pop up later like a helium balloon pulled to the ground and refusing to stay there) and focus on parenting the girls. Right now, I have to concentrate on getting through this echo so I can pick them up from Bridget's.

I sign in and wait for my name to be called. The waiting room is a good size, and there are quite a few families already waiting. Several have infants still in carriers, their tiny bodies already burdened down by disease or defect. This will be me . . . should baby boy live. We'll be visiting the cardiologist on a regular basis. The thought is overwhelming, but the alternative is worse. I wonder how those parents feel about this place. Sad they're here, or happy to have such good doctors? Or both?

Dr. Donofrio is awesome. She's professional, yet personal; optimistic, yet realistic. A great match for Henry and me. We both love her—well as much as we can love someone we've only met four times.

Amanda is my technician again. She moves the ultrasound probe over my uterus like a kid driving cars across the floor, in slow, steady patterns, moving it this way and that. Dr. Donofrio reads the echo and informs me nothing has changed. They still can't get a full picture of the right ventricle, the pulmonary arteries are still tiny and stretched and the tricuspid valve is not visible. The good news is that there isn't any change with the function. The heart seems to be doing enough of its job to keep the baby alive. She warns me once again that this is not an easy fix.

"Your son will probably be in the hospital for up to the first year of his life. There's no real knowing how long it will take. You need to prepare for the long haul."

"I've been thinking about the lengthy stay," I say. "I'll be able to bring the girls with me to the hospital, right? I can't just leave them behind."

She takes a deep breath. "Life is going to be difficult for awhile. You may not be able to make visits to the hospital and keep on top of the girls at home. You'll feel like you aren't doing a good job at either. Many moms face this situation, and end up bringing siblings for short visits. You'll need to line up help. You can't be in two places at once. You'll work out a routine, things will fall into place and it will get done.

"I'd like you to contact the OB we use to deliver our heart babies. His name is Dr. Downing. Tell the receptionist you're being referred by Children's. He'll contact your OB to transfer any files he needs, and will work with you and them as to when he wants to start seeing you."

The thought of leaving my daughters for extended periods of time doesn't sit well with me. In my car, I dial Bridget to let her know I'm on my way.

"What'd she say?" she asks.

"Nothing different. Everything's the same, including the plan," I say.

"Then, what's up? What aren't you telling me?" she says. She knows me well. There's no use trying to hide anything.

"We talked about the hospital stay. She warned me it's not a place for the girls. That it'll be too boring for them," I say.

"She doesn't know the girls. And she doesn't know you," she says. "You know we're all here to do anything you need. Heather, Katie, Willa, me . . . between us, we'll be able to handle the girls."

"I know. I know. I really want them with me, though. I think it's the best thing for them. Can you imagine a year—A YEAR—of your mom being gone all the time, without you? I think it's much better to try it at least. I want to take their craft things and books and some Polly Pockets. I can change the stuff out when they're bored."

"They'll do fine, Leighann," Bridget says.

"Speaking of which, how'd they do today?" I ask.

"Ainsley needed a few snuggles. Natalie's fine. You know her. She and Maggie disappeared all afternoon and are probably somewhere in the basement, organizing a neighborhood school. Those two . . ."

This is what I need—real conversation about something other than what's coming full steam ahead in eight short weeks. I spend enough time worrying about what I won't be able to do.

CHRISTMAS. WHAT CAN I say about Christmas? It came and went like all the others. We spent time with family. Laughed, played games, ate too many cookies. We measured my girth, compared it to Henry's and found that once again my husband's still bigger than me even when I'm in the third trimester. In all fairness to him, I still have several weeks to go. We should also note that he's a giant. A giant that produces large children. I've gone from feeling like a fat, but still graceful whale, to a walrus hefting her weight across the sand with every move. Sometimes I even bellow when rising from the couch. If I get any bigger, there's danger the males may start bellowing, too, and throwing their tusks around. I have faith in my husband, though. He's huge and has large incisors. He's bound to be the winner.

Natalie told people I was pregnant long before I actually was. This proved for several awkward and embarrassing conversations. For example, when she told my mother-in-law at a family dinner, "My mommy's having a baby," you can imagine everyone's excitement and surprise. When I explained I wasn't actually having a baby, they looked at me through tiny slits of eyes and pursed lips. *Sure, right, no baby. Gotcha. Just let us know when we can tell the news to everyone. Until then, our lips are sealed.* It took quite a bit of convincing for them to understand it was the child, not the mother who was in denial.

Or the time she told a little old lady behind us in line at the grocery store. I mean, really, what do you say to a smiling old lady? My child's really, really wanting another sibling, but we mean parents just aren't ready yet. When we did get pregnant, Natalie was ecstatic. Her prayers (yes, she was praying for a baby) were being answered! We told her before the diagnosis, way back in August. We told her all the family birthdays and holidays we had to get through before he'd be born, ending with Valentine's Day. She knows we only have one more holiday to go, and has been preparing non-stop.

The other day, she was piling things onto her dresser. "Mom, these are little pieces and baby boy can't have them," she said. I assured her it'd be quite some time before he'd get into her stuff. Later, that day, I overheard her saying to Ainsley, "When baby boy gets here, no hitting. Be gentle. And no telling him he can't come into your room. He's little."

We were all hanging out in my bed this morning since I'm still as sick as a dog. Natalie was singing into her toy microphone and rubbing my belly. The baby moved. Her eyes lit up. I've been trying to let her feel him move for quite some time. This is the first time we were successful. She kept trying to get him to move again. She leaned down and said loudly into her microphone, now pressed against my tummy, "Are you ready to come out here, baby boy?"

Natalie knows the baby has a boo-boo on his heart. She hears me pray for God to heal the baby . . . that he'll be all right. When I tell her that he'll be in the hospital longer than mommy, she nods as if she understands. It's clear she doesn't. Bridget and our friend, Heather, are due within two weeks of me. I tell Natalie their babies will come home with them. That seems to register for her. "Why do they get to come home and baby boy doesn't?" she asks, making me wonder if she thought all babies stayed longer than their moms.

"Because their babies don't have boo-boos, sweetie. Our baby does. He'll have to stay where the doctors can help him, and make him better. We'll visit him every day and take him cards and gifts."

This is the hardest part for me. Knowing this pregnancy will have such an effect on my four-year-old. Ainsley's too young to really get what's going on. At two-and-a-half, if the baby doesn't make it, it'll be a tiny blip on her screen. It will bring Natalie to her knees. With her age, and how much she's already bonded, she won't understand at all. I'm afraid she'll think it's her fault. I wish I could encase her into an emotional bubble for the next year, and pop it only when things are okay.

I'm kind of wishing for a bubble for myself, too. Planning out the number of kids I want is just the tip of the iceberg. I plan everything. I'm someone who, when traveling, takes a notebook containing numbered tabs, corresponding to each day we'll be traveling. Behind each day, there is a printout of our hotel reservations, driving directions between stops, suggested sightseeing activities (must-sees, top 10 lists, area highlights), and anything else I think pertinent to the day.

I'm the same person who numbered her moving boxes and made an excel spreadsheet with the corresponding numbers and a list of contents inside the box. Time consuming, but considerably worth it when you're looking for the blender a week after the move.

I also plan out my menus a week (sometimes two, or possibly a whole month) in advance, so I can grocery shop once a week and know exactly what I'm having for dinner on any given night.

I sound fun, don't I? Unlike Forrest Gump, my mama never told me a life was like a box of chocolates. She taught me how to make the chocolates, and plan exactly what I wanted in each spot.

I don't know that person anymore (me, not my mother). I've lost all ability to plan. For one thing, it's hard planning when the future's so, obviously, up in the air. We have no idea what's going to happen at birth, let alone how many months we'll be tied to a hospital room after that. I can't make any plans for traveling, or visiting friends, or deciding if I need to get a new car with the pending arrival of the new baby . . . because it may be pending forever.

It's not just the big decisions either. I haven't made a weekly menu in months (gasp!). All my mental planning energies are being used up to make decisions and plans for the baby's arrival. I don't like the new me, but can't muster the brain cells to find myself.

Here I am facing the final month of planning before our son's birth day. We meet once more for a routine echo with Amanda, and a consultation with Dr. Donofrio.

"Okay, guys," Dr. Donofrio says as she comes into the conference room. "This is it." She takes out her pad of paper and her pen and draws a heart. By now, we know the heart parts by memory. Right atrium, left atrium, left ventricle, dotted line where the right ventricle and tricuspid valve hopefully are, the mitral valve, the aorta and the pulmonary arteries branching off to each side, like arms stretched out wide to embrace someone.

"I'm having a hard time seeing the ductus—the blood vessel that allows blood flow in utero and closes within forty-eight hours after birth. In and of itself, if the ductus isn't present it may not be a big problem. We see that sometimes. It actually eliminates an entire set of scenarios surrounding the ductus, and whether we'd have to try and keep it open with medicine.

"Instead of a ductus, I'm seeing a web of extra vessels. When the blood has nowhere to go, the body makes new vessels to give it a place to flow. These are called collaterals. They may help supply blood to the lungs. If we don't need them, we have ways of dealing with them in the cath lab that aren't invasive.

"I'm also still unable to see the right ventricle. We really tried to get it today just to have a clue what's going on, but the chest wall is in the way. We're either looking at a perfect unseeable right ventricle, Tetralogy of Fallot, or a hypoplastic right ventricle with tricuspid atresia. Unfortunately, we won't know until birth. Right now, the plan is to deliver at Washington Hospital Center. However, if it's okay with you, I'd like to change that and have you deliver here at Children's. I keep going over every detail in my head, and we've eliminated every possible danger, except transport. I'm confident we'll be able to stabilize the baby after birth, but it'd be much easier on him to not have to transfer hospitals, exposing his heart to the air." She looks at me expectantly.

"Sure. We trust your judgment. Let's do it here. What does that mean?" I ask.

"It means that we'll have to fill out paperwork for the city. We aren't a labor and delivery hospital, so we have to file for a special permit. It's no harder for you, we do all the legwork. You'll sign some releases today. Because we're a pediatric hospital, it means we don't have the facilities or staff to work with adults, so Washington Hospital Center will send a team over here, instead of us sending a team there. They'll work out of one of our ORs and will bring anything they think they need that we don't have. We'll go over every possible emergency that could happen to you during the surgery, and Dr. Downing will prepare for each one.

"When the baby's born, he'll immediately be put on a breathing machine and assessed by a team of specialists. I'll do an echo to try and figure out how big the right ventricle is. From this less invasive test we'll be able to determine what questions remain, and choose from a list of other tests, as to what the best next step is. This could include anything from MRI, CT scan, or catheterization. These tests will let us know whether the baby needs any cardiac intervention or surgery. If not, it'll just be a matter of protecting the heart. We'll push heart surgery off as long as we can to get him bigger and stronger. Stacey, our guest services liaison, will take you up to the CICU to show you around. It's the specialized Cardiac ICU I told you about."

We walk with Stacey to the third floor of the other wing of the hospital and come to a set of locked doors. Stacey badges us in. We arrive at the nurses' station. "This is Miss Toni," she says waving her hand at the lady behind the desk. "This is Henry and Leighann Marquiss. Their baby will be staying with us in a few weeks."

Miss Toni stands up and extends her hand. "It's so nice to meet y'all," she says.

"Thank you," I say. "Can you tell us a little about the unit?"

"Our unit's special because it's an intensive care unit especially for heart patients. There's one nurse to every patient. If we're real busy, a nurse might have two, but no more than that. We get kids of all ages, but we're especially fond of the babies. We bond with them quickly and love on them as much as we can. The nurses take such good care of them."

My fears of my child lying by himself in an empty hospital room are answered. Tears of relief run down my cheeks. I look around quickly for a tissue. Miss Toni hands me one from a box on the desk without missing a beat.

"I'm sorry," I murmur. "I don't know why I'm crying."

"It's okay," she says sweetly. "You've got a lot going on."

"Why don't we walk down the hall so you can see what the rooms are like. The charge nurse can tell us if there's an empty one right now," Stacey says.

AFTER TOURING THE CICU, we make our way across the parking lot to the physicians' offices at Washington Hospital Center to meet Dr. Downing. He's extremely friendly, with a great bedside manner. He knows why we're here and goes out of his way to make things easier. He looks over my medical history, including the past pregnancies.

"Is this your first c-section?" he asks.

It is, so he goes over what happens during a routine c-section and how mine will be different. "Typically, we make the smallest incision possible in the uterus and then push and tug until we get the baby out. Because of your son's condition, we don't want to do any pushing or tugging, and I want to make sure to alleviate any kind of stress on the heart. I plan to cut a bigger incision, so I can get my hand inside to cup around the baby's heart, and protect it on the way out. Did you have an epidural with either of your prior deliveries?"

"With my second," I say. " I've heard the dad can't be in the room during a c-section spinal block. He was there for my epidural. Is there any way he can be there this time?"

"I don't see why not. Also, once you're admitted to Hospital Center, you'll be able to go back and forth between the hospitals. For safety reasons, you can't go until you're able to use your legs, but as soon as the spinal wears off, I'll clear you. You can either call for an escort, or Henry can wheel you across the parking lot in a wheelchair.

"I need to see you once a week for the remaining two weeks to make sure everything's proceeding as planned, and I also need you to go downstairs to have a Biophysical Profile (BPP). In fact, I'll walk you down today, and see if they can fit you in while you're here. It's a lot like an ultrasound, where we're able to look at different physical signs of life—like movement, heart rate, diaphragm movement, muscle tone, and the amniotic fluid level. Let's head down there now if you don't have any more questions."

He walks us down to radiology, and somehow gets them to squeeze us in. On his way out, he hands me a business card for the radiology department and says, "Ask them what their availability is next week and the week after and take appointments that suit your schedule. Then, call my office and make appointments on the same days so you don't have to drive down twice. Is there anything else I can answer for you today?"

"I think we're good. Thank you," I say slipping the card into my wallet. Only two more weeks of doctor appointments before the big day. I can't believe we're almost there.

I lean into Henry's body while we wait. I feel all the energy leave my body through my toes, as if I'm a bathtub whose plug was pulled. Henry puts his arm around me and kisses my head. "Just a little bit longer," he murmurs.

Henry's sawing logs peacefully beside me as if we aren't standing on the edge of a cliff about to jump. It's the night before our son's birth day. I'm having a hard time falling asleep. My day was filled with mixed emotions. All my planning ended up on the editing room floor, as we worked out what needed to be done. I envisioned driving the girls to my sister, Johanna's, and saying good-bye there. I forgot I had a pre-surgery appointment at Children's, so Henry ended up convincing me to let him take them. At the last minute I wasn't ready to let them go. I suddenly felt panicky and rushed. I hugged them hard to my chest as if I were saying good-bye for the last time. I knew the next time I'd see their cherub faces our lives would be changed forever. It wasn't so much them I was saying good-bye to, but to life as we know it. I wasn't ready to let go.

Henry and the girls headed west while I headed east into the city to sign consent forms, rehearse the birthing plan once more, and have my blood drawn so my type is on file in case I need a transfusion. Now, lying here in the darkness, I have nothing more to think of than my babies, who are far from me tonight, and the one who is ever-close, about to make a dramatic entrance into this crazy world. In the last week two people asked if I'm excited. Um, no. I'm scared to death. As long as I'm pregnant, the baby's alive. He doesn't need oxygen right now and he's perfectly protected in my womb. Emotionally, I wish I could keep him inside an extra month. I vacillate between holding firm to the belief that God is going to intervene and believing the medical community's prediction that he has a slim-to-none chance. Even if God did tell me the baby would live, He didn't say how long.

WHEN THE ALARM sounds I feel as if I've just closed my eyes. It's 4:30 A.M. on February 19, 2009. It's go time!

Our tires are warming the pavement by 5 A.M. We drive the same car we drove to the hospital to deliver Ainsley, and the same one Henry drove when Natalie was on her way (he was out of town when I went into labor). I gulp back bile the entire ride, hoping I can get through the next two hours without vomiting.

I'd be surprised if I needed all my fingers to count the number of cars in the parking garage at this hour. The hallways seem dim, as if even the lights know it's too soon to shine brightly. We make our way to the surgical check-in on the second floor. One lone receptionist awaits our arrival. Although I spent time yesterday filling out paperwork, there are still a few things that need done. "When you filled out the birth certificate, you didn't list a name. What should we put on the crib?" the receptionist says. I look at Henry. After many discussions and short-list of boy names other than Henry Ernest, he still hasn't decided.

"Just put baby boy," I say. "We haven't named him yet."

Nausea sweeps over me again overtaking my entire body like a giant tidal wave. Beads of perspiration dot my forehead. My arms and back, which were cool just a minute ago, stick to my shirt. "Do you have a trashcan handy?" I ask haltingly.

"Are you okay?" the receptionist asks, simultaneously reaching under her desk, and producing a plastic bin.

"No. I'm still having morning sickness. The quicker I can lie down the better," I answer.

"Dad, why don't you stay here and finish the intake and we'll let Mom go back and lie down in the prep room." She picks up her phone, "Mel, can you come up here and get Mrs. Marquiss? She's not feeling well."

Within seconds, Mel, my OR nurse, is opening the big wooden door a few feet away from the reception window. I waddle through the door and follow her down the hallway. "We're here on the right. Just lie on the bed and I'll get you a gown. We'll get started," she says. I lie quietly on the bed hoping the contents of my stomach stay put. Henry comes in a few minutes later, and sits in a chair beside the bed. "You feel better yet?" he asks gently.

"No, worse. Can you find me something . . . anything . . . as fast as you can?" I feel the gag start in my lower abs, and ripple upward with brunt force. Henry scrambles to find something.

"Nurse!" he calls. "Do you have something my wife can use? She's sick!"

His name comes out of my mouth in a garbled fashion. It's hard to talk and try not to throw up at the same time. Last night's salsa and tacos find their way to the surface. Henry throws his hands under my mouth as the first of it comes out. Mel shoves a mauve half-moon basin under my mouth as the second round starts. When it's over, I lie back down exhausted and clammy.

"Dad, you can wash your hands over here," Mel says leading Henry to a sink mounted to the mint green tiled wall.

"I'm sorry, honey," I say.

"No problem. That's what I'm here for." Henry smiles at me, while scrubbing cilantro and tomatoes from his fingers.

After Mel gets my vitals and weight, Dr. Downing and another OB come to my bedside to go over the procedure. "This is my colleague, Dr. Fries. She's one of the high-risk pregnancy obstetricians at Washington Hospital Center. She's going to assist me with the surgery. After you've gotten your spinal, we'll check you to make sure you can't feel anything. Once we're sure you're numb, I'll start the incision. I'll cut through your skin and then your uterus. As I explained before, I'll make a slightly larger than normal incision in the uterus so I can cup my hand around the baby's heart, and bring him out with as little stress as possible. Once he's out, we'll hand him to the pediatric team and stitch your uterus. It'll probably take about an hour for the whole thing, with most of it on the backend. Do you have any questions?"

"No. I think I'm good. Thanks," I say.

"Great. Just sign here to say you understand everything and you give consent to go through with the procedure," he says. I sign on the dotted line.

"Hi, I'm Dr. Cartwright, Director of Anesthesiology at the Washington Hospital Center. This is Dr. Moody. He'll be assisting me. We'll be performing your spinal block today and manage your vitals during the procedure. As far as the procedure itself, if you feel like you need it, we'll have sedatives available. We'd really like to try not to use them because they'll transfer to the baby. Since he's going into a procedure himself, we'd like him to be clean. However, if we get in there, and you need something, you tell us. It's okay. His team will account for him having a little something on board. Do you have any questions?"

"I've heard dads have to wait until the prep and spinal are done before coming into the room. Can my husband please be in there during the spinal?" I hold my breath for the answer.

Dr. Cartwright hesitates. He looks at Henry and then at me. "We really hate to have the dads in there. It makes a lot of people woozy to watch the procedure."

My heart starts racing at the thought of being in the OR without Henry. "He watched my epidural and didn't get woozy. This kind of thing doesn't bother him. I'd like him there."

"Why?" Dr. Cartwright presses.

Because I'm scared to death. Because my baby might not live. Because he's my husband. I can't say any of that because I feel myself crumbling from the inside out, like a building detonated from within. Without Henry by my side I, too, will be a mess of debris, lying haphazard on the floor. "He's my rock," I manage to eek out with tears in my eyes.

Dr. Cartwright exhales audibly torn between compassion and protocol. "Look," he says talking straight to Henry. "If you feel the tiniest bit woozy you need to excuse yourself from the room. This is a pediatric hospital. There's no one here to help you if you go down. We're here to take care of your wife and child, not you. We can't afford to lose any staff to support you. Do you understand what I'm saying?"

"Sure," Henry says, "not a problem."

"Okay, you can come in." Turning back to me he says, "Any other questions?"

"No, I'm good. Thank you," I say in a shaky voice.

"Great. Sign here that you understand the procedure and agree to have us treat you," he says. I sign the consent form.

Dr. Cartwright and Dr. Moody leave, but are quickly replaced. "Hi, I'm Dr. Levy, Director of Cardiac Anesthesiology here at Children's. As soon as your son's born, Dr. Downing will hand him to me. I'll walk him into the adjoining OR and immediately put him on a ventilator. I'll make sure he's stable and then watch his vitals, while Dr. Boyajian and his team perform surgery." Catching on, I reach out my hand for the pen to sign yet another consent form, this time for a procedure on my child. I'm starting to feel like a deli owner who should hand out numbers as more doctors line up to talk to us. The plastic surgeon is next.

"Hi, I'm Dr. Boyajian. I'll be placing a Gortex cover over your son's heart today to protect him from infection. I believe Dr. Donofrio went over a lot of the reasoning behind this, but do you have any questions for me about the procedure itself?"

"No, thank you," I say.

"Okay, we'll see you when we come upstairs to check his surgical site," he says shaking my and Henry's hands. I sign his consent form, too.

"Hello!" Dr. Donofrio says cheerfully. "How are you feeling this morning?"

"A little nervous," I admit. "But it's time."

"Yep, just a few more minutes. You met the team, right?"

"I met a lot of them!" I say.

"There's quite a few fantastic doctors on hand to make sure we have everything we need to make today a success. There'll be about ten personnel in your room and twenty more waiting in the adjoining OR to work on your son. Your team's mostly from Washington Hospital Center, and your son's team is ours. After the procedure, we'll try to bring him through here on his way upstairs, so you can catch a glimpse of him. Otherwise, you'll have to wait until you can use your legs and come over to visit. Okay, this is it. I'll be going between the rooms. See you soon." She squeezes my hand before leaving.

I look at Henry and smile weakly. Then, I remember. "Hey, my mom is on her way. She has no clue where we are. We should let someone know she's coming."

"I'll find someone," he says and takes off down the hall. About a week ago, my mom called, offering to be here today. "Mom, I'm okay. I don't need you there. I'll have Henry. Really, I don't want you to have to take off work," I said.

"I know you're private and hate feeling vulnerable," she said. "But think about it and let me know. I want to take off work to be with you. Work is the last thing on my mind. Henry will probably be at Children's with the baby. You might like having someone with you in your hospital room while you're waiting on your legs." After a few days of thinking about it, I decided she was right. I made sure Henry was okay with it, then called her back to accept her offer. Willa offered to be here, too, but came down with pneumonia a few days ago and doesn't want to take any chances. We'll keep her updated by phone.

Mel is working through her checklist, making sure we're ready to go when they call for us. Henry returns and sits quietly beside me to wait. We chat idly to pass the time. The hospital is pretty quiet still. We've been scheduled before any of the other procedures, so we'll be done and out before things get busy. There's literally no one else in this department except our teams and us. It's quite surreal. All this fuss for one little baby. Our baby.

"Can you get me that basin again?" I say. My stomach lurches. I sit up, just in time to vomit into a waiting plastic half-moon made.

"Better?" he says. I nod.

"Okay, we have the green light. You ready?" Mel says coming to the side of the bed.

"As ready as I'll ever be," I say.

She raises the railings on my bed and unlocks the wheels. Dr. Cartwright and Dr. Moody roll me down a long white hallway, with gurneys parked along one side. We pass one big door and then come to a second. They carefully swing my gurney into the room and roll it up beside a clean surgical bed. The room is completely white with silver metal accessories. Cold and plain . . . exactly how you think of a hospital OR. Medical cabinets full of equipment and supplies line one side of the room. A sink and more cabinetry fill another side. *This is so unnatural,* I think. *This isn't the way it should be. I never want to do this again.*

"First, we're going to give you the spinal. Once you're all set, we'll move you into place for the surgery," Dr. Cartwright says. "Do you remember how to sit?"

"Yes, I think so," I say. Henry helps me move into the sitting position. I turn to face him with my legs dangling off the side of the gurney. He's sitting on a stool. I brace my shoulders against his chest. We clasp hands in my lap, under the bulge of my stomach. Our heads are bowed in toward each other, ears practically touching.

"Okay, now arch your back like a scared cat and stay as still as possible," Dr. Cartwright says. "I'm going to sterilize the entry point. You might feel a small prick, followed by pressure in your spine."

I arch my back and try not to breathe, but the anxiety is getting to me. I try rhythmic breathing to slow my heart rate. As I'm breathing, I feel the tears I've been holding back all morning burning at the sides of my eyes. I'm breathing audibly now, like a train huffing up a track. Tears run down my cheeks.

"I'm scared," I whisper in Henry's ear.

"It's okay," he says in mine.

"Not of the needle. Of what will happen next. There's no going back. He's either going to live or die and we find out soon," I say. The tears are falling faster now, bouncing off his hands. I've always loved his hands. Twice the size of mine with smooth, round fingertips.

"It'll be okay. It's no big deal," he murmurs.

No big deal! We're only just about to have a baby with his heart sticking out of his chest!

"You can lie down now," Dr. Cartwright says. He and Henry help me down and I stare at the ceiling. The tears have stopped, but those that remain on my face itch my cheeks and eyes. I reach up to brush them away. Dr. Cartwright and Dr. Moody come to my sides. "On the count of three," Dr. Cartwright says. On three, I'm moved to the surgical bed, just like you see in the movies. I stretch my arms out to the side, and they strap my arms down for safety— possibly theirs, in case I go crazy and try to hit someone. Or, perhaps, so I can't escape by army-crawling my way out of the room.

"Okay, Dad," Dr. Moody says, "You're going to sit on a stool right here above Mom's shoulder. I think you'll be out of the way." Henry grabs a rolling stool and perches over my left ear.

Now that the spinal is complete and I'm in place, the rest of the team begins entering the room. I hear cabinet doors clang open and shut. Drawers slide on their tracks. Dr. Cartwright and Dr. Moody hook me up to various instruments to record my vitals. My chest tightens. My breathing picks up a little. *If this baby was healthy, I'd totally roll off this table right now. This is ridiculous.*

I can hear my heart beating on a monitor to my right. I notice it starting to beat faster, then faster. I'm running a marathon.

"How we doing?" Dr. Moody says from behind me.

"Anxious," I say. There's an edge to my voice. "Very anxious. I don't think I can do this and I'm not kidding. Get me off this table. NOW!"

As I say the words, my stomach lurches again. I turn my head, managing to vomit over my shoulder. Henry puts his hands up in time to catch most of it, but a little splatters on my gown and hair.

Dr. Cartwright and Dr. Moody move quickly to assist Henry and stabilize me. After I'm done, I turn my eyes to the composite board-tiled ceiling. *This sucks.*

"Okay," Dr. Moody says turning up a dial on his medicine-dispersing machine. "You should start to feel better now. That's a normal reaction to the anesthesia we just put in your spine. Some people have a panic attack. How are you feeling now?"

"Actually, I feel really good," I say and I mean it. I hear someone offer to take Henry to wash his hands in the sink down past my feet at the far end of the room. "Are you sure?" he says. "I don't want to get in the way."

"It's okay," the voice says. "We still have time and those paper towels aren't going to cut it. I'm one of two anesthesiologists on hand to help the Hospital Center personnel. I don't think they'll miss me for a few minutes." When he's settled back in, he wipes my shoulder and hair as best he can. "You okay?" he offers quietly.

"Yeah. I think I am. I feel a lot better now. That was weird. I'm not doing very well handling the pressure."

"You're doing great," he says. "You just reacted to the medicine. Don't worry about it." He massages my shoulder. I watch the nurses put up a blue paper curtain at my chest. I can no longer see more than a foot in front of me.

Dr. Fries and Dr. Downing approach the side of the bed. "Okay," Dr. Downing says. "We're ready to start. I'm going to do a test cut and you tell me if you feel anything." He pauses. "Anything?"

"Absolutely nothing," I say. It's really strange and a little scary, because I don't even feel him touching me.

"Dr. Downing, can you tell us when it's about time to pull the baby out? We brought our camera and I want Henry to take a picture."

"Sure!" Dr. Downing says. "It's going to be about twenty minutes."

I look back up at the white ceiling tiles, amazed that not five minutes ago I was having a panic attack and vomiting on my husband (again!), and now I'm lying here being sliced open like a watermelon without a care in the world. I'm so calm and warm. I imagine myself lying on a desert rock like a lizard sunning itself. Relaxed. Calm. Drowsy. I'm cognizant enough to know that it's not normal, but relish the reprieve from all the worry over the last few months.

"Okay, Dad. Get the camera ready. He's coming out," Dr. Downing says. "Definitely a boy!" Suddenly there's urgency in the footsteps around the room.

I hear three tiny mews like a kitten; sounding a little hoarse and weak. Then voices:

"Got him?"

"Yeah."

"Who has the cord? The cord! Who has the cord?"

"I have it!"

Then the banging of double swinging doors.

Henry sits back down on his stool. "Did you get pictures?" I say anxiously. "Any good ones?"

"Yeah, I got a few." He smiles, "You want to see your son?"

I nod my head. There are no words. Tears stream down my face. I heard my son cry, which means he took breath into his lungs. He was born alive!

It seems like just a few minutes later, when Dr. Donofrio comes rushing back into the room. She's dressed in blue scrubs. I can tell she's excited as she comes up beside the bed. "Okay," she says. "There were a few surprises today . . . your son's heart is definitely outside his chest, as we suspected. However, it's not open to the air. There's a thin skinlike material the body made to cover the heart. Dr. Boyajian says it's not typical skin. At this point, we don't know much more. What we do know is that your baby does *not* need surgery to put on a Gortex cover. This is amazing news.

"The other surprise is that he was born with something called an omphalocele. It's when part of the gut forms in a sac outside the body. These are more common than ectopia cordis. We deal with them a lot. For whatever reason, it didn't show up in any of the sonograms. It's really small in comparison to what we normally see. Dr. Sandler, the general surgeon, will take a look at it, but it really isn't going to be an issue. The biggest issue will be if your son's right ventricle is big enough. We'll be able to start running some tests later this afternoon. For now, we'll take him upstairs. It was a little sticky at first, but Dr. Levy stabilized him. He's now on a breathing tube and has good vitals. We'll let you know more as we go along."

"Hand me the camera so I can see what she's talking about," I say after she leaves. "Did you see the omphalocele?"

"Yeah, I noticed something below the heart when I was taking pictures. I guess that's what it is," Henry says.

We flip through the three pictures Henry took, trying to get a good look at the heart and omphalocele, while Dr. Fries talks about her veterinarian's real estate to Dr. Downing. They're stitching my uterus closed behind the blue paper curtain.

"How you doing?" Henry says over my shoulder a few minutes later.

"I'm okay," I say. "But you know how when someone rubs your hand in one spot over and over it gets annoying?"

He nods.

"That's how I feel right now. They just keep stitching and stitching and stitching. I mean come on, already."

"We can hear you," Dr. Downing says in a teasing tone.

"Oh, my gosh! I totally forgot. I can't see you because of the curtain, so I guess I didn't think about the fact that you can hear me."

Henry reaches up and flicks the curtain with his finger. "It's paper. Of course they can hear you."

"I'm also on drugs. Can we chalk it up to drugs?" I say completely embarrassed. Everyone laughs.

"It's kind of a tactical error to rush your surgeon," Dr. Downing teases.

The stitching finally ends, and I'm wheeled back down the long white hallway to the same room where I was prepped pre-surgery. It becomes my post-op recovery room. We soak in the stillness, as Mel takes my vitals. I smell the vomit on my gown from earlier. I can't wait to change.

"Surprise! Surprise!" Dr. Donofrio's voice comes closer as she walks into my room. There's some commotion as a team of nurses and physicians bring a hospital crib on wheels into the room. "Help me sit up," I say to Henry. I'm still paralyzed from the spinal and want to make sure I have a good view. I know the visit won't last long.

My first glimpse is of a tiny baby who looks to be sleeping. His nose and cheeks are covered with tape, securing a breathing tube in his nose. I try to memorize everything I can in the twenty seconds they have him in the room. I gaze at his wavy light brown hair, soft and wispy like a duckling. His lips and chin resemble Ainsley, but with half his face covered, it's hard to know for sure how far the resemblance goes. As they wheel him from the room, I realize I'm holding my breath. I let it out slowly.

"He has hair," I gush to Henry.

"He looks like Ainsley," he gushes back.

"Did you get a picture?" I ask. Henry nods. Were it not for the drugs, I might be able to come up with something else to say, but nothing comes to me. My baby is on a ventilator in an ICU somewhere several floors above me.

Mom arrives soon after the baby's visit. We all agree that Henry should stay with the baby and mom will come with me. We can let him know later where my room is across the street. We'll use our cell phones if there's an emergency, or a decision we need to discuss. Dr. Downing, as my physician, and Dr. Moody, as my anesthesiologist, supervise my transfer. We roll out of the surgical area into an elevator that goes down to the parking garage. A security guard holds the door open at the parking garage exit and walks us across empty parking spaces a few hundred yards to a closed door. As we get closer, he speaks into his walkie-talkie, "Patient approaching." As if on cue, the closed door opens with the help of another security guard. "Yours from here," the first guard says to the second. A slight nod of the head and I'm now another hospital's charge.

Forty-five minutes later, I'm settled in my room on the post-surgical floor. Since my baby isn't in this hospital, they don't put me with the labor and delivery patients. I'm not sure how I feel about this. In one sense, it'll be nice to not have little babies in view, as I worry about my own, but, in another, it feels weird to totally ignore the reason I'm here.

"Did you decide what to name the baby?" my good friend, Bridget, says over the phone. It's about three o'clock in the afternoon. My head is in the clouds still from the painkillers I'm taking around the clock.

"No. Can you believe it? Henry kept saying it was a game-day decision. I asked him this morning and he said he still isn't sure. I honestly think he's waiting to see if the baby is going to make it through the day. We're still calling him baby boy."

"It may take time . . . Jason's about to leave here. He should be to you guys in about an hour. Call me if you think of anything you need. There are plenty of people chompin' at the bit to help."

The sky's dark. Jason and Henry spent the greater part of the day over at Children's keeping a watchful eye on the baby. They're out getting me Pad Thai, because we all know a good meal is the best medicine for a nervous mother. That and oxycodone. My mother is about to take her leave. She's been a trooper, keeping me company all day. It's past visiting hours at Children's and I've yet to use my legs. Not having gotten my hopes up that I'd get over there today, I'm only a little disappointed. I can see his hospital from my window. He's lying over there somewhere, separated only by a few hundred yards of pavement, without his mommy to hold him. I can't imagine what it's like for mothers who don't find out until after birth about their baby's heart defect. Many times, babies are flown here before the mother is cleared for discharge. She must wait several days to get here. Sometimes, by then it's too late.

THE SUN STREAMS through my window early Friday morning. I'd like to say it's this wonderful fact of nature that wakes me from a peaceful slumber. Instead, I must admit it's another fact of nature—a full bladder. Even more pressing than the fact I have to pee like a racehorse, is the apparent fact that the nurse didn't wake me in the night to give me pain meds as I requested. Every inch of my sagging and deflated middle region is on fire. The only solution I can think of to eliminate one aspect of my pain is to wet my pants. This seems like an amazing idea until I come to the logical conclusion that I'd then have to sit in my own pee or move so the nurse can clean me. Since moving is what I was trying to eliminate in the first place, I quickly talk myself out of the ridiculous idea.

"Henry," I whisper. He's curled haphazardly on a pull-out chair by the door. He rigged himself a longer bed by propping his feet on an extra sitting chair. The nurses stumbled past him all night, making it impossible for either of us to get good rest.

"Henry," I say louder.

Nothing.

"Henry!" I practically shout.

"Huh?" he says, his voice thick with sleep.

"Come help me out of bed. I can't do it myself."

After a toe-curling trip to the restroom, I buzz the nurse for meds. Aside from the pain, my mind is focused on one thing—how quickly I can see my baby. Dr. Downing clears me for takeoff mid-morning. Henry snags a wheelchair from the hall. I'm still too sore to walk. He pushes me through a labyrinth of hallways that make a shortcut to the connecting parking lot. After lying still for nearly twenty-four hours, doped up on drugs, my brain struggles to adjust to the movement of the walls and pictures as they race past my eyes. I feel like we're going 80 miles an hour.

As we exit through a back door, the February wind hits me in the face, knocking the breath from my body. I squint in the bright sunlight and pull my coat tighter to my chest. Three cold and painfully bumpy minutes later, we enter our son's hospital. Henry flashes his visitor badge at the security desk and keeps moving toward the elevators bypassing the security line.

Henry wheels me into the CICU and to our baby's room. The lights are dimmed. A constant beeping from the monitors and ventilator keep time with his heartbeat. He's lying in a warming bed, the orange light from the heater giving him an unnatural glow. There's a monitor on the left, and under it a series of pumps with lines pushing medications into his veins, keeping him sedated and comfortable. On the right is a ventilator with its own screen, tracking his breathing. Without this machine, my son wouldn't be here. It seems crazy, all the things necessary for one little life.

Henry rolls me over to the bed, and I get a glimpse of a swollen face. Well, half of it, since tape covers his nose and cheeks still. I stroke his soft skin and hair. Moving slowly through the pain, I stand up to get a better view. The nurse retrieves an elevated desk chair from the hallway, so I don't have to stand.

"Do you want to hold him?" she says.

"Seriously?" I say. I anticipated it would be weeks before I could hold him. While the nurse goes to find extra hands, Henry helps a second nurse situate a recliner beside the crib. I hobble like an old lady, with bad knees and a crooked back, into the recliner. The respiratory therapist and charge nurse arrive to help with the transition. The respiratory therapist keeps the vent tube secure, while the nurse grabs all the lines and leads and situates them as the charge nurse lifts my son into my lap. The vent tube, leads, and lines are then clipped to the pillow my son lays on. I'm now holding my baby for the first time.

I can't believe how fat he is. The girls were long and thin with frog legs. Especially Ainsley. Man, that girl was skinny. You would think the daily root beer floats would have packed on the pounds. But no, she let me do the packing for both of us. Little baby boy did his job and sucked it all out of me. At two weeks early, he's a good eight and a half pounds. His arms and thighs are padded with Michelin-man rolls that make you want to blow raspberries all over him, and he sports a double chin you could store nuts in for winter. "Is this puffiness from his heart condition or is he just fat?" I ask.

"He's just fat," the nurse says. We all laugh.

Dr. Donofrio comes in during the afternoon. "There's good news and there's bad news," she says. "The bad news is that your son's right ventricle is very small. It's called Hypoplastic Right Heart Syndrome (HRHS). We talked about this as a possibility before he was born. If you remember, hypoplastic means underdeveloped, and because of this it doesn't pump blood into the lungs. We fix this with a series of three surgeries, from now until he's between two and four years of age.

"The good news is that he won't need the first surgery. Typically, we do what's called a BT shunt within the first few days to allow more blood flow to the pulmonary arteries. However, your son doesn't have a ductus. His body's compensating in other ways. What's great about this, is that he's able to grow bigger and stronger before going into a major surgery. The stronger he gets, the better his chances are of surviving the surgery."

Henry and I are devastated by the news. We were praying for no heart defect. It lowers the chances of survival from 50/50 to zero. I look at our son, sleeping soundly in his crib. "We need to name him," I say quietly. "I completely understand if you don't want to give him your name." Knowing that eye contact can signal aggression to some mammals, like cats and men, I avert my eyes, giving Henry the space he needs to make a decision.

He sighs. "I think we should name him Henry the Fifth."

Now my eyes are on him. "Are you sure?"

"Yeah. I've been thinking about it. I want to name him Henry. He's my first son. I can't seem to call him anything else. Look at him. He looks like a Henry, right?"

"Yep," I nod. "Definitely a Henry. Look at those broad shoulders and thick chest. He's a bruiser."

"We should probably give him a nickname, though. It's already confusing when we're around Dad. There'll be too many Henrys and we can't call him Baby Henry for very long."

"Okay, let's find a nickname that means king, referring to him being the fifth," I suggest.

Henry does an Internet search and starts reading through lists of names. "Ryan!" he says excitedly. "Ryan means 'a little king' in Gaelic. It could be after my brother, too. What do you think?"

"Ryan it is, then."

WHEN DR. DOWNING tells me I'm ready for discharge, I resist the urge to tie myself to the bed and refuse to leave. I'm not ready to leave this place. First of all, my nurse, Gloria, gives the most amazing sponge baths. Secondly, I haven't had to cook or clean for three whole days. I think this deserves noting. But, most important, the thought of leaving the only place where I can sleep within seeing distance of my son is about as appealing as cutting off my big toe. Can I do it? Yes. Do I want to? Heck, no.

Unfortunately, Washington Hospital Center isn't a hotel. Kristen, our social worker at Children's (we are now lucky enough to have our own social worker!) suggests trying the Ronald McDonald House, where Henry's been the last few days.

My first glimpse of the House is a little after 10 P.M., the day of my discharge. I stand looking up at a large white mansion in northeast D.C., a convenient ten-minute drive to our son. I feel a bit like Maria in *The Sound of Music* when she first arrives at the von Trapp home, completely intimidated and a little out of place. I'm supposed to be taking it easy. I wouldn't call sitting and standing by your child's hospital bed for the last eight hours taking it easy. "Limit stairs," Dr. Downing's advice echoes in my mind as I look at two full sets of stairs connected by a landing leading to the front door.

Hunched over from muscle fatigue, I take them slowly. Like a toddler, I put one foot on a step and then the other foot. Both feet hit each step. My body won't do it any other way. By the time I get to the top, my abs are screaming and my groin aching from overcompensating. Henry's holding the door open, his arms weighted down by my bags.

Henry leads the way to our room: up the elevator, down the long hallway, to the very last door in the corner. I collapse on the bed and never want to move again. I nearly fall asleep with my coat and shoes still on. Henry arranges my clothes in the closet, and toiletries around the sink. This is his domain, his home for the last three days. He knows the drill, and the people. I know nothing but the need for more Percocet. I'd doze off right now if it weren't for the fact that I have to pump in an hour. Henry walks my breast milk down to the freezer for the 11 P.M. feeding, and then again for the 4 A.M. feeding. He rocks. The freezer is three floors below us in the basement. At the 7 A.M. feeding, he pries open the taped-shut storm window and puts the milk on the ledge.

"I wish I would have thought of that last night," he says, grinning at his ingenuity. I smile at him, silently hoping a bird won't knock the milk off. Doesn't he know I'm working hard to provide the liquid gold our son needs to grow strong?

He jumps—literally—back in bed. It's now I should tell you the mattress we're sleeping on is a strange sort of air mattress instead of one made with springs. For the record, get the one with springs. Please, just believe me on this one. When Henry lays on his side, my side inflates super high with his displaced air bouncing me up higher. Maybe it doesn't matter with couples more matched in size, but since he's over a foot taller, and more than double my weight, it's not only annoying, it's also very uncomfortable. We try going back to sleep, but it's useless. We give up and start getting ready.

The days at the hospital are full of activity. Kristen comes in every day to make sure we have what we need and that we're doing okay emotionally. "Just wanted to make sure you have your parking sticker for today and remind you that there's a support group meeting this Wednesday in the Heart and Kidney Unit's (HKU) library, just down the hall. It's a great way to meet other families going through the same thing you are, and hear about their journeys."

"Thanks," Henry says taking the flyer. "We'll try to make it."

As Kristen is walking out, Tracey is walking in. Tracey handles all the insurance issues for Ryan's case. "I spoke with your insurance and everything is settled. Your policy is amazing. I've never seen one quite so good. Usually, there's a lifetime cap per person, which means once you reach one, two, maybe three million, you're kicked off the plan. You can imagine, in cases like this, it happens rather quickly. Yours has no lifetime cap. All you should owe is the family deductible."

As Tracey heads out, the child-life specialist, Judy, walks in. She helps families deal with hospital life. "Good morning, I love the music you have playing," she says referring to the classical music coming out of the computer. "It's great stimulation for Ryan, even though he sleeps a lot. Babies love soothing music. Have you thought of when you'll bring your daughters in to meet their brother?"

"We're hoping to bring them in a few days. Maybe Sunday or Monday," Henry says.

"If you wait until Monday, I can help you prepare them to come in. We use pictures and baby dolls to explain everything to small children, so they aren't shocked. It's good for them to have time to process everything first," she says.

Judy leaves. The fellow Kitty, comes in. "Hi, Mr. and Mrs. Marquiss. I just wanted to give you an update on Ryan. As you know he doesn't need the BT shunt procedure. His oxygen saturation levels are staying stable at about eighty. He's breathing over the vent which means that he's initiating more breaths than the ventilator settings require, and is on the lowest setting possible before we turn the machine off. He's doing really well. We want to take him off the ventilator completely, to see if he can breathe on his own. It can be hectic so we're going to ask you to step into the family lounge. We'll come get you when we're ready."

It quickly becomes apparent Ryan needs support to breathe. His little brow is furrowed, like an old farmer whose face gets forged by the sun, and he's breathing through an open mouth. Even with my lack of experience, I can see he's working hard. The team intubates him, which basically means putting the breathing tube back into his nose, and begins doing CPAP trials.

During a CPAP trial, the ventilator settings initiating the breaths for the patient are turned off, and the patient initiates all breaths. The machine responds with a burst of positive pressure to fill the lungs upon inhale. Ryan starts with one hour on CPAP and three hours off (with the vent initiating the breaths). The goal is to get him to three hours on CPAP and one hour off. At that point, he'll be strong enough to try coming off the vent again. CPAPs are much like the training a runner does to get ready for a race. Thus, these CPAP exercises are called sprints.

While Ryan works on his breathing, I continue working on providing nutrition necessary for him to grow. It's been almost a week since his birth, and my milk is coming in today. I've been pumping the tiniest amounts of colostrum up until now. I feel the milk—not in my body, but in my emotions. It's been drama, drama, drama all morning. Everything is either annoying, or the end of the world. I spend the majority of the morning either crying, or trying not to cry. Time tends to mesh together these days, but it's Wednesday. I know, because today, the support group for the CICU parents Kristen told us about is in the HKU library.

"Let's go to group," Henry says. "It starts in five minutes."

"I don't really feel like going today," I mumble.

"Come on. It's good for us to go," he says.

I'm having a hard enough time with my own emotions. A support group is the last thing an introvert needs on a day like today. I'd rather stab myself in the eye with a fork. "I'm going to be here for the next twelve months. I really don't feel the need to go the first week I'm here. If you want to, you can go," I say flatly. There comes a time in everyone's life where the fight or flight mechanism kicks in. Henry intuitively knows flight is the right choice in this situation. He takes wing toward the library.

I move to Ryan's bedside, grateful for the quiet, and let my tears soak his blanket. I was raised in a suck-it-up household so the presence of tears signifies weakness and vulnerability. I still have too much pride to show my husband how weak I'm feeling. I'm not sure why I feel the need to hold my tears back even from my husband, but I do. With him at group, I'm able to open the dam I've saved up all morning. A housekeeping employee comes into the room and begins sweeping the floor. She's middle-aged, with dark hair and a sweet face. She sees me crying and offers words of encouragement. I smile at her and nod. She continues talking about how the baby will get better, and not to worry, but her Spanish accent is so thick that I can hardly understand her. In fact, I almost want to laugh. It makes sense that she thinks I'm crying over Ryan, but I feel pretty optimistic about him. He made it through the first couple days and is holding his oxygen levels pretty high. It's these stupid hormones flooding through me. If she knew why I was really crying, she'd probably laugh, too.

Thursday morning, Henry starts talking about picking up the girls. "I miss them so much," he says over breakfast. Still popping pain pills every four hours, and spending every possible waking moment in an 11 x 11 space filled with machines and tubes and a son fighting for his life, I can't even think about adding two preschoolers to the mix. Henry devises a plan to make everyone happy. He spends the night at Johanna's so he can see them a day early, and brings them home Friday evening. We line up my dad to help me Thursday night and Willa to get me home on Friday.

The girls get home before I do. I get their call in the car. The first thing Natalie says is, "I want my mommy." It's been eight days since she's seen me, so I don't blame her.

"I'll be home soon," I tell her. When I arrive, I hug the girls and take them to the living room. "Do you notice anything different about my tummy?" I ask.

"There's no baby!" Natalie says. "Daddy told us baby boy came. He's here!" She's beyond excited.

"Yes, he came while you were at Aunt Johanna's. And he has a name. We named him after daddy, but we're going to call him Ryan. Remember, Ryan has a boo-boo on his heart?" They nod their heads. "He had to stay in the hospital so the doctors can help him get better."

"Can we see him tonight?" Natalie begs.

"Not tonight, sweetie. It's almost bedtime. We'll go see him tomorrow. I promise." I glance at Henry and see he's nodding his head. We considered taking Judy up on her offer of Monday, but know Natalie won't wait that long. We pull out my computer and show them the pictures of Ryan's room and equipment we took for this purpose. "This monitor right here, that looks like a TV with different colored lines on it, tells the doctors and nurses important things about Ryan, like how fast his heart is beating, how well his heart is working and other things. This, right here, has food in it that travels through that tube and into his stomach. And this machine helps him breathe until he is strong enough to do it on his own."

As we finish up, I realize it's time to pump again. Although I wear a nursing cape, Ainsley's curiosity gets the better of her. Being two, she has no couth. Walking over to me, she puts her head under the blanket to figure out what the noise is. Her eyes are as big as saucers as she sees the milk filling the bottles. "Milk!" she exclaims and points.

"Yes, milk," I say smiling.

"What are you doing, mommy? How are you getting milk? Why do you need it?" I feel like I need a flak jacket as Natalie barrages me with questions.

"You know how you see other mommies nursing their babies?" I say. "Our baby can't eat like other babies right now. He's too sick. He has a tube in his nose that goes down into his stomach. Mommy pumps the milk out of my body and the nurses send it down the tube to fill Ryan's tummy." She nods her head with understanding. It will become a reality for her in just a few hours.

SATURDAY DAWNS BRIGHT and early, and with it come two little hobbits into our bed. It's good to feel them close by again. I hug them tightly, being careful not to let them anywhere near my incision. We laugh and cuddle and play as a family. It isn't long before the girls are clamoring for us to get up so we can take them to meet Ryan. After a week of not seeing the girls, they seem grown-up to me. As we're getting ready, Ainsley comes into our room wearing a backpack and carrying a tote bag (she's totally into accessories).

"Do you like my backpack?"

"Yes, I do like your backpack."

"Thank you," she says and walks out.

AS WE PULL into the parking garage, Henry preps the girls. "Listen, when we get to Ryan's room, we're all going to wash our hands. It's very important we wash any germs off that we bring in with us. Your brother is not the only baby there. Use your inside voices. We don't want to wake anyone up."

"Okay, Daddy," they say.

The girls enter the room. We all head straight to the bathroom washing our hands together as a family, making it a big production to help the girls remember the process. Then we head over to the crib. We forewarned the nurse that we were coming. She covered up Ryan's sternal defect at our request. We're unsure how the girls will react to it.

They oooohhhh and aaaahhh at him for a few minutes while also trying to steal a glimpse of whatever is under his bandage. We let them touch his feet. Then they're ready for something else. Other nurses on the unit come by to meet the "little voices" reverberating off the walls and down the hallway. They play with the girls and dress them up in isolation gowns and masks. The girls love it. Soon they're settled into watching a movie on our laptop. Henry and I are relieved the girls haven't batted an eye at anything they've seen today. They act as if everyone goes to visit their new baby in an ICU.

Ryan responds well to the girls, too. When we first arrived the nurse was on edge. She explained he'd been irritable all morning and sensitive to noise. I watch his numbers as the girls play around him. His blood pressure decreases fifteen points and stays there our entire visit. It seems his sisters are just the medicine he needs.

Ryan's beautiful oxygen saturation levels of eighty have disappeared like snow on warm pavement. Over the last few days, they started trending down into dangerous territory. Today, we saw numbers anywhere from sixty, clear down to thirty. If I could capitalize a number I would. Thirty is dying. The plane is on the way down, the ship hit an iceberg and is taking on water, the house is on fire. Twelve days into this thing and I'm quickly learning that plans in an ICU are fluid. They change course as easily as water rolls from one side of a desk to another.

Dr. Donofrio schedules a cardiac catheterization immediately to find out what's going on. A heart catheterization involves a specialized cardiologist threading a catheter (thin plastic tube) into a vein or artery from the groin or neck and into the heart and blood vessels. Catheters are then used to measure pressure and the amount of oxygen in the various chambers of the heart. In addition, other catheters can be used to obtain pictures (angiograms) of the heart's anatomy and to perform interventions such as balloon angioplasty.

As expected, we find Ryan's pulmonary arteries are small, very small, but the kicker is that he seems to be getting very little blood flow through the pulmonary valve. Most of the blood isn't getting into the lungs via the traditional route, but rather from collateral vessels (extra vessels branching off the veins and arteries that close and open in response to blockages on the original vessel). We knew the collaterals were present, but didn't realize that there's one primary collateral doing basically everything. It's possible he had other collaterals earlier. They aren't predictable and can close down or pop up unexpectedly, causing the oxygen saturations to fluctuate.

Dr. Donofrio and Dr. Kanter, the cardiac interventionist who performed the catheterization, walk us through the pictures taken in the lab during the cath and graciously answer all our questions as we wade into a Cardiology 201 course. All the answers point to one thing: Either we attempt surgery to increase pulmonary blood flow to the lungs with a shunt or we do nothing. "What happens if we do nothing?" I ask.

"Then we make Ryan as comfortable as possible and allow him to struggle until he can no longer sustain enough oxygen to live," Dr. Donofrio says gently.

I look at Henry, "Do you want to do nothing?"

He doesn't miss a beat, "No way. We've come this far. Why would we quit now?"

"Okay," I say to Dr. Donofrio. "When would we do a surgery?"

"This week," she says, "as soon as possible. Tomorrow."

"Tomorrow?" I burst into tears. It's too soon for me! I need time to process. To get used to the idea. The reality is there is no time.

"We need to do something soon," Dr. Donofrio explains. "His sats tell us he needs surgery now."

"Okay. Tomorrow then," I say wiping away my salty response.

CONSISTENT WITH PROTOCOL, we meet with the cardiac surgeon to go over Ryan's surgery. The staff warned us he's extremely realistic and not to be too scared. Dr. Jonas is a world-renowned pediatric heart surgeon. Dr. Donofrio told us about him pre-birth at one of our many consultations. He's the author of *the* textbook used for pediatric cardiac surgery, and one of the best. He walks into our room to go over the risks and get the consent form signed. We introduce ourselves and get down to business.

In his Australian accent, he says, "Ryan has a unique heart configuration that makes things very complex. The placement of his aorta's different than most, so I won't be able to make my usual connection." He goes on to tell us how the shunt will work, and starts going through the risks.

"There are no statistics on this complication. I don't know of any documented case of ectopia cordis with single ventricle and pulmonary stenosis being successful. If you wanted to try and construct the worst combination of problems, you couldn't go much further. He already has two strikes against him. However, that being said, I think it's reasonable to try the surgery tomorrow. He'll survive the actual surgery, but I'm not sure what will happen afterward." Although he paints a bleak picture, we really have no other option. Ryan's body won't sustain life without intervention.

Henry's parents come to visit Ryan that night and take the girls back with them for a few days. "I don't want to leave," Natalie says. She's only been home four days, and this is all unexpected.

"I know, sweetie," I say. "I don't want you to leave either, but Mommy and Daddy have to be here very early tomorrow for Ryan's surgery, and it's going to be a long day. We don't know what time we'll be home. It's better if you and Ainsley are at Marmi and Pop's house playing. You'll have a lot more fun. We'll come get you as soon as we can."

It's scenes like this that I've been dreading since Ryan's diagnosis. I feel like I'm tied to a torture rack in the Tower of London having to decide which child's needs to meet. I quickly consider having her stay, but know it's not the best thing for everyone. I don't want her to witness something going wrong, nor do I want her to have to sit through a twelve or sixteen-hour day at the hospital.

We arrive a little after 8:30 A.M., just in time to see Ryan off to pre-surgery. We're inundated with information and the heaviness of the past two weeks. There's a surgical waiting room, but we choose to stay up in Ryan's room. It's quiet and we're able to take the time to rest. We're told the surgery should last up to three hours. When it's wrapping up we'll be paged to go downstairs to talk with Dr. Jonas. We make ourselves comfortable in the recliners and settle in for a short nap. This is where anyone with half a mind would wonder how in the world parents could sleep during something this earth-shattering. All I can say is that when you're under enormous emotional pressure, added to getting up in the night to pump, fatigue sets in and you can sleep almost anywhere.

An hour and a half later, the pager buzzes. "Henry, the surgery's over. Time to meet with Dr. Jonas," I say, shocked it took so little time. Is this good or bad? As I'm reaching for my bag, Dr. Jonas walks into Ryan's room. He shakes our hands and gets right to the point. "Ryan had his first big break today. We found a good place on the pulmonary arteries to connect the Gortex tube. Now, we need growth. They're closing him up now. You should be able to see him before too long."

They keep Ryan heavily sedated, to allow his body time to rest and recover from the trauma. Ryan sleeps most of the afternoon and into the evening. Henry and I watch the monitors and get a crash course on post-surgical norms. Ryan's satting in the eighties. By the next day, he's tolerating lower vent settings. He no longer needs supplemental oxygen; the vent's initiating only fourteen breaths per minute. Ten is the lowest they go before weaning the vent off totally. Ryan's doing a lot of his own breathing.

With Ryan stable, Henry drives the hour and a half to pick the girls up from his parents. Our life is becoming a bit surreal. I've only held Ryan twice in the last two weeks. When I'm at his bedside, I feel very connected. When he cries, I cry. When he sucks, my breasts let-down milk. Yet, when I leave and I'm home by myself, or taking care of the girls, I feel disconnected. I don't miss him unless I think I won't see him that day. I don't feel heartsick until the noise stops.

Bonding with a baby you don't care for day-to-day is much like trying to learn to type without a keyboard. I try changing Ryan's diaper as much as possible, because it's really the only way I'm contributing other than providing breast milk. That, too, is in a sterile environment. No skin to skin contact, only skin to plastic, the pump pulsing with a rhythm all its own. No snuggling, no hugging, no new baby smell. I come and go, just like his nurses do.

He seems to know us, though. Several times he's fought through the meds when I'm talking to him. I see his little eyes moving behind his closed eyelids and then, Bam, he opens his eyes and looks around. He moves his eyes in my direction, even though he's unable to focus through the meds.

They told us it could be up to a year before they close his chest. A year! Where does that leave us? I just want him home. I feel like the kid who goes to camp and is excited for the first day. Once nighttime comes, and the excitement wears off, she just wants her mama. CAMP IS OVER! I want to shout. I want normal. Not this new version of normal, but the life I had before.

Our personal campsite is the Ronald McDonald House. When Henry and I checked in three weeks ago, we left our checkout date open. We've been living here pretty much every day since.

The House is like a hotel, except with a common kitchen with several refrigerators, a laundry facility and several play rooms. The girls love that they have a whole new set of toys, other little kids, and that we all sleep in the same room. There's a shuttle to the hospital that we take most mornings, and Henry can catch it back to the House when the girls get antsy or Ainsley needs to nap. He's been their primary caregiver and I notice they're starting to cling more to him than me. He knows I'm focused on Ryan and is being sensitive to let me call the shots as to who, when, and where all of us are at each moment in time. Sometimes I ask him to take the girls out of the room because I need a break from their chattering. Other times, it's the girls who need to get outside the confines of the hospital walls. Every so often, I ask Henry if he wants alone time with Ryan, but more often than not, he's happy to get outside. Sitting inside makes him feel like a bird with clipped wings. He'd much rather be able to fly on a regular basis.

We meet other families at the House who are in heartbreaking situations. I read once that if we all threw our problems into one big pile, we'd pick our own to take out again. I think of this often when I meet another House family. One family comes up from North Carolina every six weeks for their son's cancer treatments. They've been coming for two years. TWO YEARS! They live eight hours away. Every six weeks, they interrupt their lives for a week and live at the House. Their son is ten.

One family had twin boys. In December of their second year, the first son drowned in a family member's pool. That January, their remaining son was diagnosed with brain cancer. They now face losing both of their children within a year.

A third family has a sixteen-year-old son with cerebral palsy. He started having life-threatening issues nine months ago. They spent a month in their local pediatric hospital in Boston and then transferred here eight months ago. They've lived in the House since then, going back and forth to the hospital taking turns visiting their son. They swap sleeping with him at night and sitting by his bed during the day. "I just took a job here locally," Tina says to me one morning. "We've run through all our savings. This is the first month we weren't able to pay our mortgage in Boston."

"Wow. I can't imagine. What do you do?" I say. We're in the kitchen. I'm grabbing a quick bowl of cereal for the girls. She's preparing a bag lunch.

"I'm a social worker. The good thing is this city needs a lot of them," she smiles. "See you tonight." She leaves to start her new job.

Other families have come and gone in the few weeks we've been here, some short-term fixes, a night here and a night there. The stories are as different as the ocean is wide, and everyone's in crisis. We're each coping in our own way.

For the moment, our family is trying to take things in stride. However, it's hard to be patient with Ryan's progress. We catch Dr. Donofrio on her daily rounds. Henry asks, "So where do we go from here? Do we have a plan as to when Dr. Boyajian will close up the chest?"

"Not yet," she says. "We're still waiting for Ryan to get stronger. He's only a week post-surgery. We need time for the pulmonary arteries to grow. The shunt will help with that. And we really don't want to move too quickly. We've never done this before. Your son's the first baby to make it this long with ectopia cordis and a single ventricle."

"We know we can't do anything with his ventricle for another four to six months," Henry says. "Why can't we close up the chest now and then go in later to fix his heart?"

"Because we don't want to kill him," Dr. Donofrio says bluntly. "We don't know how his body's going to react. We're going to take things slowly and only move when we're comfortable he can handle it. Right now, he can't.

"Let's focus on the positive things, though. Your son's stable. He made it through a very difficult surgery. He's tolerating food and gaining weight. We haven't talked about it much, but many omphalocele babies don't tolerate feeds. Ryan's doing great. He's practically fat," she says with a wide smile. "It doesn't seem like we're doing anything right now, but we are. We're working on lung strength, weight gain, and nutrition. All these things are extremely important for Ryan's success."

Henry and I are driven people. In all the ways we're different, we're the same in that we're always headed somewhere. We're the type who needs a weekend after our weekend and a vacation after our vacation. We have high expectations for progress in ourselves, and in others. It's hard to *feel* like something is happening right now.

The girls, on the other hand, haven't complained once. They have their own little hospital routine. They come into Ryan's room, run straight to the bathroom to wash their hands then climb on a chair to say hi to their brother. Once that's over with, they get on with their plans. Natalie's typically includes the hospital TV or a DVD. Ainsley, whose attention span is as big as a gnat, engages in pretend play. Today, she's a doctor. The nurse lets Ainsley wear her ID badge. Ainsley says, "I a doctor." She makes her doctor house behind my chair and walks in and out, treating her patients. "My tummy doesn't hurt," Natalie insists from her seat in front of the TV where Ainsley's trying to treat her malady. "I don't want to play doctor," she tells her sister for the fifteenth time. Ainsley gets the hint and moves on to other patients . . . the nurse and me. She goes between us, putting on pretend Band-Aids. At one point, I call her by name. She looks at me sternly and says, "Call me doctor!"

We make a point of going home each weekend for a change of scenery and to recharge. I can't stay away both days, so I sneak down Sunday afternoon while Henry stays home with the girls. The drive to the hospital takes me over Key Bridge. I love this bridge. I drove over it five days a week for the first three years of our marriage, working my way through college as an executive assistant at an engineering firm in Alexandria. We lived in the District, where Henry was in school on a basketball scholarship. We were so poor if we had five dollars to rent a movie on the weekends we thought we had hit the jackpot. I grew up in a middle-class family so frugality was nothing new to me. I'd catch the George Washington Parkway and take a route five minutes out of the way to watch the sunrise over the Washington Monument.

Georgetown University sits on the hill looking out on the Potomac. The tall spires from one of its buildings reach toward the blue sky. The water looks peaceful, even when traffic is heavy. The Hoya crew is rowing on the river. I always wanted to row. It, too, looks peaceful; rhythmic, hard, yet satisfying work. These sights are comforting and familiar. I watch pedestrians stream down the sidewalk toward M Street, making their way to the shops and cafés lined up all the way to the Four Seasons at Pennsylvania and M. I wonder how I'll feel about this bridge after Ryan's released from the hospital.

My anxiety level rises as I turn onto Whitehurst Freeway. As I enter the hospital I wonder how Ryan's doing. Ryan's been on CPAP trials for the past week. Today he's weaning from his sedation in preparation for coming off the vent. I watch him moving in his sleep. He isn't fighting the vent or holding his breath, something he's been known to do. Apparently, he was awake this morning for two hours looking around and happy.

"Hey, baby," I coo. "Mama came to see you." I talk to him in a sing-songy voice. He opens his eyes and looks at me. "Do you think I can hold him?" I ask Stephanie, his nurse. I want to take advantage of him being awake in my arms.

"Sure," she says brightly. She calls the charge nurse and respiratory therapist in to help us get situated. Ryan's little face contorts into a silent cry as we move him into my lap, but quickly relaxes once in place. He promptly falls asleep.

"He's happy because you're holding him," Stephanie says.

"Yep, that's mommy therapy," says the charge nurse.

They're happy because their patient is happy. I'm disappointed. I know I should be excited to hold him—this is only my fourth time in almost a month—but I really wanted to play with him up close in my arms. It seems like all I do is watch him sleep, either naturally, or because of sedation. For once, he was awake with the girls not here. I hesitate to hold him when they're with me. He has a ton of wires and IV lines running to his body that the girls could easily pull. It's actually sort of dangerous. And, because of the lines and especially his vent tube, it's a big deal getting him onto my lap and off so I don't want to be stuck in the chair with the girls running wild. When he was awake and acting happy, I thought this would be our chance to play together. Instead, I sit back and relax, breathing in his smell and counting his perfect toes.

LATER THAT WEEK, the team decides Ryan is ready to try extubation again.

"Hey, baby. How you doing? You look so happy with that tube out of your nose. Does it make you happy?" I sit cooing at Ryan who has just been extubated for a third time. Two prior attempts ended in failure, so I'm trying not to get my hopes up for this one. Instead I focus on playing with him while he's off sedation and happily awake. He's a completely different person when he's off drugs (aren't we all?). His eyes sparkle. His only breathing apparatus is a tiny nasal cannula blowing fresh oxygen into nostrils.

There's a knock on the door. After the briefest pause, a rather friendly looking lady steps into the room. "Are you mom?" she asks.

"Yes, I'm Leighann."

"I'm Cathy, from OT. I'm here to make a chest shield for Ryan. The doctors ordered for him to start OT and PT now that he's off the vent. We want to make sure we protect him. Do you mind if I work on it while you're here?"

"Not at all. Come on in," I say, glad to hear Ryan will have therapy.

I watch in amazement as Cathy starts by measuring Ryan's chest just like a seamstress would. Out of a large white sheet of hard plastic, she cuts out a template with only the measurements, no pattern. She dips the rigid plastic into a large silver metal vat of boiling water, making it pliable. She takes her time molding it into the shape she wants—something of a cross between a turtle shell and a breastplate from ancient Rome. As she works she continues to dip the plastic periodically so it's still workable. Going back and forth between molding and trying the piece on Ryan's chest for fit, she works her magic. Finally, she's satisfied. It cools into a hard plastic shield.

She then fits it with sheepskin and foam to keep the plastic from irritating Ryan's skin. Next comes the measuring and securing of Velcro straps, which cross over Ryan's back like suspenders keeping the shield in place. We don't want it to shift and push on his heart or omphalocele.

Ryan isn't sure what to do with his new accessory. He doesn't mind it once it's in place. It's the getting it on that's the problem. He cries until we have it secured. It'll be a few days yet before Ryan's approved to wear the shield for any length of time anyway. The attending wants to make sure he's able to breathe long-term off the vent before we start strapping something around his ribs and diaphragm. For now, we just try it on for size.

Henry's been back to work for two weeks. We're living back at home, and trying to get into a good routine. I'm still adjusting to being a stay-at-home mom who commutes an hour each way to take care of my son.

Wednesdays are turning out to be my hardest day. I have this crazy need to wake up and try to leave the house early to get to the hospital and I'm seeing a trend. Most of my days are stressful. It seems as though Wednesday is my hump day. The last two Wednesdays I've been weepy and on the brink of panic. PMSing every week is not going to work for me.

I have a knack for making a To-Do list a mile long and thinking it's reasonable. I remember when I first started staying home when Natalie was born. I'd get a ton of things done each day. It's easy when you only have one and she sleeps so often, or sits and coos in one spot on the floor. When she started moving it was a wake-up call for this project-oriented mama. Now I've been known to make a To-Do list then cross out the word *Today* and replace it with *This week*. I'm realizing I need to do the same thing now.

Before Ryan was born I had big plans for our visiting rotations: I'd take the mornings and Henry and I would switch out the evenings. We'd all be there as a family on the weekends. Reality hit home when the two-hour roundtrip, not including the Washington, D.C. traffic, makes it impractical to drive back and forth multiple times a day. Already I don't see Ryan as much as I'd like. It looks like I need to scale back my expectations even further. Settle down, maybe take Wednesdays off. This is a marathon, not a sprint.

Some stress is alleviated when Bridget offers to take the girls on Tuesdays and Thursdays. We meet in the preschool parking lot as we're both dropping off our four-year-olds. Ainsley jumps into her van. Bridget picks up her daughter and Natalie when preschool lets out just after lunch. I swing by to pick them up at her house on my way home in time to heat up dinner. It makes a big difference for the girls and me. It's two days for them to run around and play with other kids and two days for me to focus solely on Ryan. Even with this, I'm barely keeping my head above water.

About the time I'm at my breaking point Dr. Donofrio suggests we start thinking of bringing Ryan home. He's breathing on his own and weaning down on his medications and the supplemental oxygen. She thinks going home—away from the germs in the hospital—would be a positive thing on the condition of weekly doctor appointments and frequent home nursing visits. Easter's a few weeks away. I set my sights on having him home in time for a family egg hunt.

EASTER– 2009: "Ainsley! Natalie! It's time for the egg hunt." We're at Henry's uncle's house for the big family Easter celebration. Most of Henry's extended family, consisting of his mom's seven siblings and their combined thirty children plus a handful of grandchildren, is here. After debating whether we should come, stay home, divide up, or stay unified, we decide it'll be good for us to have a day to focus on family and fun. While Henry's sisters, Sarah and Lexi, help the girls find eggs I steal away to the car to pump. The quiet envelopes me while the sun melts any reserve I have left to ward off emotions I've wrestled with all morning. Tears and milk leave my body at about the same pace.

I'm exhausted. The glimmer of hope I had a few weeks ago is dimming like a candle running out of wax. I'm literally being used up by this roller coaster. I really, really wanted all of us to be here today. Sadly, Ryan's status is much the same as it was two weeks ago. He hit a roadblock while weaning from the supplemental oxygen. He's sitting at 5 liters (you can't leave the ICU until you're under 3 liters) and desats when that little *oomph*'s taken away. I watch the children running, hoping to get to the candy-filled eggs before the others, and wonder if Ryan will ever join his sisters at play.

THE MONDAY AFTER Easter an echo shows Ryan has a membrane in his heart that's cutting off blood flow (called a cor triatriatus membrane). Typically Dr. Jonas would perform open-heart surgery on the left atrium and physically cut away the membrane; however, the team wants to try a heart catheterization to see if Dr. Kanter can balloon it open. Although the membrane would eventually grow back, this would buy us some time to getting Ryan stronger before having an invasive heart surgery.

The day before the scheduled cath, Dr. Kanter comes for a visit. The girls are running around Ryan's bed as if they've drunk two five-hour energy drinks apiece. Earlier they were lining up their animal figurines and playing house with them on the tray table. The animals still stand at the ready like soldiers waiting for the battle command. We've made Ryan's room into our family room with two recliners side by side and the tray table in the middle. In the patient's closet I set up plastic stacking organizational drawers, a set of three for each girl, and stock them with crafts, small toys, puzzles, and books. I change them out frequently so the girls don't get bored. Additionally, the girls bring small toys from home in their "hospital bag" and play anything from Polly Pockets to doctor. We try to limit the TV as much as possible since it seems to suck all the creative juices from their little minds and replace it with the phrase, "There's nothing to do."

Dr. Kanter comes in to all this mess and makes himself at home. "Hello, girls," he says cheerfully. "How are you today?" A father of three small children roughly my own children's ages, he's in his element.

"Good," they chorus.

"Which one do you want?" Natalie asks grabbing a sheet of Little Mermaid stickers from her hospital bag.

"That one," Dr. Kanter says pointing to Ariel singing on a rock with the water splashing behind her windblown hair. I have yet to figure out how to look that good when surfacing out of billowing waves. Heck, I have yet to figure out how to look that good period. Natalie removes the sticker and punches it onto the lapel of his white lab coat.

"Which one?" Ainsley echoes, holding up her sheet of Little Mermaid stickers.

"Um, how about that one?" Dr. Kanter says choosing another Ariel pose. Not to be outdone, she slaps it on next to his first sticker. He smiles and pulls open a sheath of papers he has tucked under his arm.

"Girls, please go play with your animals. I need to talk with Dr. Kanter a minute." Thankfully they listen.

Dr. Kanter is instantly likeable. The first time I met him was when he came to get consent for Ryan's first catheterization. He gave me the option of sitting in a waiting room outside the cath lab or staying in Ryan's room. Henry couldn't be there and I didn't like the thought of sitting by myself in an empty waiting room so I chose to stay upstairs on the unit. Dr. Kanter never made me feel that was a bad choice.

The second time was when he and Dr. Donofrio gave us the results of that heart cath. Henry and I sat in a conference room while Dr. Kanter patiently went through each picture of Ryan's heart and answered our questions. Now six weeks later we meet again.

"I wanted to go over the risks and get your consent for tomorrow's cath," he says. "We'll do much the same as we did before. I'll use the instruments to thread a catheter up through a vein in Ryan's groin and into his heart. I'll wind a wire with a balloon up through the catheter and into the pulmonary vessel sack. It's fitted with miniscule razor blades on three sides on its end. I'll inflate the balloon and work it through the cor triatriatus at the opening of the sac to perforate its sides. After removing this balloon I'll insert another wire-and-balloon combo. This time the balloon will be smooth and when it's pushed through the perforated membrane, the hope is the membrane walls will break open leaving a flap instead of a rigid wall. Theoretically the blood will flow freely through the flaccid membrane flap and oxygenate Ryan's body properly.

"We've never done this before on an infant with a cor triatriatus membrane. We do this sort of thing in adults all the time for different reasons. Having said that, it's a reasonable thing to try in this scenario. I think there's a real possibility it'll work and save Ryan from having to go through open-heart surgery.

"Now on to the risks. As we talked about before there's a chance of stroke, clotting, bleeding, hemorrhaging, damage to vessels, and emergency surgery. Do you have any questions?"

"What time will he go down?" I say.

"He's on for first thing so probably somewhere between 7:30 and 8 A.M.," he says.

"Okay. I'll be here," I say and sign on the dotted line. Even though the risks are scary, I don't really have much of a choice.

"HI, THIS IS Dr. Su from the CICU." The call comes in around dinnertime. "Ryan was struggling so we just finished intubating him."

"Okay," I say.

"We think he needs support right now. Putting him on the vent allows his body to rest. We want him to be in the best shape he can be when he goes to the cath lab," she says. "Oh, and he's been bumped from the cath lab for a more urgent case. Kanter added him for Thursday so just two extra days to wait."

I hang up with Dr. Su and continue serving the girls dinner. I feel like a hot air balloon that just got snagged on a tree limb. We were finally moving in the right direction and now we're on pause. Again.

TUESDAY MORNING I drop Natalie at school and kiss Ainsley good-bye as she hops into Bridget's van. I look on the bright side about the cath being on Thursday. It means I can have a good visit today, the girls can visit tomorrow and then they'll be with Bridget again for the cath on Thursday.

I walk into the unit around 11 A.M. As I'm handing a bag containing several bottles of breast milk to the receptionist the fellow approaches me. At the same time, the charge nurse sees me and says, "They moved Ryan to a new room. Did they call you?"

"They called me to tell me they reintubated," I answer.

"Okay, I'll see if they're ready for you," he says.

I turn my attention to the fellow, Melissa. "Ryan took a turn for the worse last night. His sats were sitting in the fifties so we ordered an echo. It shows the membrane is putting more stress on his heart. The blood is building up more rapidly causing his heart to work harder to push it through the blockage. He needs to go to the cath lab as soon as possible. We put a call into Kanter to see when he can get him on the schedule," she says calmly.

Unfazed and actually a little relieved I walk to Ryan's room. You'd think being met at the door by a doctor would be a clue something is up, but honestly, I'm used to Ryan "being sick." That's the whole reason we're here. I'm already prepared for him to have a cath, and I'm happy it's happening sooner than later.

When I notice a group of people whispering in the hallway outside Ryan's room, the seriousness of situation hits me. I hear the echo Doppler recording Ryan's heart rate. I move past the whisperers into the doorway. As if bouncing off an invisible shield, I stop dead in my tracks. I haven't seen Ryan since before the reintubation the previous night. My last vision of him was awake, happy (although working hard to breathe) and active lying in a crib. Just yesterday I held him comfortably on my shoulder as he drifted into a peaceful sleep. I have to look twice to make sure I have the right room.

My son's lying listless in a big-boy hospital bed looking small and weak. His face is swollen to twice its size, an indication of poor heart function. He's heavily sedated with the addition of a paralytic making him appear lifeless. His heart and stomach seem larger than they were yesterday—protruding from the middle of his frame like coal buttons on a snowman. The biggest difference is his color. He's extremely pale with a grayish hue. The color of death is something anyone can recognize when hit in the face with it.

A drum starts pounding somewhere deep in my chest. It gets faster with each beat, drowning out any sound in the room. The casualness with which the team talked to me over the phone and in the reception area doesn't match what I'm seeing. They were perhaps a bit solemn, but certainly didn't say anything to cause me alarm, nothing to indicate the toll the last twenty-four hours has taken on my baby.

Casey, his nurse today and many times before, sees my shock. She's comes to my side and lays her hand on my arm. "Are you okay?" she says quietly.

"Yeah," I manage to eek out. Justin, the fellow, and several other team members are working around me trying to finish the echo and whispering about next steps.

"Justin needs to put in an A-line," Casey says. My brain isn't firing on all cylinders. There's so much I want to say but can't get the gears in my mouth moving. I look at her speechless. I don't want Justin to put in the A-line. Ryan's a hard stick and I know he'll need to go to the lab to get one. That's what has happened the last two times he's gotten an A-line. I can't imagine it'll be different today. Justin sees my hesitation. He says, "I can wait a few minutes if you need some time with him." I nod. I don't know if I need time with Ryan or just need space, but I'm grateful for the privacy.

The room clears and it's almost peaceful. A polar opposite of how I'm feeling. The only sounds are the soft hum of the ventilator and the controlled sobs wracking my body. I reach up to stroke Ryan's head. He opens unseeing eyes. They can't sedate him enough to keep him from opening his eyes when I come. His eyes are dead and unfocused. He keeps them open searching for me. *He's not done fighting.* I don't talk for fear of losing it all together so I simply rub him. I want to sing him the song Henry taught me and has sung to our babies from the time Natalie was just a bean inside me. I sang it to him before he was born but haven't been able to sing it since. It says, "Go to sleep, little baby. Go to sleep, little baby. And when you awake, we'll patty-patty-cake. And ride the shiny little ponies."

I sing it now in my head wishing he could hear me and praying he'll wake up. That he'll really wake up and not need this stupid ventilator anymore or these intrusive wires. I can't sing it though because I know he may never see a real pony in his lifetime. He may never leave the confines of these walls. And it reminds me we drug him to sleep more often than not. Kissing his head I whisper, "Everything's going to be okay," and pray to God it's true.

"Leighann, we need to start," Casey says softly from the doorway. I turn to her and nod my assent. The team comes back in and starts prepping Ryan's equipment for the move to downstairs.

Dr. Levy, the anesthesiologist who assisted with Ryan's delivery and every procedure since, walks into the room. I'm immediately relieved to see his familiar face.

"Why is it every time I see Mr. Marquiss it's because he's acting up?" he jokes as he gently touches Ryan feeling for pulses and checking his vent to see what levels of oxygen he's on. He then joins me at the door to give Justin the space he needs to place the A-line. Since an A-line goes straight to the heart placing one is considered an in-room procedure. The area must be sterile and parents aren't allowed to be in the room.

"How are you doing?" Dr. Levy says.

"Okay," I say tentatively knowing if I tell him the truth I'll most likely start sobbing again.

"It's a little dicey, but we'll do our best," he says. "It could be his shunt or the cor membrane. We'll know more once we get him downstairs. If he has to go to surgery, I'll be with him the entire time to watch over him."

I inhale deeply and nod. Casey's phone rings. The cath lab's ready. Justin hasn't gotten the line in. "We'll do it downstairs," Dr. Levy says. It takes half a dozen people to push all the equipment and bed. I'm left looking at an empty room. I take the opportunity to pump. When I'm done, I make my way to the cath waiting room and call Henry at work. His phone rings several times before a voice that isn't his picks up the line. "Hello, Henry Marquiss's line." I recognize the voice as our long-time friend and Henry's coworker, Eddie.

"Hey, it's Leighann. Is Henry there?" I try to keep my voice even.

"He's not. Can I take a message?" Eddie says seriously. I have no idea what to say. What kind of message should I leave? "Your son's taken a turn for the worse." Or "Ryan's not doing well." Or "Call me." I'm silent.

"I'm kidding. He's right here," Eddie says and hands the phone to Henry.

"Hey, what's up?" Henry says chuckling.

"Ryan isn't doing well," I whisper, breaking into sobs.

"Should I come down?" he says immediately serious.

"No. It's okay. I didn't expect it, that's all. He's going to be fine. He's in the lab right now. Dr. Kanter and Dr. Levy are on the case. Kanter will open the membrane to see if that's the issue." My voice is stronger now and the tears have stopped. I always feel better when I can turn the conversation to the clinical and live above my reality.

"Are you sure I shouldn't come? Even though Ryan'll be okay, do you want me to come be with you?" Henry says.

"No, I'm okay now. It's the first time I've voiced it so I'm still processing. I'll be fine. Can you plan to pick up the girls from Bridget's? I'm not sure what time I'll get out of here."

"Sure. I'll give her a call now and tell her you're tied up. You sure you're okay?"

"I'm good. Really. I'll call you with an update when I know more." *What if I had to call Henry and tell him Ryan was dead?* I immediately push the thought aside. That's a dark alley I'm not prepared to walk down just yet.

The cath waiting room is separate from the surgical waiting room. I'm the only one here. My body aches. It's most likely the stress coupled with all the driving I've been doing. I decide to string Ryan's Beads of Courage. Purple, black, silver, light green, rainbow, and yellow. He gets one of each every day. Sometimes two black or two silver.

Beads of Courage is a program using art therapy to help kids visualize the invasive procedures that happen to them throughout their illness; a visual reminder of how brave they are and how much they've had to endure. There's a list of eligible procedures such as pokes with a needle, dressing changes, X-ray, respiratory therapy, overnight hospital stay, surgery, line insertion or removal, and so on. Ryan's a complex case so he gets a lot of beads.

On an easy day, he receives one for his IV meds, blood-gas draws, dressing change, X-ray, respiratory therapy, and overnight stay. On a hard day he's received beads for such things as TPN (nutrients through IV), heart catheterization, heart surgery, blood transfusion, and intubation.

His best beads thus far are the two beads representing the day he met his sisters (the social worker let each of them choose a special bead for his strand); and, the bead representing his birth at Children's Hospital. I can't wait to explain them to him.

I decide to count the beads. I want to know how many he's accumulated in his short seven and a half weeks. I get to bead 100 and coincidentally it's his heart bead for the shunt surgery—two weeks into life. I string up to his seven-week mark and count over 300 beads. Good grief! I gently coil the string of beads and place it in my bag.

The fellow walks out of the cath lab and toward the waiting room. I can see her through the glass walls. "It went extremely well . . . better than any of us expected and better than anyone could've imagined. Ryan tolerated the procedure beautifully. They're getting an echo right now to get a picture of the membrane and then they'll be done."

While I wait for Dr. Kanter, I move to a child-size table in the center of the room. I straddle the pint-sized chair to relieve the pressure in my back and bum. Dr. Kanter comes out of the lab, grabs another little chair, and joins me at the table. He shows me pictures from the cath. The membrane was closed up all but a hole the size of a pinhead. He shows me the balloon size he was able to get through the membrane before and after the perforation.

I'm tired and I briefly think how funny we must look to a passerby. Here's a man and woman sitting at a tiny table discussing life and death issues. I almost smile, but manage not to as I realize Dr. Kanter's telling me Ryan has a fever and it might indicate an infection. It's not the time to be smiling. I refocus and ask if the events of the morning could've caused his body to react with a fever. We discuss fevers, antibiotics, and more.

THE CATH PROVES to be the magic bullet Ryan needs. He successfully comes off the vent the next day and weans off oxygen five days later, the day after his two-month birthday. He moves to the Heart and Kidney Unit (HKU) meaning for the first time in his life he's no longer critical. The HKU is the step down unit from the

CICU lovingly referred to as "the floor." The fact Ryan's here has me hopeful.

The team hasn't given us a timeframe for going home, however, I notice they start talking about things other than Ryan's heart function, like weaning his medications and learning how to eat. We were just starting to work on getting Ryan to eat orally before he needed the cath. We start up again with occupational therapy twice a day to see if he'll suck a bottle. I also start exposing him to nursing any time I can.

Feeding is a common problem with heart babies. It takes a lot of energy even for a healthy baby, which is why most babies fall asleep shortly after or during eating. Most heart babies can't eat a full meal because their little bodies can't generate enough energy to sustain the suck-swallow pattern for long periods of time.

Another obstacle is that he has a nasogastric (NG) tube making him feel like he has a strand of spaghetti at the back of his throat. It's a very uncomfortable feeling and actually discourages him from swallowing. Swallowing will most likely be an issue anyway since he was intubated within minutes of birth. A vent tube blocks the airway and therefore, the patient is unable to swallow anything, including spit.

It's hard to teach an old baby new tricks. Learning to eat comes slowly. Painfully so. Ryan starts by taking a few ccs of milk and by the end of the week is taking 11 ccs. For perspective, he needs approximately 120 ccs to make a full meal. He must do it eight times a day. So far, he's refused anything by breast, but I still offer it if my visits correspond with his mealtimes.

The third week in April I sit down to try and nurse once more. It's about 1 P.M. and Ryan's getting fussy. I figure he might be hungry. I sit comfortably in a recliner by his bed and cradle his head in the crook of my arm. He plays around for a second or two before latching to my breast—as if he's done it his entire life—and starts sucking and swallowing and breathing—all at the same time. Not for one suck either, as he's been doing on a bottle nipple. I start counting his swallows to report to the OT. I lose count at thirteen. I remember the OT saying she didn't want to exhaust him and I also know the team wants to keep track of how much he's eating. How am I supposed to not exhaust him if he's full-on nursing and how exactly do I know how much is coming out? Most importantly, the OT mentioned aspirating (food going into the lungs) as a common problem with feeding tube patients. How do I know if the milk is going to the right place? I push the emergency button. Who else pushes the emergency button when their child starts nursing?! "Can you page OT and see if Ryan's allowed to nurse?" I ask frantically. "He's nursing and I'm not sure if I should stop him."

The nurse comes in the room a few minutes later smiling, "OT says it's fine to nurse for as long as he tolerates it. Don't worry about if it's going in the right place or not. He'll choke if it's going in the wrong place."

Ryan nurses for a full four minutes. Then, just like that, he unlatches and plops his head back on the pillow looking quite satisfied and drowsy. His little hands move up beside his head, he gently closes his eyes. He's done. He's happy. I'm happy. We're all happy.

"Mrs. Marquiss?" the HKU nurse practitioner comes into the room. "Hi, I wanted to chat with you about the possibility of Ryan coming home this week."

I nearly jump out of my chair but don't on account of the sleeping, milk-drunk baby in my lap. "This week?"

"Yeah, we think he's ready. In fact we're really just waiting on medical supplies to arrive to be able to send you home. He needs a feeding pump and some wound care supplies, but other than that he's ready."

"So when are we talking? I never got anything ready at home so I need to install his car seat and wash his clothes," I say.

"Let's plan for Tuesday. We should have all his equipment by then."

Tuesday. That's four days from now. We've hinted of home before; however, we never planned a specific day or ordered supplies. I'm a little hesitant to get my hopes up until he's actually in his car seat. My biggest concern is that Ryan will come home with a feeding tube. The team assures us we'll be fine with the tube; that many families are nervous but end up without issues. The nurses will teach Henry and me how to insert the tube and check to make sure it's in the right spot. Additionally, we'll see the pediatrician and the cardiologist on a weekly basis. Ryan's scheduled for an echo on Monday to get another read on how his membrane is faring. It will give Dr. Donofrio an idea of how often she needs to see him. We'll also have a nurse visit our home two to three times per week.

"Don't you think having someone see him five times a week is overkill?" I ask Dr. Donofrio as we go through Ryan's home plan. She shakes her head. It's obvious to her I'm in denial. "There's no way this is overkill. Ryan's fragile. He needs to be seen. It'll give everyone peace of mind knowing he's stable."

That settles it. As I process the schedule I'm okay with all the visits. I remember at Natalie's one-year appointment the doctor said, "Okay, we'll see you next year." *Next year?* I thought. *You're kidding right? I've been coming every two months for twelve months and now you're just going to let me have her for a full year without any check-ups? How will I know if she weighs enough?*

So yes, we're freaking out a little at the thought we'll have Ryan all to ourselves with no doctors, nurses, or monitors letting us know what his numbers are. While I haven't relied on his numbers for weeks now it's still reassuring to look up and be able to see his respiratory rate, heart rate and oxygen saturations at the drop of a hat. After Ryan's shunt surgery way back in the beginning I questioned Dr. Jonas and several other staff members what Ryan would do should he be in distress. I'm working on "looking at the patient and not the monitor." Easier said than done.

Over and above the overwhelming thought of being Ryan's primary medical care giver, it's exciting to think we could settle into life as a family and no longer have to choose between visiting Ryan in the hospital over doing normal things like going to the park or playing in the snow or having a quiet day at home. In the weeks Ryan's been hospitalized it's been a tug-of-war keeping things normal for the girls and maintaining a balance of having time to rest. I purposefully tried to be home for family dinner and keep a consistent bedtime routine so the girls had stability to their days. We also made Saturday our day away from the hospital as a family and focused on doing fun things with the girls. It never felt right to me to have us off doing family things while Ryan was lying in the hospital, but it became important for us not to be consumed by hospital life.

We can now transition to truly having three kids at home. We have some new waters to chart. Will Ryan sleep through the night? Will Ainsley be willing to give up mommy's lap? Will we be able to go out places or stay in for fear of germs? No matter what, I know we'll be fine taking it one day at a time. If there's one thing the CICU taught me it's that plans should be flexible.

HE LOOKS AROUND dumbfounded by all that he sees. There isn't a monitor or white lab coat in sight. His little eyes register confusion. He searches for me and finds me standing above him cooing. His little arms and legs are pulled in tight to his torso like a turtle missing his shell. He doesn't make a sound. It's as if the vent has trained him that trying is a waste of time. The only time he makes a peep is to cry . . . but even that's rare. He tends to express himself through his eyes or facial expressions. It's all he's ever had to communicate with. Even his hands were of no use being tethered to the sides of the bed so much.

I try to make him comfortable. "Hey baby, mommy's here. You wanna come up with me?" I situate him carefully in the baby sling my neighbor loaned me. Ryan's been home three days, but still gets concerned when he can't see me. This new place without beeping, constant light, and multiple people coming in and out of his room has him feeling lonely and afraid. When he sees me though, he visibly relaxes. If he wasn't eating practically around the clock, I'd hold him all day long. As it is, I hold him for the brief fifteen minutes or so he's off feeds. Sometimes he falls asleep in the sling, swayed gently as I walk through the house doing my chores. I hold him, too, when he's eating if I have things I can do sitting down. There's pumping and charting, wound care, medications, and paperwork. I'm not sure I'll ever wade through the river of paperwork that comes with having a medically fragile child.

The girls are adjusting to having a new baby in the house. "I like it better when Ryan's in the hospital," Natalie said this morning. "You have time to play with me." She got mad when I was pumping, playing paper dolls with her, and talking to Willa at the same time. I thought I was doing well because I was multi-tasking. She couldn't stand that she didn't have my full attention. She cleaned up her dolls and stormed off to her room. I finished pumping and went to find her.

"Remember when Angelina's mom had a new baby and Angelina was sad because her mommy was busy?" Natalie's face softened and she nodded her head. "Do you feel like that a little?" She nodded again. "It's okay to feel sad that I'm busy. I love you very much and want to spend time with you. Right now I'm learning how to have a new baby. I have to practice a little and soon I'll be better at having more time." I give her big hugs and kisses and we cuddle on her bed for a while.

I seek out Ainsley. She's struggling, too. She sucked a pacifier today and climbed into Ryan's swing. She refuses to listen when I ask her to do something and is pushing all of Natalie's buttons. The poor girl is trying to figure out her place in the family and discover if everyone still loves her. I pull her aside. "I love you, sweet girl. Do you see me taking care of Ryan and think I don't love you any more?" She looks at me blankly. "I like taking care of you, too." I get no reaction. She goes back to playing. I leave her room wondering if I got through.

Growing up in a big family, I know kids can get lost in the crowd. When I was in second grade the school informed my mother and father I was being punished for forging my mother's signature on my reading homework. Second grade!! The kicker is I'd been doing it for at least a month before I was caught. Our teacher would have us show our parent's signature to the person sitting next to us. It wasn't until it was my turn for her random check that she realized the cursive writing was that of a novice.

When the principal asked me why I'd done it I said, "My mommy is busy with a new baby. I read to myself every night and then sign the paper." It made total sense to me. Why would I bother my mother if I knew I was capable of the job?

My mother never told me she was too busy to read with me. It was something I decided myself. In my case it was harmless . . . but I don't want my kids thinking I don't have time for them.

"Girls, get your shoes on!" I shout up the stairs. I strap Ryan into his infant carrier and set him in the foyer. I grab the diaper bag from the coat closet and quickly look through it—a bottle, diapers, wipes and a bottle of water for me. I set it beside Ryan. "Girls, let's go!" I head to the kitchen to pick up Ryan's bottle of breast milk from the fridge, a can of formula, and empty bottles, which are drying on the counter, to go with my pump. That would have been devastation if I had forgotten them, more so for me than him. Can I get a nursing-mother's amen? I circle back to the living room grabbing my pump from beside the couch and meet Ryan back in the foyer. Still no girls.

"Girls, what's going on?" I yell up the stairs.

"We're coming," Natalie says. Sure enough they round the corner hand-in-hand decked out in their finest.

"Okay, to the car," I say. I grab Ryan, his diaper bag, and my breast pump. Shoot! I forgot his feeding pump. After securing him in the car and depositing the bags, I run back into the house to grab his pump. As a precaution I quickly grab an extra NG tube, skin prep wipes, skin tape, and tube lubricant—all supplies I'd need if his tube needed replacing during our trip.

I'm sweating by the time I settle into the driver's seat. I pull up to Bridget's house fifteen minutes later and practically throw the girls inside. I resist the urge to say, "Tuck and roll!" They're too young for my humor.

"Hey!" I shout. Bridget's in the kitchen cleaning off the counters. "Hey!" she shouts back, and I'm off, running back to the car.

Ryan and I arrive a few minutes behind schedule to his first heart clinic appointment since coming home. We're four days into this thing and it's time to see if we're doing a good job. We're at the Fairfax clinic where I came for many of my ultrasounds and fetal echos. I remember the stomach butterflies that accompanied me each time I pulled into the parking garage. No butterflies today. This will be the first of many visits to see the cardiologist with a child in tow.

It's time for Ryan's feed. I discreetly take his bottle from its cooler pouch and add two scoops of formula before shaking it. The nutritionist has recommended from birth that we mix formula and breast milk for added calories. Heart babies burn calories faster since their heart has to work hard to be efficient. I pour the contents into the feeding pump bag. Taking the cord hanging from the bag, I remove the cap and put the end of it into the bottle I just emptied. After powering up the pump I push the buttons corresponding with the type of feed, feed rate, and feed amount before getting to a screen that prompts me to prime the pump. I watch as the remaining few ccs that are in the line drain into the bottle. To remove the air, I take the end of the pump line and put it up into the top of the feed bag. I continue priming the line, watching as the new milk snakes from the bag down the feed cord until it drops from the tip into the bag. I connect the tip to Ryan's NG tube and press the START FEED button.

I can't tell you how many times I saw nurses "waste" milk as they were performing this process. Or throw breast milk away because they were too lazy to measure out what they needed. Being the one working hard to provide the nourishment, you can bet I figured out the most efficient way to save every last drop.

Amanda pops her head into the waiting room. "You ready?" she asks. We make our way down the hallway to the echo room, my stroller laden down with two different pumps (each feeding Ryan in their own way), a diaper bag, a drink for me, and my precious son. I pull Ryan up onto the examination gurney and into my lap, feeding tube and all. Dr. Donofrio comes in toward the end of the scan. "How's it looking?" she says to Amanda.

"Pretty good. Here you want to take a look?"

Dr. Donofrio takes Amanda's place and deftly moves the ultrasound probe across Ryan's heart scanning for his pulmonary arteries and trying to get a good read on his cor triatriatum membrane. She told Henry and me that the first time they performed an echo on the day Ryan was born they were surprised to find they could put enough pressure on his exposed heart to get a good picture without causing any changes to his numbers on the monitor. It's truly amazing how strong the heart really is.

"The cor membrane is still flaccid. The PAs are small but hopefully will grow with all the blood flowing through them from the shunt. How are his sats?"

"Sixty-five. Sixty-eight, maybe," I answer.

"Not great, but baseline. Let's see him next week to keep track of the membrane. I want to be certain it's stable before spacing out the visits."

I CALL MY mom from the car to check in, "How'd it go?" she asks. "Does everything look normal?"

"Sure!" I laugh. "As normal as a heart with a missing ventricle, two superior vena cavas, a cor triatriatum, a central shunt coming off a tilted aorta, small pulmonary arteries, merged pulmonary veins, twisted slightly to the side and sticking up through the chest wall can look!"

"Okay, funny." She says. "You know what I mean."

"Yes, I do. I'm just teasing you. Everything looks fine."

"I wish I could help you with the girls next week. I feel like I haven't done much," she says.

"Mom, please. You work full-time. Don't worry about me. I have tons of friends helping me right now. I get three meals a week, I have friends who take the girls anytime I need them to, Willa's been coming down some, Katie's cleaning my house and doing my laundry. I'm fine."

"I know. As your mother, I want to help. Are you guys busy this weekend? I can come cook and clean for you."

"We'd love to see you. You don't have to cook and clean though."

"I'll see you this weekend rain or shine," she says.

THE GIRLS DON'T want to leave when I get to Bridget's house. "Mom, that wasn't long enough. We never see Maggie and Rebecca anymore. Can't we stay longer?" Natalie whines. How wasteful for me to worry those weeks in the hospital that my girls felt neglected with me gone!

"Nope, to the car. You'll have plenty of other times to see them. Right now your brother is waiting in the car and I have dinner to cook. Let's go."

"Moooooommmmmmm," she starts.

"Yes, mom," I say firmly.

"Yes, mom," she repeats and walks, shoulders hunched like Quasimodo, to the car.

At home, I take Ryan out of his carrier and put him in the swing. He loves movement. Even in the hospital he preferred a bouncy seat over lying still. I position him so he can watch me in the kitchen. Ainsley and Natalie run off to play in the recesses of the house.

"Mommy, Ryan's pump is beeping. I think it's done," Natalie says. She and Ainsley appear on the stairs. They've changed into princess clothes complete with clear and pink plastic shoes. "Can I turn it off?"

"I'm just drying my hands off. Let me make sure it's finished, honey," I say. We both reach the pump at the same time. Before I can get a good look at the screen, she presses the OFF button. "Natalie! I said to wait. Now I don't know if it was done or if there's air in the line," I scold. I look at the bag, which is basically empty, but I can't tell if he got all his ccs. "Next time wait until I tell you to turn it off. I have to keep track of the food he's getting."

"Sorry, mommy," she says softly. "I was just trying to help."

"I know. It's okay," I say rubbing her head. Natalie *is* a big helper. She volunteers to fetch diapers, clothes, or blankets. She'd change Ryan's diaper if I let her, but I think four years old is a little young for the task. Ainsley likes helping in other ways. Her favorite activity is shaking the bottles once I add the formula. She's also constantly trying to put socks and shoes on Ryan or cover him up with a blanket. Poor Ryan! The doctors told us his heart has to work so hard that it's like he's constantly running a marathon. He's always sweating as it is. I follow behind Ainsley and remove whatever warm accessories she's added.

Natalie likes being in charge and has a hard time allowing Ainsley near Ryan. She complains Ainsley's going to hurt him. I notice Ainsley's very gentle. I make it a point to split the "helper" responsibilities with her and work with Natalie on sharing her brother.

We get into a rhythm of visiting the cardiologist and pediatrician once a week. In mid-May we consult with the plastic surgeon and the general surgeon to plan for closing Ryan's chest wall. The optimal time to do it is when Ryan has his Glenn procedure (heart surgery) in August. Dr. Jonas will probably cut through Ryan's skin membrane and the plastic surgeon is unsure how well it will heal. It's important we take steps to prepare new skin for Dr. Jonas to pull across the incision.

I meet with Dr. Boyajian in the plastic-surgery clinic. It's in a different wing in the same building where Ryan was born. Walking through the hallways I have flashbacks. The cafeteria smell as the elevator opens to let someone off at the second floor. I called Henry to tell him about Ryan's emergency cath from the windows right there. The hallway that leads away from the plastics clinic on the third floor and toward the family services office. The girls always hugged the paper cutout of Dr. Bear before heading to see Nadine for a parking sticker. Today I head to the left and sign in with plastics.

Dr. Boyajian is one of the most creative people I've ever met. It's fascinating to meet the various doctors and see which personalities are drawn to the different specialties. Dr. Boyajian is definitely an artist behind a surgeon's knife. The first time I spoke with him in depth was when Ryan was only a couple days old. We chatted about Ryan's case for over an hour. Dr. Boyajian must have thrown out five different ideas on how to close Ryan's chest, most of the techniques never having been used on an infant or for this particular defect, but all within the realm of possibilities.

"Mrs. Marquiss, how are you?" he says extending his hand.

"Hanging in there," I say. Ryan and I are seated near the exam table in a chair along the wall. Dr. Boyajian takes a seat across from us. "I've been doing a lot of thinking and the safest course of action is using tissue expanders. Tissue expanders are silicone bags—they come in all different sizes, but we'll probably use the one hundred cc size. They're placed between the skin and fat and gradually filled with simple saline solution. Over time, the tension created by the growing bags causes new skin cells to develop, in effect growing new skin. Tissue expanders are frequently used with breast reconstruction for cancer patients or with any patient who has scar tissue needing to be stretched. Unlike cancer patients or burn patients, in Ryan's situation there's no scar tissue. I've used them extensively with older children who tell us there's no pain so I don't want you to worry.

"As far as I know nobody has used them in infants. There are inherent risks. Tissue expanders grow in as well as out which means there'll be compression on Ryan's lungs. How much, we don't know. Cardiology is concerned how the tissue expanders will affect Ryan's breathing mechanism. We realize, because he doesn't have a chest wall, his body has adapted by using the muscles we use in respiratory distress. They're what you and I use when we've run a race or chase a ball. So Ryan has no reserve to fall back on. I'm not convinced they'll affect him much. But we won't know until we try."

"What happens if they compromise his breathing?" I ask.

"He ends up back here on the floor or in the CICU. Best case he's on supplemental oxygen. Worst case, a ventilator," he says.

"Okay. And you think this is the best way?"

"We talked about breaking his ribs and putting in metal expanders, but that'll be too painful. I don't want to put him through that. This is the least invasive and the least painful. And it'll work. We've done it countless times with other kids. The only unknown is how much pressure the lungs will tolerate," he says.

"Where do we go from here?" I say.

"We're going to need several months to grow enough skin. I'd love to give him injections twice a week so . . . let's see . . ." He rubs his chin while doing the math. "If we're really conservative and only do ten ccs at a time we need about eight weeks. When's his Glenn?"

"August twenty-seventh."

"Well then, let's book it for mid-June. He'll come in for surgery that morning and go straight to the unit for observation afterward. Call the surgery line and tell them I asked you to set it up," he says. We shake hands and he's off to reconstruct someone else's child.

Several days later I'm back on the same floor, in the same clinic, to meet with Dr. Sandler, the general surgeon, to go over putting Ryan's omphalocele into his body.

Dr. Sandler checks out Ryan's stomach. He squeezes the area around the omphalocele and pushes it in a few different places. He says, "This is a nothing. His stomach feels great. There's no hardness. It seems like his bowels are working fine. His omphalocele's tiny in comparison to what we see. It's just a matter of pushing it back in and stitching the skin over it. With Pentalogy we usually see a herniated diaphragm. I'll put a prosthetic patch on the diaphragm to cover the hole while I'm working on the omphalocele. What are Boyajian and Jonas saying about timeline?"

"Jonas is doing the Glenn August twenty-seventh and I've just scheduled the tissue expanders to be inserted for June seventeenth."

"With Ryan's particular anatomy, cardiology should have first shot at him. We need to make sure his heart is stable. I can do the omphalocele during any of his upcoming surgeries as long as his vitals are stable and he can tolerate an extra thirty minutes on the table. If Boyajian inserts the expanders in June we can do the omphalocele either during the Glenn or anytime after that. Let's touch base closer to August when we know how Ryan's faring."

My conversation with Dr. Sandler is reassuring. The omphalocele seems like a breeze compared to everything else. A nurse once asked me how we handle holding and caring for Ryan. I described it as "casually careful." I don't walk around on eggshells with him nor do I shoo the girls away. I treat him as if he were a healthy baby with the addition of meds, feeding tubes, and all that jazz. Believe me, I know he's not healthy!

Yes, he's fragile. He *could* hurt himself should he fall on his exposed heart. I already know it'll be hard to push him when necessary and let him go when appropriate by the way I respond to working on his feeds.

Now that he's home and off oxygen I work several times a day to get him to take feeds by mouth. I gave up breastfeeding after a few weeks because he cried every time I offered him my breast. It's much easier to coax a rubber nipple into his mouth so I switched exclusively to bottle feedings. He takes between five and ten ml by mouth twice a day. Not much, but enough to keep him in the habit.

Ryan cries most times he sees the bottle and fusses when I try to give it to him. I hold his chin firm and work the nipple on the roof of his mouth. He plays with it and sucks on it some. After a few short minutes he cries full-throttle and I stop. It's a no-win place to be. I don't want him associating eating with bad feelings, but I also don't want to be so lax he stays comfortable letting the tube do the work for him. After each session, I feel like I've wrestled an alligator.

The past few days he's started refusing the bottle altogether. His nasal passages are congested . . . possibly from irritation from the NG tube. The pediatrician says the nasal membranes create lubricant when they have constant rubbing, which is why Ryan sounds congested. There's no drainage in his sinuses or lungs to speak of so we have no other explanation. This means oral feedings are out for now. I place a call to the occupational therapist that taught me how to work with Ryan and is known for being able to "get a rock to eat."

"Hi, this is Ryan Marquiss's mom," I say. "You worked with Ryan in-house and I'm wondering if you can help me set my expectations." I explain about the nasal congestion and our progress or lack thereof this far. "Should I try getting him to accept the bottle and if so, how much should I expect him to eat at one time?"

"I'm not surprised he's refusing the bottle. If he's congested he can't breathe through his nose while he's sucking. Besides that, it's normal for heart babies to have feeding tubes for a long time. Don't be surprised if he goes straight from the feeding tube to a sippy cup," she explains. "Even if the congestion goes away, he won't have the energy to establish a consistent suck-swallow pattern. I see a lot of heart babies go to a sippy cup without ever having accepted a bottle. It doesn't hurt them developmentally at all. It's just the way it goes."

Hearing this is both a relief and a disappointment. My goal was to get rid of the feeding tube and now it looks like that's unrealistic. I'm learning goals and expectations should be as flexible as plans.

IT'S MID-MAY. Ryan's been home for two weeks. He's being checked over by Mary, the home nurse assigned to check on us twice a week. This is only her fifth visit.

"Ryan doesn't seem right today. Has he been acting funny for you?" she says.

"He's had diarrhea for three days now. Eight diapers last night alone. The pediatrician convinced me to give him the rotavirus vaccine on Friday. I think it made him sick. I called her and the cardiac hotline yesterday, and both told me to give it another day," I said.

"I think you should take him in," Mary says. "I know he's a baby and really just lays around, but he's not his peppy self. I'm really concerned."

"Okay. I'll call the cardiologist now," I hurry off to make the call grateful for the professional advice.

"HEY, GUYS, COME on in," the nurse at the pediatrician's office says as she holds open the door between the waiting room and exam rooms. I barely have a chance to sign in before she appears in the doorway. "Girls, follow the nurse," I say.

"We're going to be down here in room one. It's typically for well visits. We don't want Ryan in a room that might have germs in it. What's going on today?" She says leading the way.

"Ryan's had diarrhea for several days now and the cardiologist wants to check to make sure he's not dehydrated," I explain.

"Let's take his vitals and then Dr. Shepherd will be right in." She takes out her stethoscope and listens for Ryan's heart rate.

There's a light knock on the door. Dr. Shepherd enters the room. "I heard Ryan isn't feeling well. Let's see what's going on," she says.

After checking him over and looking at the numbers she says, "He doesn't look terribly dehydrated and his vitals are okay. Do you want to wait one more day and then if he's not over the diarrhea go in for lab work tomorrow?"

"I'd rather go in today if you don't mind," I say. "He's been losing liquid for the last three days. I can replace it pretty easily since he's fed through the tube, but his home nurse was really concerned about him this morning and I've been concerned for a few days. I'd rather put my mind at ease by finding out his electrolyte levels sooner rather than later."

"Okay, sure, I'll write you a script for the labs and we'll call over to Reston Hospital and let them know you're coming. I don't want him waiting with the general public and chance picking something up," she says.

The kids and I trudge back to the car not more than ten minutes after arriving. It's the quickest trip to the doctor's to date.

We cover the distance of the few blocks to the hospital fairly quickly. "Give me a minute, girls. I'm going to start up the feeding pump here by the car. Can you come stand next to me so I know you're not in the road? There are big cars in the parking lot and they might not see you. Here, each of you put a hand on the stroller."

"Can I shake it, mommy? Can I? Can I?" Ainsley asks bouncing up and down as if on a pogo stick.

"Sure, sweet girl. Hurry up though. Mommy's in a rush." I start the machine and get it ready for the milk.

"Can I push the buttons, mom?" Natalie asks sweetly.

"Okay, but let me help you. I don't want to waste any of the milk." Natalie and I prime the pump and start the feeds. Soon we're headed for the building.

"I'm here to have my son's blood drawn. The pediatrician said she was going to call ahead." I say to the receptionist at outpatient services.

"What's your son's name?" she asks.

"Henry Marquiss," I say, signing our name on the registry.

"Oh!" she says jumping up from her seat. "Come down to window three."

I follow her down the row of cubicles and enter the one marked THREE. She's standing behind the desk. "This is Mark. He'll get you registered and then I'll meet you in the hallway and take you to the lab. We don't want you waiting long."

"Thank you," I say confused by all the hoopla, but loving that I don't have to get in line behind the thirty-plus people in the waiting room.

Mark starts entering Ryan's insurance information into the system. When he's done he says, "If you'll go back to the waiting room door, I'll meet you in the hallway and walk you down."

I gather the girls and we meet Mark at the other side of the waiting room. He walks us back toward the hospital entrance and knocks on a door marked LAB.

"Come in," a man's voice says from behind the closed wooden door.

Mark holds the door so I can push the stroller through. "Hi, I'm Mike. I'm going to be taking your blood today. Or is it his?" he says smiling down at Ryan.

"I'm Leighann," I say returning his smile and shaking his hand. "It's his." Turning to the girls I say, "Hey, why don't you guys color a picture while Mr. Mike helps Ryan." I pull out a coloring book and crayons I brought for busy work.

"But there's no place to sit," Ainsley chirps like a bird begging for food.

"You can sit at my desk," Mike says kindly. "See, one of you can sit here and the other one there. How's that?"

With the girls situated, Mike begins the process of drawing Ryan's blood. "He can be a hard stick," I warn him.

"All right then, I have my work cut out for me," Mike says. I wonder if he's ever melancholy. Since the moment we walked in he's been incredibly kind and upbeat. He's perfect for this job. He deftly inserts the needle and immediately gets blood flow. I'm impressed.

"Okie dokie. We're done here," he says snapping his rubber gloves off and marking the tiny vials of dark purple blood. "We'll get you the results as soon as we can and fax a copy to the doctor. I heard there's a rush on these. Anything else I can do for you today?"

"Nope, that's it," I say. "Girls, let's go. We're all done here."

"But I didn't finish my picture," Natalie says surprised.

"Me either," Ainsley echoes.

"You'll have to do them in the car. We're all done and Mr. Mike has more patients."

"Awwwww, can't we just stay a little longer?" Natalie says.

"Come on, guys. Let's go." I can't believe I'm begging the girls to leave the doctor's office.

AT HOME, I change another yucky diaper and cuddle with my sick baby on the couch. The girls sit at the table and finish their coloring. Soon they're off playing something else and I'm dozing. Ryan cries every time he has a bowel movement so with an average of eight diapers each the last two nights I haven't slept much. The shrill ring of the phone wakes me.

"Hi?" I hear Natalie say. She comes running into the room holding out the phone like it's a pariah about to chew off her chin. "Somebody's on the phone for you, mommy."

"Hello?" I say into the receiver.

"Hi, Mrs. Marquiss. This is the pediatrician's office. We got the blood work back from the lab and the numbers don't look good. Dr. Shepherd put a call into the cardiologist and they both feel you should take Ryan downtown to Children's. Since it's closing time for the clinic, they'll admit him to the floor through the ER."

I sigh before saying, "I'll take him right in." I hang up the phone devastated. The familiar sinking feeling returns to the pit of my stomach. Back to the hospital for admittance. We spent so long trying to leave the place I'm in no hurry to return. I really wanted Ryan to be home the full eight weeks before his tissue expander surgery. Yes, I'm setting goals again because I obviously haven't learned my lesson. I exhale slowly before dialing Henry's cell phone number. He answers on the second ring. "Hey, I'm in a meeting can I call you right back?"

"Actually, you got a minute?" My voice catches. "I just got off the phone with the pediatrician's office. I need to take Ryan downtown. He's severely dehydrated. Dr. Donofrio's admitting him tonight to the floor."

"What can I do?" he says.

"I need you to come home earlier than you probably can. I'll call your mom to see if she can come down for the next few days to watch the girls. If she can't, I'm sure Bridget or Katie will watch them. You'll have to drop them on your way to work. I'm guessing he'll be there at least overnight."

"No problem. I'll work it out. I'm supposed to be at one more meeting after this. I'll call Josh to go in my place. Will forty-five minutes be soon enough?" he says.

"Yeah, it'll probably take that long for me to pack up and get the girls acclimated anyway."

"Okay. See you soon. Love you," he says.

"'Love you, too." We hang up. "Girls! Come here a second," I say loudly. They come in and sit beside me. "Hey guys," I say pulling them close. "Ry-ry has to go back to the hospital for tonight. He's not feeling well and his doctors and nurses need to help him get better. I'm going to stay with him to make sure he isn't lonely or scared."

"But I don't want him to go back," Natalie wails. "We just got him." Her eyes fill with tears. She crosses her arms over her chest defiantly. Ainsley tugs my arm and says quietly, "Can you stay here? I don't want you to spend the night." Her thumb immediately goes into her mouth.

"I know, guys. I don't want Ryan to go either. It's what he needs right now though. And it won't be for as long as when he was born. Do you want to help me pack?"

"No," they chorus, but tag along after me anyway. They sit on my bed watching me throw clothes and toiletries into my overnight bag.

Henry and I do the switch off exchanging a long hug at the door. He slaps me on the rear and gives me a weak smile as I head to the car. Willa will come down late tonight and care for the girls until I can get back. I have no idea what we'd do without her. I think about how the specialist recommended we stay local. It was excellent advice. I can't imagine having Ryan in one part of the country and my girls in another. I feel torn between the two as it is.

AT CHILDREN'S ER, I wait in a small line to register. The room is only about a third full. When it's our turn, I roll Ryan in his stroller up to the triage nurse and take a seat across from her. She gets my insurance information and general demographics before taking Ryan's vitals. As she raises her stethoscope to listen to Ryan's heart I quickly say, "Um, before you do that, can I tell you to be careful? His heart's exposed. Let me open his shirt so you can see where to place that."

Without skipping a beat, the nurse picks up her phone and says into the line, "Do you have a private room back there? I have a patient with an exposed heart and I'd like him to come back immediately."

"Oh, you don't have to do that . . ." I interrupt. I realize she thinks Ryan's heart's open to the air, something that's common up to a few days after open-heart surgery, but a situation you'd never go home with. (I don't think!)

"No, it's better this way. You can step over to that desk. A nurse is on her way out to get you," she says.

Ryan quickly becomes the talk of the ER as doctors and nurses come by to look at his anatomy. For most in the medical profession, ectopia cordis is seen only in textbooks and even more rarely with the patient living. This is a once-in-a-lifetime opportunity and something they'll turn into folklore. I welcome them all. I'm happy for this chance to have them learn from Ryan's case. I joke about charging twenty-five cents per view like the little Chinese ladies in San Francisco who make fortune cookies.

After a harrowing forty-five minutes of trying to place an IV line, Ryan's finally hooked up to intravenous electrolytes and admitted to the HKU.

We spend two days in the hospital. In that time his temperature stabilizes as do his bowel movements. It takes a full half hour for his facial expression to relax once home. Even then, he keeps his eyes on me for reassurance. At one point, I have him sitting on my lap facing forward, but he cocks his head back to continue looking at me. I hold him until he falls asleep. When I put him in his crib, he opens his eyes and his little lip quivers. "I have to put you down sometime," I say gently. I pat his back until he surrenders to a deep sleep.

I feel light for the first time in a long time. I'm in the garage cleaning up from an earlier painting project. It's the first day of June. I know a lot of people consider painting rooms or furniture to be a tedious job. The peace and quiet gives me a chance to clear my head and re-energize. It's easy to lose myself in the project because I'm forced to slow down and keep a steady stroke. My breathing slows . . . it's almost like meditating. Yes, I get all this from painting an old hutch! Depending on the size of the project, it's a cheap form of therapy.

After many months of living on the edge of panic, I feel balanced. I finished my project, played with the kids, and even have dinner in the crockpot, definitely an A-game type of day. The phone rings as I'm wiping my hands on a towel. "Hello?" I say. There's no answer. "Hello?" It must be a solicitor whose computer hasn't clicked over yet. I'm about to hang up when I hear a faint "hello."

"Henry, is that you? I can barely hear you," I shout into the receiver thinking somehow if I shout I'll hear him better.

"I'm in the ER," he says a little louder but still faint.

"What? In Reston? Why are you at the hospital? Are you okay?" I ask bewildered.

"My appendix. I have to have it taken out," he says. "I'm in a lot of pain.'"

I take a deep breath. "Do you want me there?"

"If you can."

My mind starts clicking through all the things that need to happen. "Okay, I'll see what I can do."

I hang up and immediately dial my mother-in-law who by now has certainly sprouted wings and has a strange glowing circle hovering above her head. "I can come down, but I probably can't get there until nine. Is that too late?" she says.

I look at the clock. 4:30. "I'll call Elayne to come watch the kids until then. I'll keep you updated." I quickly dial our regular babysitter's number.

"Hello, this is Janna," Elayne's mom says.

"Hey, Janna. This is Leighann. Henry's in the ER and I was calling to see if Elayne can watch the kids until my mother-in-law gets here. . . . I'm just now realizing she isn't trained to take care of Ryan. It's not going to work. Let me think."

"Is Henry okay?" Janna asks.

"It's his appendix. They're going to take it out tonight, most likely. I'd like to be there if I can," I say.

"I totally understand. What kind of caregiver are you comfortable with for Ryan? I'd come, but I have to get two different kids to baseball tonight. . . . You know what? Our neighbor is a nurse. She goes to our church. You probably don't know her though because her kids don't babysit. Do you want me to call her and see if she can come?"

"That'd be perfect. She really doesn't have to do much except know how to administer meds and work a feeding pump," I say relieved.

Janna's neighbor arrives within a half hour. She tells me her name, which quickly takes flight with all the other information my brain can't be bogged down with. I show her Ryan's food and medication schedule.

"Is this his normal color?" she asks politely.

I look at Ryan's little blue nose. I'm so desensitized I hardly notice it anymore. "It's normal. He sats in the mid-sixties and is always cyanotic. And he's always slightly in respiratory distress. If he looks any worse than that over the next few hours, which I don't expect he'll do, call me. My cell number's on the pad on the fridge. Dinner is in the crockpot and as long as the girls are happy, I'm happy. They go to bed at seven thirty. My mother-in-law should be here around nine. Thank you so much." I run out the door with my breast pump in one hand and a small overnight bag in the other.

AT THE HOSPITAL a nurse leads me back to Henry's triage room. He's lying on a gurney writhing in pain, sweat beads on his forehead. I look up out of habit for any sort of indication of his vitals, but the monitor isn't on. "Do you need anything?" I ask.

"I could use something to drink," Henry says through clenched teeth. "I think the nurse is getting me pain meds, but she's been gone awhile."

Poking my head out the door I see a nurse doing paperwork. "Are you my husband's nurse?" I say as politely as possible.

"Yes, can I help you?"

"He's thirsty. Is he allowed anything by mouth?" I ask.

"He can have clear liquids for now," she says. "Also, the orders just came through for his pain killers so I'll bring them right in along with some water."

"Awesome. He was asking for those, too," I say.

Back in Henry's room I sit beside him quietly to let him rest. "Who's with the kids?" he asks after a few minutes.

"A nurse friend of Janna's," I say. "I called to see if Elayne could come before remembering about Ryan. Janna called her neighbor who also goes to the church."

"Good thinking. I wouldn't leave Ryan with very many people right now. How long is she staying?"

"Your mom's supposed to get here sometime tonight after the kids are asleep. She can stay the next few days if we need her. How's your pain level?" I ask.

"On a scale of ten, about a fifteen. They wanted me to wait in the waiting room so I laid down in front of the receptionist desk and said I wasn't moving until they brought me back. It didn't take long after that. I wish they'd bring me pain meds though," he says.

As if on cue, the nurse walks in with water and two white pills. "Here you go," she says cheerfully. "The doctor should be around within the next half hour or so."

The doctor verifies it's Henry's appendix, and by the time he goes back for surgery it's nearly nine o'clock. "It's going to be about an hour, Mrs. Marquiss. I'll come out and let you know when we're done." He leaves me in a deserted surgical waiting room. You would think I'd be lonely or bored however it's amazing to sit in the quiet with absolutely nothing to do but wait. Well, almost nothing to do. I set up my breast pump and pull my nursing cape around my front. I look like Madonna on her Blonde Ambition tour trying to be modest. In a room with no one in it, it really doesn't matter. I pull a snack from my bag (I always have one on hand) and pick up the book I brought to read. Just as I turn the first page my phone rings. "Hey, where are you? I'm in the ER waiting room, but don't see you," Bridget says.

"Are you kidding me? What are you doing here?" I say, shocked.

"Do you think I'd miss the chance to spend some quiet time with you? These days I only see you if you're coming or going so I figure now that you're trapped you have to talk to me!"

She laughs when she sees me. "Are you seriously pumping in the middle of the waiting room?" she says.

"I'm the only one here!" I say. "Do you want me to find a more private spot?"

We spend the next hour drinking each other in. I can't remember the last time I just sat and talked to a friend with nowhere to be, no kids pulling on our arms or clothes to get our attention. Just us. The hour goes too fast.

"Mrs. Marquiss, your husband's getting closed up," the surgeon informs me. "I'm surprised he didn't go toxic. His appendix is one of the worst I've seen. It was riddled with infection. I think he's been feeling pain for some time and ignoring it. There's a good chance he'll get a post-surgical infection or run a fever tomorrow. We'll give him antibiotics tonight and then you'll take a prescription with you. For now, the nurse will come get you when your husband's moving to a room."

"I guess that's my cue," Bridget says. We hug good-bye. An orderly comes out a few minutes later and leads me to Henry's room. I watch as he's rolled into place. The nurse hooks up his leads to a monitor and hangs his bag of IV antibiotics. It's 11:30 P.M. For the next half hour she asks him questions like how many years he completed in school and if he'd classify himself as Caucasian or African American because these questions are *so* important they cannot wait until morning. We finally turn the lights out at midnight. As I pull the blanket up around my shoulders my cell phone rings. It can only be one person.

"Hello?" I say.

"Hey, it's Willa. I'm so sorry, but I pulled Ryan's feeding tube out. I'm afraid to put it back in," she says.

"It's okay. I'm only five minutes away. I'll be right there."

The house is dark when I arrive. After grabbing some lubricant, a skin prep pad, tape, scissors, and a sterile feeding tube from the hutch in the kitchen, I head upstairs. I find Ryan and Willa in the nursery. "I'm so sorry. I don't know how it came out. I was trying to lift him from the crib and the next thing I know his tube was out," she says.

"It's fine. I do it, too. It's long and catches on things. I'm going to need your help though. It's a two-person job."

"Okay, just tell me what to do," she says.

I lay Ryan on the floor and sit next to him. I pause for a moment trying to remember which nostril his feeding tube was in yesterday. It's good to rotate it so the nasal passages get rest. I open the skin prep pad and rub a stripe of it across his right cheek like an Apache dressing for war. The residue's clear but sticky. "This helps the tape stick to his face better," I explain. Then I cut two strips of tape about 1.5 inches by 1 inch and set them to the side. I only need one, but sometimes I mess one up during the procedure so now I always cut two just in case. I also cut a very small strip to use as a marker.

The tube is yellow and about the thickness of a piece of spaghetti. It has numbers on it measuring 1 to 45. By taking the tip of the tube and placing it at the patient's earlobe and then snaking it over to the tip of the nose and curving it down to the belly button, you can find out how much length you need to end up in the stomach. I measure Ryan every third or fourth tube insertion to make sure there are no changes. I don't bother measuring tonight. Pulling the new tube from its sealed plastic bag I take the marker strip and wrap it like a Band-aid around a finger at the number 36. Some people mark the spot with an ink pen. I prefer the tape method so I can easily see it hasn't moved in or out with his coughing just by glancing at him. If it was a pen mark, I'd have to inspect the tube more closely, and sometimes the ink rubs off.

I dip the tube into the lubricant making sure it's fully coated on the last two inches. "Okay, here's the hard part," I say to Willa. "You have to hold his head still. This is a really yucky feeling so he's going to squirm and cry. Press your palms on either side of his head near his ears, but don't cover his cheeks. I need to put the tape there."

"Okay," she says taking a deep breath while stabilizing Ryan's head in her hands.

"Here we go," I whisper more to myself than her. *Please let this go in right*, I pray silently. Holding the tube as close to the end as possible without touching the lubricant I guide it into Ryan's right nostril. I point it the slightest bit up to follow the shape of his nose then apply a little bit of pressure as it hits the curve at the back of his nostril. With the pressure, the tube hooks down. Ryan is crying, his face beet-red. He gags as the tube moves from his nasal passages into the back of his throat. There's a slight pushback on the tube as the gag reflex rejects it. *Please, Lord, help me.* I pause a moment letting his body adjust. Pushing through the gag only makes him gag more and longer. As his gag lets up I use both hands, index fingers and thumbs pressed together with the tube in between, moving them quickly over the tube as if I'm shimmying up a tiny rope. I push it millimeter by millimeter down into Ryan's stomach. When the tape marker hits the tip of his nostril I stop pushing and pull the remaining length of the tube across his cheek and lay it onto the sticky patch of skin prep. Holding it there with one hand I grab a piece of tape with the other and secure the tube. The nurses at the hospital told us to check placement before taping, but we've never been successful at doing that without having the tube move so we tape first and then check placement.

"Are we done?" Willa asks.

"Almost. I just have to make sure it's in the right spot," I say. I grab the stethoscope and an empty 10 cc syringe. I take 3 ccs of air into the syringe and then connect it to Ryan's tube port. Placing the stethoscope right below Ryan's omphalocele (for most patients right on or around the belly button) I push the 3 ccs of air quickly into the tube. I hear a small *whoosh*. This means the air went into his stomach and the tube is in the right spot. I pull the 3 ccs of air back out of the tube to remove the air I placed in Ryan's stomach. Closing the top of the port I look at my mother-in-law. "Now we're done. Thanks for holding his head. I know it's a rough job. Henry hates it. He can't stand how Ryan looks at him and cries."

I lay Ryan back in his crib. My head hits the pillow by 12:30 A.M. on my little cot in the corner of Henry's hospital room. He's breathing heavily, the details of a long and torturous day a distant memory.

I ARRIVE HOME with a recovering Henry a day and a half later. After greeting the kids and getting Henry settled, I sit down to pump. I take advantage of being forced to sit still by checking my email. I haven't been at my computer for a few days. Among the spam and greetings from friends, I find the following email from my dad: "Uncle Bill passed away this morning. I'll send funeral information soon." It's dated yesterday.

I quietly go up to the bedroom where Henry's resting and sit on the floor. "Uncle Bill passed away," I say.

"You okay?" he asks.

"Yeah . . . no. I mean . . . I'm really, really sad. Is this the way you felt when Rob died? Just sad?"

"Come up here with me. I can't reach you and I want to hug you," he says. Careful not to jiggle the bed too much, I creep up beside my husband and lay in his arms. He kisses me on the head and squeezes me. I fold into his side and stain his shirt with mascara as I wash away my sadness with tears.

MY SISTER, AMY, comes up from Florida to attend our uncle's funeral and our baby brother John's, high school graduation, which coincidentally fall within a few days of each other. She and Johanna descend upon my house for a day. She immediately starts cleaning and helping me get little things done that I haven't had time to attend to. (She actually cleaned the animal poo off my tennis shoe that sat on my porch for two weeks. Seriously. She rocks.) As I watch her take charge—cleaning, doing laundry, doing dishes—I almost feel offended and territorial. I'm used to being the one with everything under control, the one taking care of everyone else. I'm used to being the helper, not the helpee. I'm not sure I like this new role. It leaves me feeling defensive . . . forcing me to admit I can't handle everything on my own. I try to be gracious and grateful.

We're standing in the kitchen putting away the clutter that's collected over the last few months when she turns to me and says, "Why aren't you having Katie (our sister) come clean your house anymore?"

"I feel bad having her come now. When Ryan was in the hospital, I wasn't here to do it myself. I'm home now and I'm like every other mom with three little kids," I say.

"That's the stupidest thing I've ever heard," she says flatly.

"Henry said the same thing when I told him. I can't have her come forever though. It's a long drive and she's got a lot going on. I'm sure every mother with three kids would love to have someone come clean their house, do their laundry, and cook them meals. I'm home now though so I feel like I should do these things myself. It's a normal part of adjusting."

"But you're not normal," she points out.

"Yes, I am," I say.

"No, you're not. You're not normal," she insists.

"Stop saying that," I say hotly. "I *am* normal."

"No you're not."

"Stop it!" By now I'm in tears and I have no idea why. I feel normal. (I'm normal, right?) Undeterred by my tears, she doesn't let up. "How many doctor's appointments did you take Ryan to this week?"

"Three, but only because he has surgery next week. Normally it's only two," I say.

"Normal mothers don't have multiple weekly doctor appointments," she says gently as if I'm a china doll that will break with heavy use. Since I'm crying it's a safe assumption.

"Look, I'm not having this conversation. This is *our* normal. It might not be everyone else's normal, but it's ours. I'm adjusting. My house isn't as clean as it used to be, dinner looks different, and my kids watch more TV. Everyone's getting what they need to survive. They have food. And clothes. And cuddle-time on the couch. So what if the toys stay on the floor overnight? Or the laundry stays in piles a few more days? Yes, I have a lot on my plate. So does everyone else. I'm assuming anyone with three kids under school age is running around trying to get everything done and not succeeding. Normal. Why have people go out of their way to bring me food and clean my house now that we're all under one roof?"

"You're still getting meals three times a week from your church, aren't you?" she asks.

"I told Bridget I didn't need them anymore and she told me to shut up and take the meals. She'd decide when I was ready to cook again," I answer.

"I knew I liked her," Johanna pipes up. She's been watching the *discussion* from the corner of the kitchen.

"Can we please talk about something else? I want to enjoy the time you're here, not feel like I have to defend myself."

"Okay, but you need to accept help. Let someone clean if they offer," Amy says.

"Fine," I say.

I try to mean it. Really, I do, but the help I need is hard to pass off. If someone really wanted to help me they could take the emotional load off my shoulders for a day or two. That's where I need the most help. Or how about pumping for me so I can get a good night's rest? Or waking up with Ryan for his early feeding. That would be lovely. Rest is always a good thing for a new mom. It's something I can't seem to get. I pump at eleven o'clock at night and then again at seven in the morning so there's no going to bed early or sleeping in. The only time I have to catch up on my sleep is during the day . . . when my three children are awake! It's a never-ending cycle. And it's about to get worse.

EXITING OFF RT. 66, I take Key Bridge into the city. I people-watch as pedestrians walk from Georgetown into Rosslyn to grab a bite to eat or catch the Metro home. There are runners, bikers, and skateboarders; students, active military personnel, and the homeless man who perpetually stands on the corner before the bridge asking for money.

The radio is on, but I'm too distracted to listen. CSPAN is my drug of choice. The Senate is debating war funding and healthcare packages. I feel my energy level winding down as the stillness envelopes me. Having the girls helps me live in denial. Denial of what's really going on, how not normal this whole situation is (yes, Amy is right). With the busyness of life gone, all I have to think about is tomorrow.

As Whitehurst Parkway merges onto K Street, it hits me. I'm driving my son to have surgery and haven't thought a thing of it until now. I'm not sure how typical it is that I'm not worried about my child's surgery. Is it weird that Henry's home with the girls at my request while I'm headed to the hospital alone with our son? *I could just keep driving. I could drop him at the hospital and keep going. No one would find me. I could disappear in an instant.*

I turn onto Twenty-First Street toward Dupont Circle, my vision blurred by tears. I feel lonely, defeated, and tired. It's like we're starting over. Driving back and forth . . . leaving my baby for others to care for. The eight-week hiatus is over. I loved those eight weeks. Life was different . . . less playing outside, less engaging the girls in educational activities, but we were a family, everyone together under one roof. We were able to play and do the things regular families do. Even through twice-weekly doctor visits, the twice-weekly home visits by a nurse and all the care that comes with a heart defect and feeding tube, I was able to get into a routine and believe Ryan was doing well.

Because of that I have to will myself to drive him to the hospital for surgery, fighting the urge to wrap ourselves in the cozy cocoon of home. My instincts are to ignore the reality of Ryan's condition. Honestly, I don't have the energy for the logistics required for a long hospital stay. I already did this for nine weeks. I dread doing it again.

I pull into the parking garage. It's late and there are plenty of parking spaces near the entrance. I sit still for a moment in the quiet. I close my eyes trying to ground myself before going in. After an hour and half of helping Ryan settle, I head down the street to the Ronald McDonald House to try getting a full night's sleep.

I toss and turn, drifting in and out of consciousness. I have yet to figure out why I feel exhausted all day, resorting to propping my eyes open with toothpicks, only to lie down and suddenly be alert. I've barely slept when the alarm goes off in the morning.

Arriving at Ryan's room before the sun pops its head over the horizon, adrenaline keeps me alert for what lies ahead. Ryan's room is dark. I expected activity since he's having a procedure shortly. An hour later a fellow brings me a consent form for the general and plastic surgeon. The process begins.

Good Morning, America is on in the surgical waiting room. A guest chef shows us how easy slow-cooker brisket is to make. I'm doing a good job distancing myself emotionally from Ryan's surgery. Driving into the parking lot I almost burst into tears at the sight of Dr. Bear, the hospital logo, but kept my composure. Is it possible to have post-traumatic stress disorder from visiting a hospital too many times? Now in the waiting room, I feel at peace.

I wonder how Ryan feels about the hospital. His little eyes grow huge every time we come. He didn't get a worried look on his face when we walked through the CICU this time. I worry about his anxiety level since he's too young to worry about it himself. I wonder if he'll be a serious little boy or if he'll enjoy life as the girls did.

Last night while I was waiting for his nurse to come ask the admitting questionnaire, I put Ryan on my lap to work his neck muscles. I've done this a couple times and he tracks me moving back and forth, side to side. I moved fast from one side to the other and said, "Where's mama?" When he moved his little neck to find me and caught my eye I said, "There she is!" He smiled—big, huge, the size-of-Texas smiles. If he could laugh he would've. He loved this new game. It typically takes a lot of work to get Ryan to smile. He doesn't make any noise except to complain or cry. No cooing or laughter. It was fun to see him enjoying something. Most of the time the feeling I have about Ryan is relief. Relief he survived birth, a heart catheterization, a heart surgery; relief he can breathe on his own, relief he's well enough to come home to us. The roller coaster of emotions thinking about his basic survival leaves little time for pure, light-hearted joy.

DR. BOYAJIAN BRIEFS me after the surgery is complete. He's pleased with the lay of the tissue expanders. They're "sitting nicely" in Ryan's chest and he tolerated the surgery well. They'll give him a week or two to recover before starting to expand them by 10 ccs twice a week.

The other good news is Ryan came off the ventilator directly after surgery and is breathing on his own—something we all secretly feared he wouldn't do. The biggest concern is how he'll breathe once his sedation wears off. If Ryan's in too much pain he'll take shortened breaths, resulting in lower oxygen levels. We'll have a better read in the next four hours.

Hours turn into days, three to be exact. Ryan cries if we move him in the slightest. We move him between his crib and the chair to change up the pressure points on his body. With oxygen levels in the high sixties, he's receiving supplemental oxygen to help his body do the work. They won't discharge him until he can maintain better sat levels on his own. I've been staying with him around the clock since he's in the Heart and Kidney Unit. Henry took off work to watch the girls.

Suddenly four nurses come rushing into the room and gather around Ryan's bed. "Everything okay?" I ask casually.

"The monitors say he's desatting but his color looks okay," one of the nurses answers. "We're just checking up on him."

I realize his monitor is alarming when one of the nurses reaches over and silences it. My brain's conditioned to ignore the beeping. It goes off so often as a result of a bad read from the probe that monitors his sats that it's become white noise.

We stand around his bed for fifteen minutes. Ryan continues sleeping, and the nurses are still watching him. His color isn't terrible. They start to disperse as it seems it's another false alarm. I take the chance to grab some dinner from the cafeteria before it closes.

My cell phone rings while I'm waiting for my hamburger. I pull it from my pocket and study the number. It's Children's Hospital. I flip open my phone, confused because I know all the doctors' offices are closed by this hour. "Hello."

"Hi, this is the HKU," the caller says.

"Is everything all right?" I say, my stomach doing a little flip. They don't usually call me.

"Ryan's working really hard to breathe," the nurse explains.

"Should I come up?" I ask.

"We think you should," she says. "The attending and fellow are on their way."

"Do you call the CICU or is that not part of the protocol?" I ask. For some reason I'm more comfortable having them involved. Probably because I've worked mostly with them and feel they know Ryan's case like the backs of their hands.

"It's part of the protocol. They'll be here before you are," she says.

"I'm on my way."

I arrive to see many familiar and some new faces. Doctors and nurses from the CICU and HKU are gathered around Ryan's crib commenting on his color, numbers, and chest movement.

"Hi, Kitty, Lauren, Lowell," I say to the three fellows. They've known and watched Ryan since birth. They know him better than I do. We talk about Ryan's breathing, trying to figure out if a boy who's always in respiratory distress is in his own sort of respiratory distress. He's awake watching us out of big eyes, through those long lashes, tracking the movement of the different doctors, latching on to them one at a time. His gaze lingers on this one and that choosing whom he wants to listen to for the moment. He takes it all in somberly. I imagine what he's thinking about the crowd around his crib. *I sure do know how to get them all in here* or *I called this meeting because . . .* or *now that's a pretty blue shirt, isn't it?*

After much debate, the doctors decide it's best for Ryan to move back to the CICU on high flow oxygen to maintain his oxygen saturation at acceptable levels.

I feel like a dog excitedly chasing a car only to be jerked back on my chain. I expected Ryan to stay on the ventilator after this surgery. I was sure the expanders would put too much pressure on his underdeveloped chest and he'd require assistance to breathe. When he came through the surgery so well and came off the vent immediately after, I got my hopes up. I allowed myself to believe he was leaving this place and in short order. Once again it's two steps forward and one step back.

I follow Ryan's gurney down the hall to the CICU, my proverbial tail between my legs.

AFTER A WEEKEND away from the girls and Ryan now under the constant supervision of the ICU, I take two days "off" from the hospital to dote on them. They're clingy and need mommy time.

It's hard being away from Ryan, but I feel it's important to fill the girls' emotional love tanks. I justify it by reminding myself Ryan's heavily sedated.

It's weird being home without him. I'll be in the middle of something and think, "Oh, I need to go check on Ryan." Or as we head outside, "I better leave the door open so I can hear Ryan." I have to stop and remind myself he isn't here. Each time is like getting sucker-punched.

I also uninstall his car seat to give the girls more elbow room and move his feeding pump to the closet. It stands in the corner like a sentry at his post waiting for his master to come home. I'm basically putting his things in storage. Having them out of sight forces me to admit he isn't going to use them anytime soon. The team isn't talking of home any longer. He's there indefinitely. Although not vented, Ryan's stuck because he simply cannot breathe through the weight or placement of the expanders. It's been long enough that we don't think pain is a factor.

I'm struck by the thought that this plan of ours might not work. This whole time I've never once considered this as a possibility—that we might not be able to grow him more skin. Then what?

The last couple days have been tough on him. His oxygen saturations are sitting lower than his pre-surgery baseline. He tires easily and has had several episodes of desatting for no particular reason.

When at thirteen weeks pregnant I felt God would heal Ryan, I moved forward assuming it meant total healing, not just surviving birth. There were times during the following months I'd question if I was reading into my experience, living on emotion or deluding myself, but I pressed on in faith.

I think God *has* already healed him in some aspects. I feel the doctors saw his heart failing and were honest with his prognosis. I believe God strengthened his heart to make it possible for him to live. I believe Ryan was born with a skin covering over his heart, something atypical of ectopia cordis, by God's design. This covering allows him to get bigger and stronger before having a major surgery. If he didn't have the covering, he would've had major plastic surgery on the day he was born. The majority of ectopia cordis patients don't live very long, one of the biggest risks being infection. We haven't had to worry about heart infection at all . . . Ryan's heart was never exposed to air. This is huge! It may not constitute healing, but it certainly constitutes protection and provision.

Seeing Ryan struggle reminds me God never promised a long life for my son. He never promised Ryan would respond to treatment or live longer than me. All He asked was for me to trust Him.

God doesn't work through fear. He works through faith. Not faith that He'll do what we want Him to, but faith that He is who He says He is. And who God is doesn't change with our circumstances. It won't change with Ryan's setbacks. I know all of this to be true. I believe it with all of my heart. Yet, this doesn't change how disappointed I am.

The day after I put Ryan's things away I'm despondent. I can't think of a single thing I want to do, including sleeping or eating or reading, my all time favorite things to do. I'm hungry, but I simply mull around the kitchen snacking without caring what it is I'm eating. Amy once told me she eats because she knows her body can't live without food, that she doesn't really *like* food. It was then I knew she was totally off her rocker. I love food. I get giddy talking about pomegranates, brie cheese melted across a lightly toasted baguette slice, strawberries and goat cheese drizzled with balsamic vinegar. Cinnamon . . . anything to do with it. Oh, and honey. And when you mix them, perhaps over a warmed pear. Oh, my gosh!

The last few days there's no food in my cabinet that inspires me. Nothing I can even think of I'd buy at the grocery store. This is enough for me to know there's something drastically wrong. Add to it that I'm not interested in reading—another passion of mine— and you have definite signs of trouble.

Henry comes home from a rare morning of golfing to find me lying in my bed. It's 2:30 in the afternoon. I still have my pajamas on. The girls are destroying the basement while watching television, and I don't care. He pops his head in the bedroom door. I look at him through red, puffy eyes.

"Will you lay with me a little?" I say craving his presence.

He lies down beside me and envelops me into the depths of his frame. I snuggle in and breathe a deep sigh.

"I'm worried about me," I say.

"Are you depressed about Ryan?" he asks squeezing me gently. Hearing the truth spoken out loud strikes a cord deep inside bringing tears to my eyes.

"Can you hug me awhile?"

He does, for a long time. Until we're hot and sweaty and breathing recycled air. "What if he can't handle the tissue expanders? He's going to end up on the vent and I don't want that. We're not even to the hard part yet. This surgery was supposed to be a nothing. An in and out is what Dr. Boyajian said. I don't know if we made the right decision." Henry lies quietly beside me never loosening his grip. He doesn't speak, just listens and lets me unload all I've been thinking the last few days. Finally I say, "Can you take over this weekend? Make sure we have food and the dishes are done and the house isn't destroyed?"

"I'm your man," he says. I know he's hurting although he doesn't talk about it. I wish he'd confide in me, but I think he sees how much I'm carrying and doesn't feel I could carry his burdens, too. He absorbs my pain and adds it to the depths of his own shielding me all he can. He becomes the mother for the weekend, making sure we all have our basic needs met, the girls are engaged, and the house kept in shape. He lets me sulk for a few hours then insists I get up and go for a walk. When I balk at having to get out of bed he jokingly says, "I thought I was in charge this weekend." He knows my body and mind need fresh air. I cry for most of my walk. I'm in overdrive and it's good to clear my head and my heart.

I'm fresher come Monday. We fall back into the routine of driving to the hospital most days of the week. The girls pick up where they left off, flirting with the nurses, setting up Polly Pocket neighborhoods in Ryan's room, and climbing on the bed to play with their brother. It's harder for them to leave him though. Ainsley, the almost three-year-old, asks on several different occasions, "Can we take baby boy home for a little bit?" or "Can we take him home for one day?" I wish I could tell her yes. How I'd love to rip him out of this hospital and bring him home. The grown-up in me knows it can't happen. On these occasions I hold her to me and hug away the tears. "Ryan has to stay here, honey. The doctors are helping him get better and the nurses are taking care of him while we're away from him." I tell her this as much to help her as to help me. It's incredibly hard to leave your baby for someone else to take care of, especially now that he's been home.

The medical team tries to wean Ryan from oxygen. He tells them through desatting he isn't ready. His oxygen levels go to a critically low level anytime oxygen's removed (forties instead of his new baseline sixties). He continues receiving a low amount of supplemental oxygen. Plastics comes twice a week to fill his expanders with another 10 ccs of saline to encourage skin growth in preparation for his upcoming heart surgery. The process is pretty straightforward.

The tissue expander is a silicone bag. It has a small tube that runs from the bag to a port that sits just under the skin below Ryan's ribcage, just above his diaper line. The port is about the size of a watch face. I watch as the fellow places a finger above and below the port, holding it in place with his thumb and index finger. He swabs the site with alcohol and then takes a syringe of injectable, sterile saline fitted with a needle his resident hands him. As he pokes the needle through Ryan's skin and into the port he explains the port is soft on the top but covered with a metal backing prohibiting the needle from going through both sides. Ryan cries from the needle stick during the procedure but calms down quickly after it's withdrawn.

The silver lining of Ryan still being hospitalized is the cardiology team can follow his vitals after having the expansions. There was some back and forth trying to figure out who should give the expansions and where and when. Lots of families do the expansions themselves at home and check in with their plastic surgeon on set dates. In Ryan's case we're unsure if unsupervised expansions are a good idea, especially since he isn't recovering quickly from surgery. For now that conversation is mute since he's in-house.

Cardiology consults with neurology and pulmonology. After ruling out sleep apnea, neurological, and pulmonary reasons behind Ryan's desatting episodes, Dr. Donofrio suggests Ryan may be outgrowing his shunt. Most cardiac patients have a terrible time gaining weight because their body burns a lot of calories just breathing. Ryan's a sixteen-pound four-month-old—the abominable snowman compared to his fellow CICU peers. It could be as simple as a shunt made for an eight-pound baby isn't supplying the blood flow necessary for double the weight.

She explains that if he continues to struggle he'll need to have another shunt put in. She won't allow plastics to do an expansion if Ryan's satting low. He has to be satting in the sixties for a full day before the expansions to give him the best possibility of tolerating the added ccs of saline. If we miss too many expansions, it'll push the Glenn a week or two. If he starts struggling on a daily basis, she'll request Dr. Jonas give him a bigger shunt to hold him over until the Glenn.

My heart leaves its cozy place in my chest and works its way into my throat; another surgery before the one that's supposed to fix him. I can't bear the thought. Tears jump ship against my wishes when I hear the news. I don't want to stay here past August. It's like the finish line for me. Yes, Ryan will need cardiac care after the Glenn, but the doctors think he'll improve significantly after the procedure. We could leave these sterile rooms and tile-clad hallways behind. If I can just get my son home we can live a somewhat normal life. Moving the surgery out isn't on my To-Do list.

"The biggest check box is getting Ryan stable," Dr. Donofrio says. "If that means adding another shunt to the list, we have to do that. I know it's disappointing. We have to keep the big picture in mind though. We'll take it one day at a time. Ryan will tell us what he needs."

For the next few days while I'm adjusting to the idea of an additional heart surgery my emotions are all over the map. Half the time I don't know why I'm crying. Other times, I want to cry and can't. I usually find solace in doing something; however, these days nothing's appealing. I go through the list in my head: Clean? Organize? Decorate? Shop? Eat? Read? Watch television? Sleep? Nope, none of that will cut it. When I sit for long periods of time I end up thinking about absolutely nothing—like how a tree is growing in my neighbor's yard or how the clouds line up in the sky. I finally know what it's like to be inside a man's brain!

I'm not the only one spent. Natalie starts acting out. At the hospital she vies for attention when I'm playing with or holding Ryan. She does things on purpose she knows are unacceptable just to get me to respond. She's interrupting and misbehaving when I'm consulting with the doctors.

Disciplining at the hospital is like performing at a piano recital—there's typically an audience. I hate correcting children in front of other people. It embarrasses the child so they have a hard time focusing on what you're saying. I, too, find myself wondering what the other person's thinking.

I learn to set expectations, and be extremely consistent. Because issues are increasing, I start laying down the law in the car before entering the building. "Okay, girls. Remember: When I'm talking to a nurse or doctor I need you not to interrupt. If you need me, you can quietly say 'excuse me' but it has to be for something really important. While I'm talking to the doctor you can play quietly with your toys, color, sit quietly on my lap, or stand beside me. If you can't be quiet, then I'll have to ask you to sit in the bathroom until I'm finished (the bathroom trashcan is our time-out stool). Understand?"

"Yes, mommy!" they chorus.

It works pretty well. If they forget, I simply say, "Remember what we talked about. Mommy's talking with the doctor right now. What quiet thing do you want to do?" This is usually enough to quiet them down. On several occasions I've had to use the bathroom, but it doesn't take too many incidents before the girls settle down.

Sometimes at night Natalie cries out Ryan's name in her sleep as if she's having a bad dream. Sometimes she's yelling it and other times it's a moan, "Ryan, Ryan, Ryan." It makes me want to let up a little on discipline, but that only makes things worse.

What helps is talking things over with her, letting her know exactly what's happening (i.e., Ryan's having surgery, Ryan's healing, Ryan's getting taken care of . . .) and lots of hugs and attention when I can give it to her. I talk to the child-life specialist at the hospital to see if she can give me any ideas. "This is all normal behavior, " Judy says. "When children are sad they don't know how to express it. They lash out in anger or misbehave. Continue setting guidelines so the girls know what to expect. And just keep talking to them."

Natalie's a time person. She needs time to feel important and loved so I start making it a point to take her out on mommy dates on the weekends. Sometimes it's as simple as running errands together, just her and me, or going to breakfast on a Saturday. The funny thing is while we're out she's constantly talking about the family. Over breakfast at a pancake house one Saturday I say, "Isn't this fun? We should come again."

"Yeah, but next time let's bring daddy and Ainsley."

"Don't you like being on a date with mommy?"

"Yeah, but they'd like it, too, so we should bring them."

I'm flabbergasted at her response, but know that the alone time is working. I notice a behavior improvement if I give her a date every few weeks.

Since the girls were toddlers, I've always brushed their teeth, put their pjs on them, read them a book, sang them a song or two, said a prayer over them, and tucked them into bed. Lately, we all lie in my bed during the books, songs, and prayer while I rub their faces and backs. They love it. Ainsley's primary love language is touch. She gets most of what she needs during our nightly ritual. I know when her tank is low because she'll climb onto my lap and sit with me until the needle climbs its way back up to full. She's the one who chases after us when we leave the house saying, "One more," meaning one more kiss and hug before you leave. If Henry rushes out the door without kissing and hugging her, she runs after him into the driveway.

Her age is a big factor, too. She's still unaware how critical Ryan's situation is; how out-of-the-ordinary having your baby in the hospital really is.

Figuring out how to balance meeting my children's need for love—all of my children—is my current dilemma. As a parent with one child in the hospital and two at home, I'm constantly torn on how to spread the wealth. I'm always choosing what will get done and what won't. Do I spend time with the girls or do I do the dishes? Do I play with the girls or do I put laundry away? I know this is normal for moms with more than one child, but it seems amplified by the fact I'm stretched thin as a pancake from traveling an hour each way to see my son on a daily basis.

Will Natalie remember a mom who crashed for an hour or two in her bed on really bad days instead of playing Polly Pockets? Or a mom who was always trying to get one more thing done before doing crafts? My girls are used to a mother who's engaged in their lives and active in creating a fun atmosphere. I feel like a failure even though I know I don't have the bandwidth or energy to be that mom. It's a reoccurring conversation in my head about how much I'm doing and how much I'm capable of no matter my expectations.

Ryan's sat levels continue to be low; however, he's stable in every other way. The team decides he can come home on oxygen support. I spent the last fifteen minutes getting a tutorial on how to move and operate the waist-high oxygen tank, and I'm just now realizing the representative isn't bringing me an oxygen concentrator, something my son will be dependent on indefinitely.

"Ryan's going to need support at home and this tank only lasts six hours. What do I do when I get home," I ask.

The rep looks at me blankly. "I don't have anything else with me. I was only supposed to bring the portable tank to get home. Someone else is delivering your home supplies."

"Can you excuse me just a minute," I say. I walk quickly a few doors down from Ryan's room in the HKU to the case manager's office. She's in charge of setting up all discharge arrangements. I'm still holding out hope she has a solution. After explaining the situation she says, "Oh yeah, they're going to deliver the home supplies at six o'clock, but someone has to be there to sign for them. I was hoping dad could do it."

I look at the clock. It's 5:30 pm. The oxygen rep was supposed to be here over three hours ago. Now I'm stuck in D.C. when I should be in Virginia. There's no way Henry can be home by six with this short of notice. Through clenched teeth I say, "Dad doesn't get off work until 7:30 P.M. Even if I leave right now, there's now way I can be there by six o'clock."

"They can deliver it up until ten o'clock tonight," she says unfazed.

"That'd be great. Is there a guarantee it will get there? I only have this one tank and it won't last the whole night if they don't arrive."

"There's no guarantee, but I can call them," she offers.

I have no idea what to say. There's no guarantee? My hope fades as I realize Ryan isn't coming home tonight because our ducks aren't in a row. I've never done this before and am kicking myself I didn't realize the equipment wasn't going to be handed to me at the hospital upon discharge. At the least, I can learn the rest of the equipment the oxygen rep has and let him get home to his family.

The oxygen tank is cumbersome on its cart. I try to imagine what it'll be like lugging that thing around in addition to Ryan, his stroller and all the stuff I need to support him. *I don't think I can do this. Maybe it's better if he stays here*, I think. After four weeks in-house though the thought of another six until the Glenn is enough to motivate me to suck it up. I sign the paperwork accepting the tank, cart, and suction machine and bid the man goodnight. I leave the hospital empty-handed. Ryan's car seat is installed and empty yet again. We'll try again tomorrow.

JULY 16 DAWNS and I can't wait to bring my baby home for the second time. Most babies only have one homecoming; we're fortunate to be able to celebrate again. Natalie jumps up and down on the sidewalk when she sees my car pull into the neighborhood. The oxygen company delivered the oxygen concentrator and several portable tanks early this morning before I left for the hospital. We set Ryan and his oxygen machine up in the living room so he's central to all our activities.

"Mommy," Natalie says, "You sleep upstairs tonight. I think I should sleep down here (in the living room). When Ryan wakes up I can take care of him." She's almost as territorial as I am. It's precious to see her run to Ryan's side when he fusses and sing to make him happy.

It's fun, too, to see the interaction between Henry and Ryan. Before he leaves for work the next day, Henry bends down to Ryan's chair and coos at him. "Good morning, Ryan. Be good for mommy today." He runs his hand over Ryan's head before kissing me good-bye and heading for the door. The last few months have been hard on him—watching his only son struggle to live. We're all glad to be under one roof again.

Ryan's new equipment takes some getting used to. An oxygen concentrator takes room air and sends it through two cylinders that magically select the nitrogen and absorb it from the air leaving the oxygen. The oxygen is passed on to the patient through special tubing called a nasal cannula. Ryan's dependent on this machine 24/7 and tethered to it by a seven-foot-long nasal cannula cord.

The supplemental oxygen helps keep the oxygen in Ryan's blood at acceptable levels . . . acceptable for a heart baby whose heart is going to be worked on shortly. Not acceptable for the general population. He's satting in the mid-sixties even with help.

You and I sat between 95 and 100 percent. This has implications for the body so the goal is to get him satting higher as soon as possible. The way to do that is to remove the expanders and do the Glenn procedure.

Ryan's a completely different baby this time around. He coughs all the time and is fussy. My theory is that the tissue expanders are pushing on his digestive track and stomach giving him reflux. He's not spitting up, but he does gag after coughing. He has to be in an almost fully upright position to be comfortable. Because he's connected to a machine, I spend a lot of time sitting on the living room floor holding him on my shoulder and patting his back. He spends his nights sleeping upright in his swing. My nights are spent on the couch so I can hear if he's choking on or vomiting his feeds. He's gone from a relatively easy baby to a high-maintenance, all-consuming one.

There's a constant emotional struggle between sitting with Ryan or being with the rest of the family. When Henry comes home at night he likes to unwind in front of the television for an hour or two. Our television is in the basement family room. Ryan is in the living room. The set up forces me to decide between being with my husband or tending to the needs of my son. No matter which way you slice it, it isn't a fair choice. I've always been purposeful not to use the kids as a justification to ignore my husband, but with Ryan's complexities it's unthinkable to leave him to fuss all alone.

Thankfully it's summer so the girls don't have anywhere to be. We spend our days playing inside around Ryan in the living room. I let them venture outside some with me watching from the window, or go out with them if Ryan's napping. I wish for the simple days when we ran off to the park or out to a farm an hour's drive from our house for the day. The only concrete things on our agenda are Ryan's doctor appointments and his tissue expansions.

We're scheduled to see plastics twice a week to get the expanders filled. Now that we're outpatient, Dr. Donofrio wants me to leave plastics and head directly to the cardiology clinic for an hour observation.

The only break I get is my weekly basketball games through a local adult league. "You playing tonight?" Bridget asks. It's Sunday afternoon. "Yeah, I think so. Henry says he can handle the kids, but I'm not so sure. Ryan's a handful these days and it's going to be bedtime for the girls. I'm still learning the ropes and I've been at it a week."

"Come on. It'll be good for you. You *need* to get out of the house. Henry will be fine. He's a big boy and great dad."

"I know. He's encouraging me to go," I say.

"Great, I'll pick you up at seven," she says, leaving no room for me to back out. What's a girl to do when her husband and best friend team up?

As I'm heading out the door I look back into the living room to see Henry sitting on the couch holding Ryan who's crying. The girls are playing upstairs. For a split second I think Henry's changing his mind . . . like a dog on a fox trail I smell fear. I pause with my hand on the door. "Look, I know what you're doing for me tonight is huge. I want you to know I appreciate it. I won't be gone more than two hours. Let the girls play. Don't worry about getting them to bed. Just try to stay sane."

"I'm fine," he says unconvincingly. "Have fun. And win!"

RYAN MAKES IT through the first week of expansions. On the second Tuesday it takes over an hour for his sats to rebound after the expansion. On Friday it takes over two. He seems to be working harder to breathe. Dr. Donofrio schedules an echo to make sure it's the tissue expanders and nothing else. The echo comes back unchanged. Dr. Donofrio stays in the room to observe Ryan for a few more minutes. The clinic's head nurse pops her head in the room and says quietly, "Do you want me to find a bed?" I hold my breath.

"Yes," Dr. Donofrio says, her eyes fixed on Ryan's heaving chest. "I'm not comfortable with this." She turns to me and says "I think we should observe him overnight. Hopefully he'll level off and you can go home tomorrow."

I've never had a great poker face. I replace my sad reaction with a look of resolve as quickly as I can, but it's not quick enough.

"You okay?" Dr. Donofrio asks. She puts her arms around me as the tears glide silently down my cheeks. "You've been so brave through this whole thing. I think this is the first time I've seen you cry."

I laugh. "It's not the first time, you just haven't seen me do it much," I say wiping at my cheeks. I exhale a few times slowly to regulate my breathing. "I'm so disappointed. I knew there was a chance he wouldn't come home at all, but it was nice having him 24/7."

"You'll get him again," she says. "Hey, you know we thought he might be on a ventilator this whole time, so it's good he's not. I just want to make sure he has the support he needs to get him to the Glenn. He's incredibly fragile. The last thing I want to do is send you home and have him turn blue." She leaves to sign the admitting paperwork. I pick up my phone to make the dreaded phone calls. The first thing I do is text Henry. Then I call my friend Katie to see if she can keep the girls until Henry gets off work. They're at her house this afternoon for a play date.

With Ryan situated in the Heart and Kidney Unit, I drive home with an empty car seat yet again. It feels like a bad joke loading all Ryan's things into the car without loading him in right beside them.

On the car ride to the hospital this morning, I was thinking about the things I love about Ryan. I love how he won't fall asleep when I'm in the room. Something he's done since he was a newborn—fighting through meds and sleep to listen to me talk or sing. He does it now whether at home or in the hospital. His eyes get droopy and a little hazy and I know he's sleeping while awake. If I leave the room only for a second, he closes his eyes and goes to sleep.

I also love how today in the car I pulled his car seat canopy open so I could watch him while I was driving. I peeked at him every once in a while to make sure he was doing okay and he was always staring right back at me. His little neck craned so he could look at me over his shoulder. I don't think he took his eyes off me one time.

Out of habit, I glance back at his seat now only to be reminded it's empty.

"MRS. MARQUISS?" THE voice on the other line says. "This is Kitty from Children's. Ryan was working very hard last night and desatted into the forties. We felt it best to bring him to the CICU and place him on high flow oxygen. He's satting in the sixties now; however, we don't feel he's ready to go back to the floor. I just wanted to keep you informed."

It's 8:30 on Saturday morning and this is the last call I want to get. It means instead of rebounding Ryan's worse. He won't be coming home today. The twenty-four–hour observation just got extended indefinitely. I brace myself for him to be there through his Glenn, scheduled for exactly four weeks from now. He's on the books for a cath at the end of this coming week anyway so he would've been admitted at least overnight for that.

July turns into August over the weekend. Accepting we'll be in-house for a while, I start talking with the team about Ryan's scheduled Glenn during Monday morning rounds. We also talk about his coughing. I explain he's had it since he came home and could someone please do something about his reflux. We consult with GI who suggests overnight continuous feeds with less volume during the day. It does the trick. Ryan's back to his happy self. I'm relieved. In the two weeks Ryan was home I spoke with four doctors about his increased coughing. It isn't until observing his behavior twenty-four hours a day that it's addressed and taken care of. It took a hospitalization, but at least he's more comfortable.

August 2009

My husband and I use a phrase in our house to describe when one of us is out of sorts to the point of being irrational either mentally, physically, emotionally, or any combination of the three. We say we're "beyond it." Growing up, my family called it "over the line."

I'm beyond it . . . for various reasons, mostly because I'm weary. Weary physically, weary emotionally, and weary mentally. I've given every ounce of myself today and been frustrated in my efforts.

I woke this morning at 5 A.M.—not a time I would choose to get up. Working on adrenaline and six hours of sleep (the most I've had in some time now), I drive the hour to the hospital for Ryan's scheduled heart catheterization. I'm alone. Henry's dream of a son died the day Ryan was diagnosed so he protects himself by not getting close to him. There are glimpses here and there of Henry's love for Ryan, but mostly there's a wall of protection. I'm trying to give him space and let him deal with his emotions, but it makes my job harder.

I arrived at the hospital by 7 A.M. Ryan's scheduled to be the first case of the day and will probably be sedated and taken to the cath lab between 7:30 and 8 o'clock. I want to spend a few minutes with him before that happens. The nurses change shifts at 7 A.M. I rode the elevator with nurses coming on shift and popped into the unit passing nurses who were still closing out night care. Many waved hello and offered words of encouragement or just plain catching up and excitement to see how big and chunky Ryan's getting. Many of them haven't seen him for two months and his growth is quite remarkable.

After turning in my breast milk at the front desk I head down the hall to Ryan's room. The nurses are giving report so I make myself at home in the recliner after sneaking a peek at my sleeping boy.

After fifteen to twenty minutes and no sign from the cath team, I interrupt to make sure we're still a go. "Yep," Molly says, "We're just waiting for Dr. Kanter to finish up with another kid." This means we were bumped from the first spot of the day and there's a family somewhere in the hospital worrying because their child's getting an emergency cath. I remember the day of Ryan's emergency cath and am thankful today is routine for us.

An hour passes. The nurse's reports are done, and doctors start peeking their heads in the door smiling at my chunky monkey sleeping in his bouncy seat. We wave and silently greet one another. I'm tired, but in a good place.

The whispering starts soon after when the residents and fellows start making their rounds. They order a CBC on Ryan. A CBC means "complete blood count" and basically counts the platelets, white and red blood cells within the blood. The results give doctors an idea of what's going on with the patient. In Ryan's case this morning, the results show an elevated white cell count indicating Ryan either has or is fighting an infection. This is enough to push the pause button on Ryan's procedure.

Dr. Kanter comes up after his first case to let me know we're being postponed. *No biggie*, I think. *I'm here without the girls, it's quiet, I'll spend the day with Ryan.*

Ryan spends the morning sleeping. I rarely leave his room trying to take advantage of every moment I'm there, but with all the sleeping he's doing, I accept an invitation to lunch with another mother from the floor. I don't know her very well, but we've passed enough times in the hallway to be on a first name basis. Her son has Downs Syndrome and a heart defect. They're in and out of the hospital often with fevers and other illnesses.

The entire time I'm in the cafeteria I can't help but wish I were back in Ryan's room. What if he wakes up? I don't have very long here and I feel like I'm wasting the time I do have socializing. For Tammy, who lives at the hospital with her son, the cafeteria and conversation are a welcome break from the monotony of a hospital room.

Upon my return, Ryan's still sleeping. "You're going to be upset, but he woke up for about an hour while you were gone. He was in a pretty good mood and played a little with his mirror. He fell asleep again about ten minutes ago," Molly reports.

She's right. I'm disappointed. I wait around until 3:30, the time I need to leave to miss rush hour, but he naps all afternoon. His body's working hard to keep his infection at bay. Sad I spent the day watching him sleep I kiss his head before heading to the car.

The girls are at Johanna's house two and a half hours away in Martinsburg, West Virginia. We planned for them to spend a few days there so I could focus on Ryan during his cath and in case there were any complications. Since the cath has been pushed back, I decide to go get them. I'm tired, my body hurts, and my visit with Ryan or lack thereof is frustrating. I almost call Johanna to say I'm not coming, but putting off the trip won't make it go away, and I'd rather not spend my Tuesday morning making the trip either.

At this point, I'm not beyond it yet. I'm still on this side of the line, working to be patient and stay awake on the drive. I arrive to get the girls and I'm still plugging along like the little engine who could. I think I can. I think I can. I think I can.

I load the girls up and drive through the nearest Chik-Fil-A. They're eating and my expectation is they'll fall asleep after filling their tummies. They don't. Ainsley stays awake the entire drive home and Natalie falls asleep about twenty minutes from home. I've overly tired now and getting grouchy, consciously deciding not to cross the line.

At home Natalie wakes up and throws a fit when I ask her to go potty before getting into bed. Ainsley's using the hall bathroom and apparently the master bathroom is suddenly scary. I feel myself start to lose it. I'm ready to punch out and the girls are gearing up for a fight. These are the moments I hate. When I'm hardly in control and I hear myself being short with the children. Hate, hate, hate it.

By the time I lay with them for a few minutes, put on a CD of soothing children's songs and kiss them goodnight, I'm over the line. There are household things to be done and I'm in no physical shape to do them. Trash to take out, dishes to be done, and bills to pay. I settle on the bills—at least I can sit in one spot to do them. Henry comes home about then and I start barking commands for him to take out the trash. He can tell I'm in a bad mood, so he retreats to the basement to watch television after dragging the trash to the curb. Days like this are rare. While caring for Ryan is difficult, most days I'm able to keep my emotions in check. I'm a big list maker so each new thing becomes a separate line item for my mental list.

The most important line item becomes advocating for Ryan's tissue expansion injections. Cardiology wants to be cautious since he's not responding well to the increased weight of the expanders. Since we're under observation, we should be able to expand them as necessary. It's critical to have enough skin in four weeks or we won't be able to do the Glenn. I desperately don't want him to get a new shunt in the interim. If we're going to open him up, let's do it to move forward. I feel like another shunt would be like walking a treadmill, lots of movement without getting anywhere.

Ryan's catheterization is moved to the middle of the week: August 5. His fever goes away and his white blood count returns to normal. The team suggests leaving Ryan on the ventilator after the cath so we can aggressively fill his expanders without having to worry Ryan's working too hard. We want to make sure his body is rested and ready in a month. Henry and I agree to the voluntary ventilation.

Ryan's cath confirms his shunt's too small. This is probably why his sats are sitting so low. It also confirms Ryan's pulmonary arteries have stayed the same size as they were in April, most likely because his shunt isn't giving great blood flow. They're small, 4mm, but the team feels that it's acceptable to go forward with the Glenn.

WHILE HE'S A candidate for the Glenn, it'll be risky. This reiterates what Dr. Donofrio told me a few weeks back during one of Ryan's cardiology clinic visits. Ryan's fragile. If his body thinks life's tricky now, it'll think it even more so once we require his pulmonary arteries to receive blood without the right ventricle (what the Glenn rewiring does). However, everyone I talk to feels it's reasonable to proceed. It's Ryan's best option and in his best interest.

The good news from the cath is the cor triatriatum membrane that was choking Ryan's heart back in April is reading at a gradient of two; a perfect reading to be left alone at this point. Dr. Jonas, the surgeon, isn't required to be in the atria during the Glenn and prefers not to mess around in there if it's not necessary. He does have to open the atria during the Fontan procedure, the final surgery in the three-phase rewiring of a hypoplastic heart. He'll wait until then to cut out the membrane for good. Ryan will receive regular echos to determine if intervention is needed before the Fontan, which typically takes place between eighteen months and four years of age. We're three weeks away from the big surgery.

AUGUST 7, 2009: It's been two days since Ryan's cath. I'm having a hard time getting out of the house this morning. As I'm working frantically to make lunches and pack up, my cell phone rings. "Unknown" flashes across the caller ID. That typically means it's someone from the hospital or a solicitor.

"Hello," I say.

"Hi, Mrs. Marquiss. This is Jodi Pike from the CICU. Ryan got an arterial line placed last night to replace his old one. He had a rough night and we wanted to make sure we had good access. Are you coming in today?"

"Yep. I'm almost on my way now. I should be there in little more than an hour," I say.

"Oh good. I wanted to make you aware of the line placement. We'll see you when you get here," she says.

We hang up and I finish getting ready. It's standard protocol for the team to contact me when Ryan has a line placed or goes for a procedure downstairs. Ryan consistently has trouble with his arterial line. It oozes blood from the placement site. The nurses try to keep it clean but at some point it has to be replaced to ward off infection and skin breakdown. I leave the house a little before lunchtime. As I'm turning from Rhode Island Avenue onto First Street, less than five minutes from the hospital, my phone rings again from an Unknown ID.

"Hello?"

"Hey, Leighann, it's Kristen. Did anyone call you to let you know Ryan got an IJ line?" the social worker asks.

"An IJ line?" I ask. "No, what's an IJ line?" We've been around awhile so I'm surprised I haven't heard of this type of line and wonder why Dr. Pike didn't mention it earlier.

"It's a central line in the neck through the jugular. Ryan's sats have been unsteady today so they just placed a line a few minutes ago to have access straight to the heart. I wanted to give you a heads up in case you're coming in to see him," she explains.

"Actually, I'm about to pull into the garage. I'll see you when I get up there," I say. Confused, I hang up the phone and pull into the parking garage.

The girls clamor over each other trying to decide who's going to pull the time-stamped garage ticket and who's going to pay the man on our way out. We decide it's Ainsley's turn to get the ticket so she crawls over Natalie and hangs half her body out of the window to reach the ticket dispenser.

I walk into Ryan's room and am immediately more confused. Ryan is lying on his bed going across it instead of up and down and it's obvious he's sedated more than usual. His arms are up over his head, limp and lifeless. His skin is ashen. Lowell, a fellow, is performing an echo on Ryan and several more doctors from the unit are milling around whispering. There are several extra nurses. I notice Ryan's puffier than normal. The more I'm able to process the scene, the more I realize he looks awful.

I quickly settle the girls in the corner with their lunch. I saved it purposefully to give them something to do at the hospital. I walk over to Ryan's bed and stroke his head for a minute. Fully sedated, he gives no response. One of the doctors heads my way. "Hi, I'm Andrew, one of the new fellows this month. Ryan's sats have been hypervolatile all morning and we're having a hard time getting them to bounce back. He has a ton of meds on board, is on 100 percent supplemental oxygen at a rate of fifteen, is on nitric oxide, and received volume (a blood transfusion). More platelets are on order. We're waiting now to see if the echo tells us anything." His tone is serious and everyone in the room looks worried so I take a stab at reading between the lines.

"Should I call my husband?" I ask.

"Ryan's really sick," Andrew says.

I look at the nurse. She's new to me, but I decide to take a different route. "I'm a little oblivious when it comes to this stuff. To me, Ryan's always sick so I'm never sure what 'he's really sick' means. I need you to tell me point-blank if I need to call my husband and if I need to have my children leave."

She looks me dead in the eye and says calmly, "If I were you, I'd call your husband and have your girls go to a friend's house. Your son's crashing and we're not sure which way this is going to go. It could go either way pretty fast."

"Thank you," I say grateful for her straight communication.

Moving to the window I dial Henry's cell number. My fingers are suddenly the size of sausages and about as useful. They shake making it hard to dial. This is the first time I've had to place a call like this. I called Henry the day of Ryan's emergency cath to let him know what was going on, but at that point in time I didn't understand the words, "very sick." I simply thought, "needs help" not "he's dying." So when Henry asked me on that day if he should come I told him no. If I'd known the docs didn't think Ryan would make it through the cath, I would've answered with a yes. Today, I'm fully aware of what's going on.

"Hey, sweetie, can I call you right back?" Henry says as soon as he picks up. It's his standard "I'm in a meeting" refrain. He's always taken my call no matter what he's doing even before Ryan was born.

"No. I need you to come to the hospital. They said you should come." I can't get the words out that Ryan's dying. My throat is so tight my vocal chords feel as if they're going to snap in half.

"I have to go," I hear him say to the people in the room. "I'm on my way," he says to me. I hear papers shuffling and concerned voices before the line goes silent.

With my shaky sausage-fingers I quickly dial Bridget's number. She answers on the second ring. "Is Jason home?" I manage to get out.

"He's working from home today. What's up?"

"Ryan isn't doing well. I just called Henry to come to the hospital. Do you think Jason would have time to drive Henry so he can take the girls back to your house? The staff suggested the girls leave," I say trying to keep my composure for my sake as well as for the girls. So far they're happily eating their peanut butter and jelly sandwiches on the hospital-provided recliners talking and laughing with each other. The words my grandmother told my mom in reference to us kids during my parent's divorce comes back to me, "They'll handle it how you do."

"Let me ask him and I'll call you right back," Bridget says. She calls back in a matter of seconds and we firm up the plan. I call Henry to let him know to reroute to their house, which conveniently is on his way to the city.

I turn back to Ryan. I can't believe I'm watching my son die. He's so innocent lying there, his sweet heart beating steadily outside his chest. He's a little over two weeks away from the Glenn. We're so close. I pray over and over to God for my little boy, almost like a chant. Not just that he'll live, but that the *best thing* will happen for his little body.

By the time Henry arrives an hour later, Ryan's sats are level and back up into acceptable ranges. Jason takes the girls as planned so Henry and I can stay by Ryan's bedside to make sure he remains stable through the next few hours. The room is suddenly quiet. With Ryan stable, the doctors have cleared and the nurse goes on a much-needed break. It's here in the stillness I'm finally able to break down and cry.

Ryan continues to remain stable overnight. We have no explanation for why his sats went haywire. He slowly weans off the nitric oxide over the next day or so and comes down on his supplemental oxygen. They continue keeping him heavily sedated since he's on a ventilator.

The ventilator is a hard machine to be on. It forces air into your lungs whether you're ready for it or not. For patients like Ryan who take breaths on their own in addition to the breaths forced upon them by the vent it can be even more uncomfortable since the forced air can catch you in the middle of your own breath. It's especially unsettling when you're in the middle of exhaling or needing to exhale but are forced to inhale. For this reason, kids on vents are usually sedated to keep them more comfortable and to keep them from automatically fighting the machine.

BY MONDAY MORNING Ryan looks much better. He's alone when I arrive. I sit on the side of his bed and trace the little patches of skin that aren't covered by tape, lines, or lead stickers. Even though he's sedated, I want him to know I'm here. I watch his heart beat under the transparent membrane and notice it looks slower than normal. I chuckle realizing there are perks to your child having his heart outside his chest. I'll never have to put my finger under Ryan's nose to see if he's still breathing or watch for a moving chest like I did with the girls. There's no mistaking whether he's still breathing—all I need to do is glance at his heart. It only takes one millisecond to get a good read on whether his heart rate is fast, slow, or baseline.

One of his nurses told me early on that being able to see Ryan's heart changed the way she treats her patients. She said that when the monitors show an elevated heart rate—say 200 instead of 120—the nurses know the baby needs meds to bring the heart rate down STAT, but when she saw Ryan's heart beat at 200 the first time, her sense of urgency tripled. She was grateful for the visual so she could respond the same way to patients whose hearts are covered.

The nurse returns and I ask her for report. "Ryan's doing really well today," she says. "His oxygen sats and blood pressure remain stable. He seems pretty comfortable. The only thing we noticed is that he's showing signs of bradycardia (low heart rate). He tends to be a little tachycardic (high heart rate) so we're watching him. His heart's also in Junctional Escape Rhythm, which is a type of arrhythmia."

"What's that mean and what causes it?" I ask.

"It means the electric impulse sent out by the sinus node to the A-V junction has been interrupted. The A-V junction takes over setting the pace causing a slower heart rate. We typically see this after open heart surgery when the surgeon gets too close to the junction, but Ryan hasn't had surgery so we're not sure what upset things."

"Is it critical?" I ask.

"No. Typically with time and meds the heart rate goes back to normal. I guess the biggest thing it tells us is that his heart is stressed. It could be a result of him crashing the other day. The fellow ordered a Holter monitor for Ryan to wear for twelve hours. It'll record his heart rate so the doctors can look at the pattern more closely. We should know more next week once they read the results."

I look back at Ryan, his heart beating slowly, his chest heaving in and out. Last night I dreamed he rolled over from his back to his stomach without any complications. He's almost six months and should be rolling and sitting up by now instead of lying in a bed paralyzed and vented. When he was a newborn I dreamed I could pick him up and cuddle him over my shoulder to soothe him. I don't hold him that way very often. I have to crook my body to cradle his heart and I'm always afraid I'll impede his breathing. In my dream it didn't bother him. Most parents dream of the abnormal, I dream of the normal.

AUGUST 19: "WE'RE having a party for Ryan!" the girls chorus. I've just come downstairs to a decorated dining room table. The girls are excitedly sitting around it. It's set with the Hello Kitty plates, napkins, and hats left over from Ainsley's birthday party a few weeks ago. There are ten place settings complete with knives, forks, and spoons. To the side is the child-sized wooden table set with six place settings although it's hard pressed to fit four children.

"Oh wow," I say. "He's six months old today, so we can celebrate his half-birthday." I'm still a little confused why they're throwing the party, but I'm not about to spoil their fun. I sit down to a mid-morning snack of grapes, banana bread, yogurt, and cheese sticks, a menu chosen by the party planners. When we're almost done eating Ainsley says, "Let's open the presents!" Natalie grabs three gift bags from the floor around her chair. "Me and Ainsley got gifts for everyone. Ryan isn't here so he doesn't get one." She hands me a gift bag laden down with a book, brush, pencil, and a Polly Pocket.

The girls don't seem to mind Ryan's absence from his half birthday party. I have a hard time grasping he's already half a year old. I remember when the doctors told me Ryan would have to wait until six months old to get his Glenn. It felt like a ship dotting the horizon. With only ten days to go, the ship is nearly to port. In Ryan's short six months he has endured two surgeries, three heart catheterizations, and three close calls. He's lived four months at the pediatric hospital and two glorious months at home. It's been three weeks since his admittance.

After the "party" the girls have a playdate with Bridget's kids so I can visit Ryan alone. I stop at Starbucks on the way to the hospital to pick up a sandwich. They have great tomato, mozzarella, basil sandwiches that don't fill me up, but taste good. Rooting through my purse for change I come across the key for Ryan's oxygen tank. Fingering it I think of my baby in the hospital and all the equipment necessary to support him. All the machinery was mind-boggling the first few days, but soon we were pros at reading his vitals on the screen.

This time around I've forgotten what the vent numbers mean and need a refresher course. It's been almost four months since he was dependent on the vent so I can't remember what numbers to keep track of.

His first visit home was easy. The only assistance Ryan needed was his feeding pump. It's so simple even my four-and-a-half-year-old can help set up his feeds. One day when Johanna and Amy were visiting they stayed with the kids while I took my car to get the oil changed. Ryan's feeds finished while I was gone. He was in his swing and somehow his feeding tube disconnected from the feeding line. My sisters didn't know what to do. Breast milk was leaking all over the floor and they were gasping and yelping at each other to figure out how to make it stop. Natalie heard the commotion from where she was playing in the basement and responded to their distress. She quickly assessed the situation— two grown women studying the end of Ryan's tube and the end of the feeding bag line. She took the feeding bag line and put it to rest in its holder below the pump. She took the feeding tube end out of Johanna's hands and put the correct cap on it to close off the leak. On her way back to playing, she hit the power button turning off the pump to stop its incessant beeping.

Ryan's brief two weeks home between his tissue expander surgery and re-admittance were a little more hectic. In addition to his feeding pump we housed an oxygen compressor in our living room. An oxygen compressor is the size of an end table and sounds like an idling 18-wheeler. It made my dishes rattle. It made it hard to have a conversation from the living room to the kitchen, something that was very easy before the low hum of the machine. It gives off heat and is heavy to move. Ryan's nasal cannula cord was only 7 feet long so he lived in that small of a space for those two weeks. There was also the pulse oximeter, a machine that reads oxygen saturations, and the portable oxygen tanks.

Even with all this equipment, it's nothing compared to what sits in his hospital room. It's amazing how much a little black key can sting as it slaps you back to the reality of the situation. I gingerly place the key in my purse and diligently continue looking for a quarter.

RYAN IS ASLEEP when I arrive. He's slept every day this week due to heavy sedation. They want to keep him calm in these last few days before surgery. For me it makes for frustrating visits. It makes me wonder if it's worth packing up the girls, food, toys, and supplies for the day just to watch him sleep. I can't bear to think of him lying alone surrounded by his entourage of machines so we go every day just in case he knows we're there.

With little else to do, I start working on Ryan's beads. I haven't started on them at all for this admission so I have quite a bit to do. Kristen counted them all out for me last night and left them in the cubby in Ryan's room. As I'm stringing them, I realize she didn't give me any aqua so I head to her office to track her down. Her office mate's the only one there . . . she's examining a large glass butterfly bead. It has bright red wings and a dark patterned body.

"What's the butterfly bead for?" I gush.

Her eyes get really big. My stomach lurches and I mouth, "For when they pass away?"

She nods. I'm not sure I understand so I mouth again, "Is it for when they pass away?" She nods again patiently letting the information sink into my thick skull. "I don't want one of those," I murmur. "I just need an aqua bead."

I grab the bead I need from the box on the desk and quickly head out the door thinking the whole time about the baby Ryan roomed with at the beginning of the week. Monday seems so long ago. . . .

Monday Bridget came along for my visit with Ryan. The last time we visited alone was during Henry's appendectomy. We talked and cooed over Ryan. He stayed awake a full two hours. In fact it's the only day this week he woke up. When he finally couldn't keep his eyes open another second, Bridget and I settled into tucking his blanket around him, rubbing his skin, and drinking him in. Molly, Ryan's nurse, interrupted our nurturing. "I need you to leave the room," she said casually. Ryan is in a room with four beds right now. He's typically in a private room, but sometimes gets bounced to the bay when the unit has more surgery patients. I grabbed my pump before following Bridget into the hallway.

"What's that about?" Bridget asked.

"I'm guessing it has to do with the other baby," I said. "She coded the other morning during an echo. Maybe she's crashing again." Being in an ICU these events, although few and far between, do happen. It becomes natural to see doctors and nurses conferring at a bedside. There were quite a few staff members by Ryan's roommate when we left the room. A few minutes later, Molly approached us again. "I'm afraid it's going to be some time before you can come back into the room. You might want to consider going home."

"Is it the other baby?" I asked.

"She's pretty sick and it doesn't look like she's getting any better," she said. "I'm really sorry to cut your visit short," her voice trailed off. I knew what this meant. "Very sick," "pretty sick," "sick"—all words the staff uses with me when Ryan's crashing.

Tears sprang into my eyes. My first instinct was to rush to the baby's side and hold her hand, stroke her head, touch her foot . . . anything to give her the assurance we were all there, helping her in her journey. The instinct lasted a split second. I knew the staff wouldn't let me. And I knew it wasn't my place. I just couldn't bear the thought of the baby not having her mother nearby. Or the thought of the mother stuck in a hospital somewhere finding out her day-old baby's dying without her. When I arrived on Tuesday I fully expected to see Ryan's roommate's bed empty and clean. But there she lay—a fighter still hanging on.

Was the butterfly bead for her family? Was it for the family in the next room over . . . the room I saw Heather, Kristin's office mate, enter with a bag of beads shortly after my visit to her office? These are answers I'll never have and probably never want to hear. One thing's for sure. Even though it's the prettiest of them all, I don't want the butterfly bead.

THE WEEK OF Ryan's Glenn procedure is hectic. Amy flies up from Florida to watch the girls. They've been shipped out a lot over the last six months and it's nice for them to be in their own home with a familiar face. Their routine isn't upset and they revel in the attention their aunt pours over them. They've only been to the pool a handful of times all summer and it's the end of August. She takes them. They take her on a walk through the neighborhood and show her where they think poison ivy grows and the park where they like to play. They point into the woods along the path to the park and tell her that's where the "creep" is. She's worried until she figures out they mean "creek." She dotes on them and parents them the way I do. Henry and I know they're in good hands allowing us to focus our energy on the second biggest day of our son's life.

All the conversations from in utero until now involved the Glenn in some way and the doctors always stressed how fragile hypoplast kids are until the surgery. In fact, the first six months until the Glenn are the most critical. Surviving it is a major hurdle for any single-ventricle kid.

During the Glenn procedure the surgeon takes the superior vena cava (SVC), two of them in Ryan's case, and connects it to the pulmonary arteries (PAs) bypassing the right ventricle all together. Instead of the blood coming up through the SVC into the right ventricle and being pumped into the PAs, when Ryan inhales, the negative vacuum in his lungs will pull the blood from the SVC into the PAs and then into the lungs to be oxygenated. Even more simply put: Instead of being pumped by the heart, the blood is pulled in by the lungs.

Ryan also faces the chest wall repair. We've talked about this forever—since our first visit at twenty-two gestational weeks— about the heart and how it doesn't like being moved around or crowded. With their past experience the doctors have no plans to force Ryan's heart into his chest cavity. Instead they'll pull the healthy skin we grew over the last eight weeks across his heart at the conclusion of the Glenn. They may conduct a bone graft during the Fontan (between eighteen and forty-eight months of age) or just allow Ryan's body to grow. The key is as Ryan's body grows, his heart will become a smaller portion of his chest and hopefully one day become flush with his body.

This leaves us with many questions. Will Ryan's body tolerate having taut skin over his heart? What will it look like? What happens when Ryan starts to roll over, walk, or run? We don't know at this point. Before he was born, it was hard for me to imagine what Ryan would look like with his heart *outside* his chest. Now it's hard for me to imagine what he'll look like with his heart *inside* his chest.

The day before the Glenn, Dr. Jonas decides Ryan's too fragile to go through both procedures on the same day. Henry and I are very disappointed. I'm especially frustrated because I advocated for the last eight weeks to be aggressive with Ryan's tissue expanders. It sounds like a week is the earliest plastics will have a chance to go in and it could be as many as two or more weeks. It makes me second-guess agreeing to the voluntary ventilation. I worry about Ryan's lungs and the damage the machine can do to them, not to mention the diaphragm, which quickly atrophies when not in use.

Dr. Donofrio and Dr. Levy call Henry and me the night before the procedure to go over our concerns and explain why the chest closure won't happen simultaneously. It's during these conversations that I realize they talk each night about Ryan's case, making sure nothing is falling through the cracks. It makes me very grateful for a team that cares so much for each patient.

WE ARRIVE AT the hospital before sunrise to see Ryan off to surgery. It's Thursday, August 27, my Papa's eighty-seventh birthday. Dr. Jonas meets with us to talk through the procedure one more time while Ryan is being prepped. He says, "I want you to understand miracles don't happen every day. It was truly a miracle we were successful with the shunt. In my experience miracles don't continue to line up one right after the other. You get some here and there, but not all the time. Today's surgery is very risky. You need to prepare for the worst."

I can't concentrate on the things I brought to do. I walk to the family library located on the same floor as surgery to see what I can find. Henry stays in the Quiet Room off the surgical waiting room. We're paged when Dr. Jonas makes the first incision and when he enters the heart. Less than four hours after shaking Dr. Jonas' hand, he's standing beside us grinning ear to ear.

"He did great!" Dr. Jonas says. "We'll watch him for a few days to make sure he's stable. Pending his status we can schedule the chest closure within the week."

We head back up to the unit to wait for Ryan's arrival. It always takes a little while for the team to finish closing up the body and getting the patient ready for transport after surgery, sometimes even a few hours.

We're finally able to see Ryan in the late afternoon. He's swollen and pale. His incision is in the exact place as the shunt surgery so it feels like déjà vu. The only difference now is the tissue expanders disfigure his chest. He looks like he has two half-moons stuffed on either side with his heart and omphalocele like buttons down the middle. He has a tube coming out of his chest to drain the natural build-up of fluid off his body.

A chest tube sounds like a babbling brook so Ryan's room sounds like a Buddhist Zen garden. The hours after surgery are quiet. The patient is still sedated and kept that way for most of the first twelve hours. These are the most critical hours so the team is on high alert, but for us parents, these hours are the quietest. Ryan's agitated any time he pushes through the meds so they're keeping him as comfortable as possible (read: pretty doped up). The team decides to keep him sedated for the next few days.

By Saturday the team is talking about doing the chest closure on Tuesday, five days after his Glenn surgery. Ryan is healing well and his vitals are good even though he's still in a lot of pain and adjusting to the venous pressure of the Glenn circuitry. It's strange to think Ryan will no longer have his heart and bowels outside his body. I'm having a hard time defining him without the chest wall defects and I feel a little sad to see them go. It's for the better, no doubt, but I feel as if we are changing something that makes him who he is.

Henry and I take up our regular spots in the Quiet Room off the surgical waiting area. It's time for Ryan's chest closure. We expect the surgery to last five to six hours involving plastics and general surgery. Dr. Sandler will start by placing Ryan's omphalocele into his abdomen and patching his diaphragm with Gortex. Until now we haven't had a good look at the diaphragm. Dr. Sandler believes there is a hole because of the way the omphalocele sits so close to the heart.

If Ryan tolerates this portion of the surgery well, Dr. Boyajian will try closing the chest wall. He'll start by removing the tissue expanders. Once it's determined there is enough skin, Dr. Boyajian will cut away the membrane protecting Ryan's heart and slowly stitch the extra skin together. He'll move slowly while Dr. Levy watches to make sure Ryan's vitals remain stable. If at any point they feel Ryan isn't tolerating the procedure they'll stop immediately and abort the closure. We'll be forced to go back to the drawing board.

The waiting is hard. I try to read and walk the halls to keep from going stir-crazy. Henry sleeps on the Quiet Room couch—his way of dealing with the stress. I have my omnipresent pump and use it twice during the surgery. I walk my milk upstairs to the unit for them to freeze. Ryan won't be able to eat until late tonight or tomorrow morning.

Dr. Sandler finds us in the Quiet Room. "He looks great and is tolerating the procedure," he says. "I'm done with my portion. I was able to insert the omphalocele without any complications. It popped right back in. It ended up being a section of his colon. The great news is the diaphragm is intact. I was surprised to find there isn't a herniation or perforation. I didn't have to do a single thing." He leaves us to contemplate how Ryan's chest closure is going.

The heart doesn't like being pushed or prodded. The longest surviving ectopia cordis patient is in his late thirties. Doctors tried fifteen times in the patient's first eighteen months of life to insert his heart into his chest. Each time something went wrong and his heart stopped beating.

Now we're waiting to find out if Ryan's heart will tolerate the tension healthy skin places on a heart conditioned to a flaccid membrane. The hours drag by before the team of physicians enters the room. Dr. Donofrio is on hand and her excitement is so tangible I feel as though I could wrap myself in it like a warm, furry blanket. Dr. Boyajian and Dr. Sandler complete the group. Dr. Donofrio starts by telling us Ryan did great, tolerated the surgery magnificently, and is looking good post-operatively. She then gives the floor over to Dr. Boyajian by saying, "Dr. Boyajian did an amazing job closing up the chest. It looks really good."

He says, "Well you did a great job keeping him alive to this point," before turning to us. "I was able to remove the tissue expanders and close the skin. Ryan showed no signs of stress throughout the entire process. There was just enough to close him up."

It's surreal to be sitting here listening to the team as they grin giddily and verbally pat each other on the back. They're on an obvious high from their success. All the planning of the past eleven months came to fruition in the last five hours. And wonder of wonders, it worked!

Henry and I head upstairs to wait for Ryan to get back to his room, anxious to see the results of his makeover. When he arrives, we stand in front of his crib and stare at his chest for a full twenty minutes our heads cocking from one side to the other like a friendly pooch. It's weird to look at him and not see his chest wall butterflied open. For several days after the surgery there's a wide strip of gauze from Ryan's chin to the top of his diaper. On Friday the surgical dressing comes off and we're finally able to see the full picture.

Ryan's skin is stitched together with black thread. The zigzag effect of the thread resembles a zipper and gives the illusion the surgeon zipped Ryan up the middle. We can't get over how good he looks. His ribs are slightly concave on either side of the incision—something Dr. Boyajian warned us would happen. The expanders don't expand exclusively in one direction so he was pretty sure there'd be some reshaping going on underneath them as well. He assures us this will correct itself over the next month.

THE CHEST CLOSURE surgery coincides with the first week of school and ballet for the girls. We go from the lazy days of summer to full steam ahead in no time flat. The days are hectic with me burning the candle at both ends running back and forth between school drop off lines, the hospital, and back to school for pick ups. Natalie starts kindergarten and Ainsley starts preschool. Thankfully my friend, Heather, offers to take Ainsley in the afternoon on preschool days for a standing playdate at the same time she gets her daughter. This gives me more time to spend at the hospital. It's a welcomed gesture since Bridget did this last spring and took the girls many times over the summer. I feel like I've used her too much, even though she'd never say anything.

Monday, Wednesday, and Friday are the most hectic. I wake early before the kids to get ready for my day. By the time they're up I'm already making lunches. We have morning boards—a simple poster board with activities velcroed in a row: getting dressed, eating breakfast, brushing hair, brushing teeth, and putting on shoes. They get to take the activity off the board as they complete it and stick in a makeshift pocket. The boards help guide them so I don't have to repeat myself all morning.

We leave to get Natalie to school shortly after eight and I arrive back home in time to pump at 8:30. Ainsley's school day starts an hour later and hopefully by that time I've put dinner in the crockpot and figured out if I have any local errands before heading to see Ryan.

The hours at the hospital tick quickly by on the days the girls aren't with me. I have to leave Ryan's room by 1:45 to be back in time to pick up Ainsley at Heather's house before swinging by the school to get Natalie at 3:20. On Mondays we head straight to ballet and then are home in time for dinner. Sometimes on Wednesdays or Fridays I leave the hospital a tad later to maximize my visit and pick Ainsley up after getting Natalie from school.

Tuesdays and Thursdays are slightly less hectic although there are still lunches to make. I pack us a lunch every day for the hospital. Natalie is on a three-day Kindergarten schedule. Having the girls with me those days forces me to eat. When I'm by myself I often wait until I'm back in the car to scarf down my food. I feel like eating takes my attention away from Ryan. When we first came to the CICU I remember the nurses talking about how casual some parents are and how they've caught some eating things like fried chicken over the child's bed. I can relate now on days where I'm so hungry I'm light-headed or nauseated. On these days, I sneak bites of my peanut butter and jelly sandwich while sitting with Ryan, hoping the nurses won't judge me.

Tuesdays we leave early enough to get Ainsley to an afternoon ballet class. Thursdays are the longest days. We're able to stay until almost four. If we leave much after that we get stuck in Washington, D.C. rush hour—some of the worst traffic in the nation—making us all grouchy by the time we get home.

WHEN RYAN WAS hospitalized in July I had the girls pack toys every day hoping it wouldn't be a long stay. Now that it's September I've given up hope that we're leaving soon and bring the crafts and small toys bins to leave in Ryan's patient closet. The girls busy themselves with their "hospital toys" and also find ways to pretend play with sterile gloves, hats, and masks. They love pretending they're doctors and nurses and make the recliners into beds for their patients. Natalie walks up to me on a regular basis during these play sessions and says things like, "I'm your nurse today. I need to check on my other baby, but I'll be right back. I'm listening for your baby." One day Ainsley decides her patient needs to move rooms and proceeds to push the recliner around the room. I set up boundaries as to where she can push her patient since I don't want her knocking into Ryan's vent or medicine pole. Playing hospital is probably one of their favorite pastimes. Ainsley's first words in Ryan's room are typically, "I want some glubs (gloves)."

When all else fails, we turn on a movie and climb up into Ryan's bed for a lazy afternoon together. My children act as if this is normal. I actually treasure the movie days when we all cuddle. I feel like a mother goose with my goslings lined up beside me in our little nest, my wings wrapped around them for protection.

However, the constant activity is wearing me thin. One weekend I look at Henry. "I can't keep going down on Sundays. It's too much. We spend Saturday hanging out and I need my Sundays to go grocery shopping and get ready for my week."

"Okay," he says.

"Do you think you could go? I can't stand the thought of Ryan being by himself two days in a row." Up until now, Henry has been watching the girls at home on Sundays while I go down alone. We'd occasionally go as a family, but mostly I went solo.

"I'm fine with that. We'll just trade places, or I can take the girls with me if it helps," he says. So just like that my visits go down to five.

Ryan struggles all of September to come off the vent. They finally think he's ready the last day of the month. When they first extubate him, Ryan's obviously anxious. His little eyes are wide and he holds tightly to my hand while his chest heaves and he breathes through an open mouth. He's done this before. When he's struggling he sucks air through his mouth, keeps his eyes closed, and furrows his brow. At least this time his eyes are wide open, almost as if the anxiety is a result of the realization he's on his own not necessarily his body having trouble. He's coming off nine weeks of intubation—a month longer than his first intubation when he was born.

I'm anxious, too. I worry Ryan will fail. I put so much stock in whether he's breathing on his own or if a machine's doing it for him. I think because it's a big indicator on when he's ready to come home. I desperately want him moving in the direction of our house. It takes me a week to shake the feeling the nurse is going to call any minute telling me they reintubated. Finally, I let my guard down like a soldier whose been told to stand "at ease."

October 9, ten days after extubation, I get the dreaded call. Ryan is struggling. They're trying to prevent intubation so they're giving him oxygen through a tube deeper in his nasal passages. It's a compromise between high-flow oxygen and full-on ventilation through an endotracheal tube. The roller coaster just sped downhill once more.

Ryan's right lung continues to be an issue. His chest X-rays have been fuzzy on the right side since extubation. The lung isn't inflating fully and therefore he's not getting the oxygen support he needs. Henry and I hunker down to learn how the lungs and diaphragm work so we can understand what Ryan's complications really mean.

The team performs an ultrasound. They find the right side of Ryan's diaphragm isn't moving when Ryan breathes. They're unsure if it's paralyzed or weak. A paralyzed diaphragm is pulled up into the lung cavity upon inhale, a place it isn't supposed to be, and can hinder breathing. A weak diaphragm doesn't move and means the patient doesn't have full breathing capabilities. There's talk about sending Ryan down to the lab to get a fluoroscopy study to determine which condition Ryan's dealing with.

A few days after Ryan's setback, I get a call from one of our regular nurses. I've just dropped the girls at school and am driving to Bridget's house to visit before a dentist appointment, which is conveniently five minutes away. "Hey, Leighann. It's Steph. Are you coming in today?" she asks.

"I probably won't make it. I have an appointment and have to be back to get the girls from school. What's up?"

"I don't know how to tell you this, but we got a memo this morning saying the hospital is tightening their visiting policy due to the surge in H1N1 outbreaks. They're only letting parents in now. When I got the memo I asked the charge nurse about your girls. She said security is instructed to turn everyone except parents away at the door, including siblings."

"Oh my gosh!" I murmur. I have no idea what to say. I pull over to the side of the road as I feel the emotion surge up my body and into my throat. It threatens to overflow in the form of bile. "How am I going to tell the girls they can't see their brother?"

"I thought of you guys right away when I read the memo. The girls practically live here," Stephanie says.

"Do you think they'd make an exception for the girls?" I croak. "I don't know many other families on the unit who bring siblings anyway."

"I'm not sure," she says. "It's a hospital policy, not CICU. I'll have the attending call you."

As I hang up, the panic that's been bubbling at the surface breaks through. I sob uncontrollably. I was doing really well managing my family and making sure we had everything we needed. This makes that almost impossible. Being able to take the girls allows me to see my kids all at once. Now, I'm being forced to spend time with my healthy kids or my acutely ill son, not both. Choosing one over the other is more than I can handle. My nightmare is coming true.

Still sitting on the side of the road, my windows fogged up, I wipe my eyes with the back of my hand. My phone rings again and I know it's a call from the hospital by the Unknown ID that flashes across the screen. I pick up on the second ring. "Hi, Leighann. It's Kristen." She goes into a full accounting of the memo. As the social worker it's her job to relate information to families and make sure we understand what's going on. "I just got off the phone with

Stephanie from the unit. I'm still trying to figure out what to do."

"I can talk to the charge nurse and see if he can arrange for the girls to come today to say good-bye to Ryan," she offers.

"Who put out the policy?" I ask.

"The Chief Medical Officer signed the memo," she says. "I'll call you back after I talk with the charge nurse."

We hang up and I dial the main hospital line. It's etched like a tattoo in my frontal lobe. I ask for the CMO's office. His secretary answers the phone. I calmly ask for the correct address to send correspondence, my voice shaking. "Is there something we can help you with over the phone? It sounds like you're concerned," she says politely.

I stammer, "I'm not sure. It might be better handled in a letter, but I'm happy to tell you what's going on and you can advise me what to do."

I explain to her my son is at their hospital and has been for six of his eight-month life. He has no discharge date and is currently in a holding pattern trying to learn to breathe on his own. That I come every day with my older children to see him and there's no way I can explain to a five- and three-year-old they cannot see their brother until flu season's over in April—six months away, double his current age. It's literally a lifetime.

I explain my children are very bonded with their brother and it'll be devastating to them and ask if there's some way I can maintain the motivation of the hospital to protect its patient population from H1N1 while keeping my family together. I suggest vaccinations, masks, and open it up to jumping through any hoop they can think of. I explain we already use ICU precautions when visiting and I never bring the girls when they're displaying contagious symptoms. She takes down my contact information and promises to get back to me.

I get a call within a few hours from the CMO's lead research assistant. She tells me the girls can come and see Ryan once they've been vaccinated and waited 48 hours (in case they get the live vaccine and are shedding the virus).

Grateful I have that in place, I call the attending for the CICU, explain the stipulations the CMO's office gave me and ask if there are any additional protocols they want me to put in place to make them comfortable having the girls in the ICU. We're a team and I don't want to alienate any of them by only going through the CMO. She says she'll get back to me.

IT TAKES A bit of legwork to find the vaccine. I call our pediatrician, the county health department, and search multiple health websites. In the end I find out the CDC hasn't issued the dead-virus vaccine to our state yet. Our pediatrician only has the live vaccine. I'm uncomfortable with the mist. I send an email to all my friends asking if they know anyone who has the H1N1 shot.

While I'm busy tracking down the vaccine, the CICU staff contacts the infectious disease department and decides I must wait two weeks post-vaccination to allow antibodies to build up in the girls' system before bringing them onto the unit.

Exactly a week after my email cry for help a friend emails me that her pediatrician has the shot. Unfortunately we aren't part of their patient roster. I promise the scheduling nurse I'll switch over but they tell me they don't have any appointments for new patients for several weeks. I can't wait that long.

I look up the lead physician for the practice and call her office directly. I leave a message asking her to call me. She's at the American Pediatrics Association conference so I don't expect to hear from her for a few days. She calls me later that evening. I gush my appreciation at even getting a call. I fill her in on our situation. My voice takes on a high-pitch as I fight the tightness in my throat. My eyes hold pitchers of tears just waiting to fall. "The CMO's willing to make an exception for our family if I can get the girls vaccinated. Our pediatrician doesn't have the shot yet and with the vaccine shortages I'm having a hard time getting them back to see their brother. I know it's a lot to ask, but I'm hoping you'll let us on your list of those receiving the vaccine. We aren't part of your practice. I'm glad to switch over though if you want us too. I'm really just trying to get my girls in to see their brother."

"Please don't cry, Mrs. Marquiss," she says gently. "I'm so sorry your family is in this situation. I can't imagine how hard it is having a child hospitalized. I'd like to help you in any way I can.

"Our office policy is not to treat anyone who isn't a part of our practice for liability reasons. I can't ask my staff to go against the policy. What I can do is give your girls the shot personally. But I need you to keep this quiet. You've seen the news. Everyone is in a panic and people are doing crazy things to get their children the vaccine. We get dozens of calls a day and parents are berating my staff when they realize we don't have enough vaccines for everyone. We're only giving the vaccine to our compromised patients. I'd say your son is compromised so by proxy your girls qualify."

I pinky-swear to keep where I got the vaccine a secret.

The next morning she calls me with an office address and the name of the head nurse there who's waiting for my call. She's decided to speed things up while she's at the conference to bend the policy in our favor. My girls get the vaccination within 24 hours. Ellen, the head nurse who gives my girls the shot, gives me a big hug when I arrive at their office. I've never met her before, but her hug is welcome. So is the vaccine.

It's a full three weeks from the time I get the call from Stephanie about the policy until the girls see their brother. On one hand it made me slow down a bit and stay at home with the girls instead of huffing back and forth every day. I chose to stay home on Tuesdays and Thursdays instead of sending the girls off to more play dates. I felt guilty Ryan was by himself several more days a week than usual. It hit me though he doesn't know any differently. He sees the same people every day. They love him. They flirt with him. He really has more people visiting him than any baby would at home. Instead of feeling sorry for him for not being with his family, I learn to be thankful for how many other people are in his life who love him. It's a new perspective for me and somewhat freeing.

The three-week hiatus didn't faze Ainsley. However Natalie started acting out at home and school and started refusing to go to ballet class. She said things like, "We have to wait a week to see Ryan so we don't get him sick." Or, "We had to get a shot to keep Ryan from getting sick." Someone suggested she may be experiencing anxiety over not being able to see him for herself. Before the policy she was able to see him on a daily basis. She could see his condition and know he was okay. Now she has to rely on my reports and can't confirm anything for herself. I'm hopeful she calms down once she lays eyes on her brother.

As the end of October approaches Natalie comes to me with a simple request. "Mommy, can Ryan come to my birthday party?"

"Honey, Ryan's in the hospital. He won't be able to be here. I'm sorry," I cringe knowing this isn't the answer she's looking for.

"It's not fair," she says. "He came to Ainsley's birthday party."

"I know," I say hugging her close. "It's not fair. I want him to be at your party, too. I want him to come home for good." She cries into my shoulder.

MY HEART GETS heavier with each passing day. Ryan continues to struggle. After allowing him to work on his own for almost an entire month, Ryan is intubated on October 28. His body is crystal clear in communicating he needs support to breathe. The team considers an underlying cardiac issue in addition to the respiratory issues. They decide to take him back to the cath lab. Dr. Kanter walks me through the procedure with the risks and benefits outlined on the consent form. "Can we skip through the risks next time?" I say half-joking.

Ryan's cath lasts four hours. Dr. Kanter finds a good-sized collateral stealing blue blood and taking it into the body before it can get oxygenated. He coils off the malicious vein with five little metal coils resembling springs found in a ballpoint pen. Ryan's oxygen sats immediately bounce back up into the seventies—his pre-tissue expanders baseline.

Dr. Kanter also gets a good view of Ryan's diaphragm under fluoroscopy. He confirms Ryan's diaphragm is paralyzed and moving up into the right lung cavity when Ryan tries to breathe in. Most of the doctors on the team have been pushing to plicate Ryan's diaphragm since the beginning of October and this gives them more fuel for their argument. Dr. Jonas is hesitant to try the plication because of Ryan's complexities, the position of his heart in relation to where most plication incisions are made and the fact plications aren't a guaranteed success. Those that are successful always have the chance of coming undone over time. Dr. Jonas doesn't want to put Ryan under stress for nothing. He's seen kids work through paralyzed and weak diaphragms and wants his patients to have every opportunity to do things without additional surgeries. He has very strong feelings in Ryan's case. His odds of survival were so low to begin with, and he has so many things going against him.

That's the exact ammunition the team launches at Dr. Jonas every day. If we know plication *can* be helpful for a kid with a paralyzed diaphragm, why wouldn't we remove an obvious obstacle? It's not like Ryan is doing stellar. Even with the recent cath he's unable to come off the ventilator. It's all very frustrating . . . to everyone.

All I've been able to think about since the Glenn procedure is getting Ryan home. Who am I kidding? That's all I ever think about! I thought the Glenn would be the magic bullet to get us out of here. I'm struggling with the idea that with all the surgeries and medical intervention my son still lives in a bubble. We're two months post-Glenn and back to square one. Ryan's in the CICU on a ventilator with so many lines coming out of him they're clipped in neat little groups to his bed. He's on IV meds and oral meds around the clock and some additional doses as needed. He's on slight sedation to keep him comfortable on the vent. His arms are restrained so he doesn't itch or pull his vent tube out. He lies in his bed smiling at nurses for more hours of the day than I care to admit.

IT'S HALLOWEEN MORNING and still dark out when Natalie enters my bathroom. "Why are you in the shower mommy? It's nighttime."

"I'm going to go see Ryan," I say.

"Moooom. Don't go see him. Stay home with us. You'll miss the treating," she whines.

"I'm not going to miss the trick-or-treating, honey. I'm going for a few hours. I'll be back before you know it." I wipe a circle of steam off the shower door so I can see her. She's pouting with her arms crossed. "Go jump in bed with daddy. It's too early for you to be up." She runs to my bed. Henry opens the blanket wide, swinging his long arm to the sky. She nestles in close to her father as he closes his arm over her protectively.

By the time I'm applying my makeup both girls are awake. Natalie finds Ainsley puttering around me in the bathroom playing with bath toys. "No one will play horses with me," she cries. She's practically writhing around on the floor with jealousy. Ainsley pipes up, "I'll play with you."

"You're too late," Natalie says, yet continues complaining. "No one will play with me, Mommy."

Annoyed with her behavior I snap at her, "Don't refuse to play with your sister and then complain no one will play with you. Why don't you say what you're really upset about?"

She looks at me quizzically. "What are you really upset about?" I prod.

"Horses?" she tries meekly.

"No. You're upset Mommy's going to see Ryan and isn't staying here with you this morning." I pull her onto my lap and hug her tight. "You feel like you didn't get to see me yesterday because you were in school and now you won't see me again this morning.

You're upset because you can't come with me and you haven't seen Ryan for a long time. You're upset because he isn't home yet and has to stay in the hospital. Guess what? I'm upset, too. I hate that I can't be with my kids all at one time. I hate that Ryan can't live at home with us. But I want to go see Ryan and I want to go this morning so I can come home and be with you the rest of the day because I miss you, too." I kiss her hair and cheek. "I love you, sweet girl. I really do love you," I murmur, kissing her head again.

She kisses me on the lips and jumps off my lap. "Come on, Ains. Let's go play horses." I sit there stunned for a split-second, surprised at her quick change. I'm not one to complain when an attempt becomes a success, so I go with it.

ON A SCALE of one to ten of important holidays, Halloween's a two. This doesn't stop me from having a pity party on my drive to the hospital. I wasn't making things up when I told Natalie I wanted Ryan with us. He has missed lots of family activities, but for some reason this one feels more important. I cry on my way to the hospital mourning our circumstances. I ignore the fact Ryan sleeps through most the visit. With the help of the nurse, I dress him in a little Halloween T-shirt I bought for him from Old Navy. We've only recently been putting him in clothes. A nurse heard me lamenting that it's so sad looking at Ryan's clothes hanging in the closet at home knowing he'll never use them. She told me as long as the outfit doesn't interfere with the lines he *can* wear it. So I dress him up and take his picture of his first Halloween. Deep down I know it's indicative of what's to come. With no improvement it's unlikely he'll be home for Thanksgiving or Christmas. After a few hours I rush home to Henry and the girls. We make a birthday cake for Henry—he's a Halloween baby—and eat it before dressing to head out for the evening. The girls dress up like a doctor and nurse in child-sized scrubs. Natalie's a trooper walking from door-to-door sulking when there are no more houses to hit up for chocolate. Ainsley hits about ten houses before indicating she's done. "Don't you want to get more candy?" I ask. Her bag only has a handful of candy in it.

"I have enough. Uppy," she says raising her arms up to me. Henry and I trade off carrying her the rest of the way. She's practically asleep by the time we're through the neighborhood.

November 2009

Natalie's Halloween meltdown is a stark reminder our kids are walking this tough road with us. One of the best things we did was to record our family playing and singing and talking to Ryan so the nurses could play it for him when we aren't there. The nurses swear by the tape and call it Ryan's audio anti-anxiety pill. I'm able to witness the affect one day in early November. He was having a rough go of it with unexplained fevers and slept most of my visit. At some point I noticed his diaper was saturated so I changed it. He silently screamed with agitation.

I turned on the tape and patted his little leg to soothe him. Within a few minutes he was fast asleep. Some time later the tape clicked off so I turned it to the other side. The audio went from the girls playing with each other in the background to Natalie talking close to the mic directly to Ryan.

"Hi, Ryan. I love you. I miss you. I wish you were home. I love your eyebrows. I love your eyelashes. I love your cute face. I love your nose. One day you'll grow up and hear me and understand me. And you'll listen to me . . ." She goes on like this for about five minutes, even making up songs like, "I love you. I love marshmallows. I love you. I love marshmallows" in a way only a little girl can.

The sweetest thing is when her lone voice came on in her crystal-clear five-year-old speak, Ryan's eyebrows crinkled. He opened one eye the tiniest bit looking over his shoulder to find her. Then he smiled a tired, droopy smile. He continued smiling on and off for a few minutes before he drifted back to sleep. To him, the girls are still here.

When the girls come back to the CICU the first week in November, Natalie immediately says, "He's bigger than he was before!" Then sets about arranging her toys and playing babies with Ainsley like she never left.

OVER THE MONTHS the illusion of control is stripped away like the layers of an onion. Each layer flakes off and once the crying from the fresh sulfur is over, I barely look back. The latest is the state of the house. A few weeks ago I was battling fluctuating hormones, Henry and I were especially disconnected, and I felt very alone. I looked around at the state of my home and realized it was easy to figure out what was happening on my insides by looking at the rooms one by one. The thought crossed my mind I should quit my bellyaching and get up and clean the house from top to bottom—I'd feel better and could cope with my heartache. This is definitely the voice of my maternal grandfather. As quickly as the thought crossed my mind it was chased out by another. My filthy house is a symptom of my out-of-control feelings and can't be solved by a good scrubbing. No matter how clean the house gets, it wouldn't change the fact my son is lying in a hospital away from his family and turning nine months old without fanfare.

I remember my mom telling me she "let go" of the house after three children and swearing I'd never do the same. Let's just say I'm becoming more like my mother every day.

The house isn't the only thing. A lot of things are unimportant now—the best dressed kids, looking perfect, a big house, a fancy car. Those are just things and putting on appearances. I have a hard time getting excited about any of that anymore. I hear people complain about mundane daily life and it's hard for me to be empathetic. It's not that I don't think they have valid complaints— these are things I complained about a year or so ago and will most likely complain about in the years to come. I just don't have the emotional energy to think those things are important right now. I'm in a very different place. I'm too busy worrying about the emotional well being of my kids, the health of my marriage, and whose needs I'll choose to meet next.

My enemies are varied: time away from the girls, the girls missing out on "normal" family activities like playing outside, going to the park, baking with mom, doing crafts. . . . All the things we used to do when being a stay-at-home mom meant I stayed at home.

Sometimes the enemy is guilt or regret or fear. Guilt over not having enough time with the girls, regret I can't be in two places at once, fear Ryan or the girls will remember this time as horrible or it will somehow make them feel less important or overlooked.

The guilt doesn't stop with the kids. I have a husband who I'm used to taking care of as well. Aside from Ryan's medical needs, Henry had the most stressful professional and financial year of his life. The economy is in the middle of the worst downfall since the

Great Depression and we haven't been immune to its devastating effects. Both of us tend to hold our emotions close to the vest, something we're trying to work on.

In the past when Henry has been stressed, I've tried to make home his haven. But this season of stress is longer than others and I'm under a lot of stress, too. I'm unable to ease his pensive moods or provide a cheery home life. It's something we're unaccustomed to, and this adds to the strain.

We try to face our weaknesses head-on. We seek a counselor to help us work through the emotions we feel but are unable to express. We're working on connecting and helping each other. Eighty-five percent of couples with special-needs kids end up divorced. We don't want to be part of that statistic.

Fatigue is the mother of all enemy ships and looms constantly on the horizon. It makes me impatient with the girls and snippy with Henry. It makes me want to be mean and ugly to people who really have nothing to do with my state of mind. After a particularly hard day I fall into bed next to Henry who's already breathing heavy in a peaceful sleep. Part of me wants to pray but the other part says to heck with it all. I've been praying for the last year and Ryan still isn't home. The thought of going through this journey without my faith in God is more than my tired mind can handle, but I'm stubborn. I curl up in a ball and sob uncontrollably. My body shakes so violently I'm afraid I'll wake Henry. I stumble to the guest bedroom in the basement and wail in the darkness. At the end of three hours I finally pray. "I can't do this without You. I need Your strength because mine's gone." It's the longest prayer I have the energy for. I fall asleep more exhausted than ever.

THE FIRST THREE weeks of November we play the game of three steps forward and two steps back with Ryan's breathing. He's able to come off the ventilator but continues to rely on high-flow oxygen to maintain his sats. My mood highly depends on how Ryan's doing on any given day. I feel like I'm on a roller coaster that has no end. The week before Thanksgiving I lie awake in bed frustrated. "I can't take anymore," I say to God. "Please let this end. Show us what we need to do to get Ryan off high flow oxygen. I need an answer." I cry myself to sleep in frustration feeling defeated.

The next morning during rounds the team tells me Dr. Sandler will perform surgery on Ryan's diaphragm the Monday after Thanksgiving.

WE ARRIVE AT the hospital early Thanksgiving morning. I can't bear not to spend a few hours with Ryan before heading to see our families an hour and a half away. He's off the ventilator so he's off sedation medication and awake. We take the opportunity to sit in his bed and play with him.

"Hey guys, let's take a family picture," I say. "We can pretend we're in a photo studio."

We cover everything we can in white hospital sheets and sit as a group on the bed. Casey, Ryan's nurse takes our picture. "Take one of just us," I say once the family pictures are done. Casey loves taking pictures, she's taken pictures of Ryan and me before at her suggestion so I know she won't mind. She plays photographer while Ryan and I pose and then play with each other. During the photo shoot he reaches up and tries to grab my hair. My baby is reaching for me for the first time in his life. I try to get him to do it again. He gets my hair and then moves his little hand to my cheek and chin. Casey snaps pictures to forever cement the event in history.

ON THE WAY to Thanksgiving dinner with Henry's family the anxiety starts in the pit of my stomach. Every year my father-in-law has us go around the table before we say grace to tell what we're thankful for. We'll do the same thing with my family tomorrow during my extended family's Thanksgiving dinner. I have no idea what to say this year. It isn't that I'm not thankful. I'm thankful for many things: the presence of God over the last year and a half, my husband and my children, my extended family and friends who've come alongside of us enabling us to continue functioning, the amazing hospital staff taking care of my son. But there's something missing this year . . . someone. I wanted my son sitting in a high chair next to me while we ate my mom's famous sweet potato casserole (with the nut topping). I wanted to slip him mashed potatoes and gravy and watch him get them in his hair.

It's hard being satisfied with life when what I'm really craving is health.

It's hard being happy he's alive when what I really want is for him to live outside the hospital walls.

It's hard to focus on the big picture of him one day coming home when right now I'm living in the details.

It's just plain hard.

And easy.

Easy to be discouraged; easy to be impatient; easy to lose focus.

I GET THROUGH Thanksgiving and the day after without having to lose my composure in front of everyone. Both families skip the obligatory "what I'm thankful for this year" game. I'm not sure if it was deliberate because of the year we've had, or if it was an oversight.

Saturday night, I'm sitting with my mom and sister, Amy, at my mother's kitchen table snacking on popcorn, an omnipresent family snack. My mother grew up eating popcorn watching Johnny Carson with her parents. She remembers the day Elvis Presley gyrated his hips on TV and her father yelled to turn it off. If he hadn't yelled, maybe she wouldn't remember. Either way, Elvis and popcorn are imprinted in my mother's memory forever.

Amy, the feeler in the family, turns to me and says, "So how are you really doing?"

I was almost through the weekend. I can see the finish line, just one more day to go. "Are you serious?" I ask. "Are you really starting this at 11:30 at night?"

She sees the look of panic pass over my face before I can recover. Her eyes well up with emotion from the pain that escaped my inmost being and rose to the surface. She cries *for* me so I don't have to. She lays her head on my mother's table and weeps. "I miss him," she says. "He should be here and he's not." She takes my pain on her shoulders because she knows I can't bear to feel it alone. I love her for it.

"Who's watching the kids on Monday?" she says, wiping her eyes.

"Willa might come down, or I can ask Bridget to do it," I say.

"I talked to Dean already. If you want, we'll stay a few extra days. He'll keep the boys at his parents' house and I can come stay with the girls."

"You don't have to do that. You already came in August," I say.

"No, I want to. It's not a big deal. We don't have any other plans," she says.

"Thank you. The girls still talk about the first time you stayed with them. They'll be excited," I say.

MONDAY, NOVEMBER 30, Ryan undergoes his fifth surgery in nine months. During the procedure, Dr. Sandler tacks down the diaphragm out of the lung space. He basically stitches it back on itself giving it less slack. This stitch may eventually work itself out or the diaphragm may stretch, but in that time, many people are able to gain strength and grow into a better breathing technique. We're hoping it's just the thing we need to get Ryan out of the CICU and on his way home.

For the first two days after surgery, Ryan's oxygen sats sit in the forties and fifties. It's nerve-wracking to know we've done everything possible and he's still satting at critical levels. On the third day, December 2, his sats jump to the eighties. It seems like the plication worked! By the end of the second week of December he's off the vent, his numbers are great, and he's almost off supplemental oxygen. He hasn't been off supplemental oxygen since June 16—almost an entire six months. I don't quite believe it yet.

The best thing is he's peppy and happy. Because his sats are higher, that means more red blood flowing through his system . . . he's practically pink instead of dusky blue. The more he comes off the different medications the more fun he is. It's hard to play with a baby who's always loopy. Yesterday I played peekaboo with him like I always do, but instead of looking at me like I'm crazy, he laughed. It really makes me wonder if when he was drugged he couldn't figure out that peekaboo was a game. He probably thought he was hallucinating.

Not only did he play peekaboo, but he also cooed when I read him books like he was reading along. This is the first time he's really cooed a lot. I've heard him coo once or twice randomly but *never* while I've been playing with him. Can I just say how utterly discouraging it is to play with a child who doesn't care for nine months straight?

He's ready to be moved to the Heart and Kidney unit (HKU) better known as "the floor" to the staff. Before this experience with Ryan, I never realized the difference between units and the different roles nurses play. The differences between an ICU nurse's and floor nurse's role are many. And since my first, real, long-term experience was with ICU nurses, the transition is a major culture shock.

At Children's the cardiac ICU nurses are assigned one to two patients. They're physically with the patient their entire 12-hour shift. They're typically assigned to the same patient(s) across the three days they work. In Ryan's case, he saw the same six or seven nurses on a regular basis. Because they spend so much time with the patient, they become extremely intimate with the patient's mannerisms and baseline; his responses to different medications and daily bodily rhythms.

They're expected to inform the doctors of every minute detail and end up driving the patient's care. They advocate for more or less medication, more or less therapy, give their opinions on when to wean oxygen or vent settings. They become the patient's voice.

What this does for the parent, especially one like me who isn't able to be there around the clock, is relieve a huge emotional burden. We know there's someone looking after our child all the time. When I call for an update the typical CICU response is to give me the same rundown they would give a doctor who stepped into the room: last gas results, what meds he's on and any wean schedule, same with oxygen and vent settings, any change to the plan discussed in rounds. When I say, "How's Ryan?" They know I'm asking first about his medical status and then about his emotional status, and respond appropriately.

On the floor there's a stark difference in the nurse's role. A floor nurse has four patients and is required to rotate between the rooms hooking up feeds, changing diapers, giving meds, and any other daily care involved for that specific patient. They don't have time to get to know the patients intimately and aren't expected to drive the patient's care. The parents are expected to be the primary caregiver and to be available as much as possible. As you can imagine, my time constraints don't change just because Ryan has moved to the HKU so it becomes harder to imagine him happy and cared for. It's easy to worry he's alone and upset or needing something. In reality, this happens far more frequently on the floor than in the ICU. It's just the nature of the beast.

When I call for an update the typical HKU response is, "He's doing great." Then I ask questions like, "What's his oxygen setting, what are his sats, does he have a fever, what was discussed in rounds?" Because the floor uses patient techs (aka a nurse's assistant), sometimes they know the answers and sometimes they don't.

The way the doctors are staffed is significantly different as well. In the ICU, the doctors are on service for a month. There may be a slight learning curve at the beginning of the month but within a few days they're caught up with a patient's needs and able to make decisions regarding care with a fair amount of information. In the HKU, doctors are on service for one week so by the time the learning curve is over there are only a few more days for them to make any sort of care changes.

For most kids, the difference between the units is a natural progression to going home. The medical staff tells us moving to the HKU is a great way to practice life at home with professional observation. The typical child coming from the CICU is home within a few days. The hard part for us is Ryan is expected to live in the HKU for more than a few days . . . it's almost Christmas and it doesn't seem we're any closer to going home than we were when we came to the floor.

Speaking to a different doctor or resident every time I'm updated (which is far less frequently) is hard, too. I have a good rapport with the CICU doctors who I've worked with day-in and day-out for the last ten or so months, whereas I only know one HKU doctor (who I worked with in the CICU and who has now moved to the HKU). Because there seems to be lack of progress, the conversations are more confrontational and leave me feeling unsatisfied.

I'm learning to be more vocal about Ryan's care on the unit. To push the doctors harder and keep at them until I'm satisfied they aren't deflecting questions. I think the perception of the CICU and HKU of me will be quite different as well, perhaps as differently as I view them. That's okay. It's a different environment and different tactics are necessary.

There's a push to get him home before the holidays. A few days before Christmas I run into a nurse from the CICU. "I hear Ryan might be home for Christmas," Steve says. "Congratulations!"

"Oh please don't say it," I cringe. "He might not make it and I don't want to get my hopes up. I already geared myself up for him to be here."

Although very close, Ryan's little body isn't ready by December 25. Instead of rushing him, we all agree it's better to allow him the time necessary to give him the best possible scenario upon arriving home. Surprisingly, I'm okay with it. I grieved about the holidays at Halloween and Thanksgiving. I refused to get my hopes up for Christmas. We spend Christmas Eve at the hospital opening gifts with the girls and Ryan. We have a few more at the house for the girls, but didn't want Ryan to celebrate his first Christmas alone.

I update my blog with family pictures and the lyrics to "Have Yourself a Merry Little Christmas." The words of the last verse especially pierce a hole through my heart.

January 2010

On January 8, 2010, we bring our son home after six consecutive months in the hospital. He's accompanied by oxygen support, around the clock feedings, and thirteen different medications needing to be administered twenty-eight times in a 24-hour period. The social worker and the in-house case manager make sure I have a night-nurse scheduled for the night we get home. I have a prescription for nursing care seven nights per week. I'm so relieved Ryan is in the car that I have little time to think through how my life is about to change. Knowing there'll be a nurse with him every night helps.

BY THE TIME I pull out into traffic Ryan's already sleeping in the backseat. He loves the movement of the car. My phone rings. It's an Unknown ID.

"Hello?" I say.

"Hi, Mrs. Marquiss. This is Dr. Donofrio's fellow, Maureen. She asked me to give you a call. Ryan had a CT scan earlier this week to get a reading on his hydrocephalus. I'm sure you've noticed his head's large in proportion to his body. Dr. Donofrio wants you to follow up on the results. You'll need to call Dr. Magge in neurosurgery and set up an appointment to have him go over the findings with you. She'd like you to make it a priority."

I just turned right onto K Street from Nineteenth. I have less than half a mile before I'm out of the city.

"Should I be taking him home?" I ask. This is the first I've heard he has hydrocephalus. Although my knowledge is limited, I'm pretty sure hydrocephalus is a dangerous condition.

"At this point, he's completely stable. Dr. Donofrio made sure of that before discharging him. However, if his vomiting increases or he gets irritable, call us right away. Otherwise, call Dr. Magge on Monday and make an appointment. Dr. Donofrio's been in contact with him so he's expecting your call. He'll get you in as soon as you can get here. And if you have any concerns, always call us. There's someone on call all hours of the day. It's better to be safe than sorry."

"Okay, thanks," I say hanging up the phone. Before the call, most my thoughts were farther out on the horizon. How long it'll take to get Ryan off oxygen? Will he have withdrawal from the last bit of narcotics as we wean him off at home? How soon can we get him eating by mouth? Now it seems we'll also be following a case of hydrocephalus.

Ryan's first night home is rough. The nurse reports he was "fussy all night and slept only in half-hour spurts." I immediately say a prayer of thanksgiving under my breath; not for him being awake all night, but because I'm hearing about it from someone else.

Ryan continues to suffer from reflux. It starts with him coughing and then he gags on his food. It happens about 50 percent of the time. Other than the vomiting, he's generally happy sitting in his chair, swing, my lap, or Natalie's lap.

I start right away trying to get him to accept water by mouth so we can work on getting rid of the feeding tube. Speech therapists at the hospital were working with him every morning and I don't want him to forget how to swallow. He opens his mouth really wide when I bring the spoon in "for a landing," which is a big difference since the last time I fed him a week ago. He swallows the tiny amount of water so I make the amount slightly bigger. He does okay. The biggest problem is he opens his mouth really wide and then doesn't close it when the spoon lands on his tongue. The liquid ends up spilling out the sides of his mouth. I begin applying pressure on his chin when I touch the spoon to his tongue and the last two tries he does a lot better closing over it.

We also work on him hitting a toy that spins and sings the alphabet. I'm trying to teach him high-five. He *is* a boy after all. It's weird to have an eleven-month-old in the house who acts like an infant. He can't roll over, sit up, or eat table food (actually he can't eat any food). The therapists at the hospital warned me to take the length of his hospital stay off his age for his "true" age. Because kids are vented, sedated, and restrained they don't develop like their peers emotionally and physically. Ryan was in the hospital eight of his eleven months, so we should expect the behavior of a three-month-old. I'd say he's pretty close to that.

Monday dawns bright and early. Bringing Ryan home on a Friday gave us a chance to breathe before jumping into school and ballet. With Ryan home we also have doctors appointments. He has two scheduled this week and a possible third if I can get in to see the neurosurgeon.

Today we'll go to Reston Hospital, our local hospital where the girls were born and Henry had his appendix taken out, to draw Ryan's blood. He's taking sodium and potassium and it's important to keep a watch on his electrolyte levels. His sodium level was of particular concern when he was discharged. We have a standing appointment at the pediatrician on Fridays to make sure he's good to go for the weekend.

We head to Reston Hospital after dropping Ainsley at school. I figure it's easier to go without a preschooler in tow and I don't know exactly how long it'll take. The waiting room is busy when we get there. I'm lugging around a tank of oxygen about knee-height that should last two-and-a-half hours on Ryan's rate of 2.5 liters a minute. We don't get the star treatment we got six months ago as no doctor has called ahead. I add Ryan's name to the long registry list and settle in for a wait. I start to get nervous the longer I sit here and by the time I'm called to register a half-hour later I'm about to pull my hair out. I ask the intake person how long it'll take to be called to the lab, but he has no idea. This waiting room covers multiple outpatient procedures so there's no telling who's waiting for what. I sit down and try to watch TV but I can't get my mind to focus on the mundane. Although I didn't think I'd be out this long, I'm grateful I grabbed an extra bottle of breast milk and the 10 A.M. dose of meds. I knew I didn't want to be caught without them.

This medicine schedule is so crazy that I sat down Friday night to write them all out. I realized he's receiving something every two hours with only a four-hour window between noon and 4 P.M. and midnight and 4 A.M. No wonder the nurses are running around like mad women giving themselves a flex-window of half an hour on administering medicine. I resolve to slowly consolidate the meds so they can be given in batches instead of one at a time. Since I have the time, I call the pharmacist at Children's to see if any of his meds are incompatible with each other. None are. I'm given the go-ahead to adjust meds up an hour or back an hour until the dosing schedule makes more sense. Unfortunately, I can't do anything with the narcotics. He's on two: Methadone and Ativan (Larazapam). The wean schedule's so complicated I have to take out a blank calendar page and write down on each day how much he should get. At his levels, you basically give the same dose for four days before minutely decreasing it and keeping that dose four days. You do this *forever* until you are down to nothing. Also you can't wean two drugs on the same day so I have to make sure I don't mess up the schedule the pharmacist set out for me.

By the time I'm called back to the lab it's been an hour and a half. I'm relieved when they call Ryan's name only to freak out again when I realize they're taking me to another waiting area. There are about ten people ahead of me. I look at Ryan's oxygen tank and see it's almost to the red warning indicator.

I push the stroller to the blood lab door and knock. "Just a minute," Mike says from inside. I'm hoping he'll remember me and let us cut in line. I vow to never put Ryan in this situation again. An older woman leaves the lab and Mike sticks his head out to answer the knock. "Well hello there, " he says with a grin.

"Hi," I say. "We're here to get Ryan's blood drawn. I hate to ask you to do this, but I didn't realize the wait would be so long and we're almost out of oxygen. Do you think you'd be able to take him next?"

"I have one lady who needs to go before you, but then I can take you after that. It'll just be a few minutes. Wait here outside the door and I'll grab you as she's leaving. Mondays are really busy, especially the morning. We have regulars who come every week and for some reason they all choose Monday morning."

"Thank you," I say. "I really appreciate it."

Ryan and I arrive home at lunchtime. I quickly switch him back to the oxygen concentrator and go into the kitchen to draw up his noon meds. When I get back to him a few minutes later, he's already asleep. One convenient thing about the feeding tube is the child doesn't have to be awake in order to eat or take meds. You can push them any time. Also, you don't have to wrestle your child in one hand, wrapping your arms and legs through theirs and gripping their head in the crook of your elbow to administer medicine only to watch half of it dribble down their chin and the rest be spit out purposefully. Nope. With a feeding tube you can sit cooing at your child watching them smile back at you while pushing nasty smelling medicine and flushing the tube with water. It rocks!

I sit on the couch for a small breather knowing I only have an hour before Heather drops Ainsley off from pre-school. I'm low on portable oxygen—I only had a few tanks leftover from last time and thought they'd last me a week. At this rate, I'll be out of them in another day or two. I go through the week's events in my head and calculate when I'll run out if I take Natalie to ballet this afternoon. I'm unwilling to tell her we aren't going because of Ryan. I grab my phone and call the oxygen company to see when I can get more in the house. Luckily, they're in our area tomorrow and can bring me more tanks. I order ten to be on the safe side.

I SPEND THE afternoon tracking down doctors, making appointments, filling out medical paperwork, and throwing laundry in the washer. I didn't expect to lose so much of my morning so by the time Natalie's dropped off at 3:30 P.M. by a friend I'm behind the eight ball. I'd planned to have everything packed up, including a snack, so we could jump right in the car to get to ballet on time. It's starts at 4 P.M., the same time I'm scheduled to pump. We're twenty minutes late and I haven't pumped. I have Ryan's feeds and my pump (I pushed his meds before we left, also due at 4 P.M.). I'm hoping to pump while Natalie's in class.

As I pull into the parking lot, the phone rings. It's the nursing company. "Hi, Leighann. It's Maria. I have bad news. The daytime nurse thought the commute was going to be a lot shorter. She's not willing to drive the hour to your house."

"What are you saying? She's not coming?" I say, shocked. Ryan's only been home three days.

"Yeah. I'm sorry," she says.

"You're kidding?" I moan.

"I'm working on getting it staffed again. I'll do my best to have you someone soon," she promises.

I hang up utterly frustrated. I'm not sure how many days I can do on my own with all of Ryan's feedings and meds. No sooner do I get Ryan and his equipment set up in the stroller than the phone rings again.

"Hello?" I say breathlessly, holding the phone to my ear with my shoulder while rushing the girls down the long sidewalk to the ballet studio.

"Hey, Leighann. It's Dr. Pike from Children's. I heard you've been trying to reach us today."

"I have a quick question about Ryan's meds. You guys put him on something right before he left to help his gut move faster in case his stomach isn't emptying fast enough causing the increased spitting-up. It's moving pretty fast now—about five loose stools a day. I'm afraid he'll get dehydrated. Can I take him off whichever one's the culprit?" I ask.

"Let me look into it and get back to you. I'll call you back in a few minutes." she says.

Finally at the door, Natalie and Ainsley rush into the ballet studio lobby. I forgot that Mondays at ballet are reminiscent of free-coffee day at Starbucks. We jostle our way to the back corner of the building where Natalie's regular class is. She hesitates at the doorway. She acted this way toward the end of ballet last semester, crying and protesting at the door for the first fifteen minutes of each class. It was very trying emotionally for both of us. I don't have the energy to handle it today. "Natalie, you need to go in the class. You can't cry and stand by the door today. We're already late. You'll miss the whole class." I say firmly.

She looks at me for a second. As if she can sense my mood she spins on her heel, entering the classroom without arguing.

I sit down in a heap close to Ryan. He's crying. I pull him out of the stroller, untangling the oxygen cord with one hand and cradling him with the other. I grab the feeding pump strap and diaper bag in one concentrated motion. Balancing Ryan across my crossed legs, I mix the breast milk and formula. "Can I shake it, mommy? Please?" Ainsley says. She's standing beside me watching everything I'm doing. "Not this time, sweetie. Mommy needs to hurry up. Ryan's hungry." I say. I pour the mixture into the pump bag and prime it as usual. Once Ryan's hooked up to his feeds, I pick him back up from my leg-cradle and gently rock him trying to comfort him. My phone rings again.

"Ains, can you get me the phone?" I say.

"Hello?" I say to the Unknown ID.

"Is this the parent of Henry Marquiss?" the caller asks.

"Yes, this is his mother."

"Hi, this is Sarah, Dr. Magge's assistant. I'm calling to schedule an appointment for your son. I got your message from this morning. When are you able to come in?" she says.

"I can come in tomorrow, Wednesday, or Thursday morning. He already has a pediatrician appointment on Friday."

"Okay, let's make it Wednesday at 10:30," she says.

"We'll see you Wednesday at 10:30 then." A few minutes later my phone rings again. I'm about to throw it out the window. Seriously. Will it ever stop?

"Hello?" I say.

"Mrs. Marquiss? This is Sarah from Dr. Magge's office again. I just spoke with Dr. Donofrio. She'd like to consult with you after your appointment so please plan to go to the cardiology clinic after coming here on Wednesday."

"Okay, I will. Thank you," I say, hanging up the phone and making a mental note. I need to make sure Heather or someone can pick Ainsley up from preschool. I'll have just enough time to drop her off, but probably won't make it back in time for pick up with two doctors appointments in one day. I text Heather before I forget to make the call.

WITH ALL THE phone calls, it seems like just a few minutes before Natalie comes bouncing out of the room. Beaming she says, "Can Miss Heidi see my brother?"

"Sure, why don't you ask her to come over here?" I say.

She looks at me shyly. "Will you ask her?"

I lead her by the hand to the studio door where her teacher is speaking with another student. We wait quietly for our turn. She looks at us expectantly. "Natalie wants to know if you'd like to come meet her brother."

"Of course!" Miss Heidi exclaims. "Is he new?"

I know she's confused since I wasn't pregnant recently. "Sort of," I say. "He's eleven months old. He's been hospitalized most his life. He just came home Friday after six months away."

Her face registers compassion. It catches me off-guard. We lead her over to Ryan. "Oh, he's so precious," she gushes. "Look how cute he is." Natalie beams. Miss Heidi looks up at me, her eyes teary. I can feel the heat radiating off my flushed face like burning coal. I'm not used to showing Ryan off, not in a *normal* baby way. I'm used to him being on display for doctors and medical students for being an anomaly, not the general public for just being a baby. My throat tightens. "Thank you," I manage to get out.

Somehow I make it though dinner, baths, and bedtime with the girls. My first full day by myself is exhausting. When the night nurse arrives to take over at 11 P.M., I crash.

Wednesday morning Ryan and I leave the house before sunrise to get downtown for the appointment with Dr. Magge. Sarah called back yesterday to say we needed to have a CT scan early and then the consultation with Dr. Magge. Henry's on point to take Natalie to school and Ainsley to Heather's house on his way to work. None of them are awake when I schlep all of Ryan's equipment and enough food and medicine for the next eight hours (to be on the safe side) to the car.

We head to radiology for a CT scan and then to the opposite side of the hospital to Dr. Magge's office. It's truly a blessing to live in an age where digital technology allows for instant results.

Dr. Magge's morning case takes longer than expected. Ryan and I wait in the neurosurgery conference room for two hours. It's a welcomed sanctuary compared to my last two days. I spend the quiet time reading Ryan the baby books I brought from home and pumping. Ryan falls asleep partway through our wait so I pull out a book of my own to read. I'm not sure when I'll have this opportunity for silence again. I'm finally ushered into the doctor's office.

"Hi, I'm Dr. Magge," he says, extending his hand. He's taller than I expected . . . at least 6'3". Being married to someone who's 6'9", I don't acknowledge anyone as tall unless they're 6'3" or taller. He has dark hair and swarthy skin reminiscent of the Middle East, but doesn't have an accent.

"Hi, I'm Ryan's mom, Leighann. Thanks for fitting us in."

"Not a problem. Sorry you had to wait. Now is your son's name Henry or Ryan? I thought it was Henry," he says.

"Oh! His legal name's Henry, but we call him Ryan since his dad and grandfather are also Henry. It helps us keep everything straight," I say smiling. "It makes it more confusing for you guys though."

"As long as I know, it's not a problem. How has *Ryan* been acting since being discharged last week?" he asks.

"He's doing okay. No signs of distress other than the vomiting. I'd say he vomits at least 50 percent of the time. His sats are pretty baseline hovering in the low seventies, but that's reasonable given his condition. I haven't seen any type of respiratory problems and his lungs are clear," I run through the regular list not sure what's important for his specialty.

"Are you a doctor?" he says, his brows knit together in confusion.

I laugh. "No, I'm not. My son just spent eight of his first eleven months in the CICU. If you give me another two minutes, you'll realize pretty quickly I'm not trained."

He smiles. "Has he been particularly fussy?"

"Not more than normal. I think his stomach bothers him but otherwise that's it." I answer.

"What about his head position? Has he been looking back over his head? Looking up at you with comfort?"

"Absolutely. He looks up over his head all the time when he's in the car so he can see me driving. Won't take his eyes off me. He doesn't cry at all when he does it," I answer.

"Great. That's what we want to hear. Do you mind if I touch him?" he asks.

He gets up and comes around to Ryan's stroller. He puts his long, slender hands around Ryan's head and applies slight pressure. He repeats this at several different angles then returns to his seat. He turns his computer monitor toward me and I see the recognizable whitish blue outline of a head with a brain inside surrounded by black. "This is Ryan's CT scan from the day he was born." He clicks another picture onto the monitor side-by-side with the first to make an easy comparison. "This is from this morning. Can you see how there's more black present in the brain here and here?" he says, pointing toward the top portions of Ryan's brain. I nod. The difference is obvious. "And here, can you see all the black around the outside of the brain close to the skull?" I nod again, not sure I like where this is going.

"Ryan has hydrocephalus. Hydrocephalus is when the ventricles in the brain responsible for creating cerebral fluid overproduce causing pressure on the brain and the skull to swell. Typically we see physical symptoms like intense headaches and vomiting. There are also negative neurological effects including destroyed brain tissue that we can see on film. If you ignore it, it's fatal."

I feel the color drain from my face.

"I believe in Ryan's case he has hydrocephalus ex vacuo. Instead of the ventricles randomly overproducing fluid and causing pressure, the ventricles increase fluid production in response to brain atrophy or injury."

"So it's an effect rather than a cause?" I ask.

"In this case, yes," he says. "We see this in a lot of cardiac kids. Their brains don't grow as large as the typical population. We think it's a result of the lack of oxygen they receive whether in utero or after birth. There isn't enough to grow the same amount of brain cells that you or I have."

"What does this mean neurologically? Will it cause any delays?" I ask afraid of the answer. Henry's biggest concern has always been how much Ryan's low oxygenation affects his mental capabilities.

"With babies there aren't neurological effects. Their synapses aren't connected yet. An adult who suffers brain cell loss as a result of trauma loses healthy synapses. This loss can take a variety of forms depending on which part of the brain's injured. Because infants are just learning everything, their neuropathways are still forming. A synapse that needs to get from point A to point B will get there. If the brain's atrophied in one spot, it will reroute and make a new path."

"Just so I understand . . ." I say. "Ryan's brain's smaller due to his lower oxygenation, causing more space in his head. The ventricles respond by producing more fluid to cushion his brain. There's no pressure or concerns physically or neurologically."

"That's right. However it is something we'll want to keep an eye on to make sure the diagnosis is right. I'd like you to come back in three months so I can look at him again. We'll do another consult and CT scan," he says. "I have to warn you though, with Ryan's anatomical defect, he isn't a candidate for a shunt. If it ends up that Ryan's hydrocephalus is the dangerous kind, I need you and your husband to understand there won't be a way for us to drain the fluid from his brain. We typically run the shunt down the neck and under the sternum. It's the bone that keeps it in place on its way to the stomach. Ryan has no bone for us to put the shunt drain behind. I'm really not sure there'd be a solution."

"Thank you for telling me. I'll make sure to talk it over with my husband. For now though it sounds like Ryan's okay."

"Yes, for now. Sarah can schedule you for another appointment in three months," he says.

I place a note at Sarah's empty desk to let her know I'll give her a call then head to the cardiology clinic. Dr. Donofrio's visibly relieved to know Ryan has hydrocephalus ex vacuo. She knew before our consultation that Ryan isn't a candidate for a shunt. "Brain surgery would be extremely risky for Ryan at this point. I was afraid we'd be facing a very difficult decision."

The course of therapy for an infant with hydrocephalus ex vacuo is plenty of playtime, interaction, and social stimulation. With Ryan home, he's getting plenty of each of these. Synapses in the human brain continue to connect until the age of two. So

Ryan's in the same boat as every other kid his age—his brain's still developing. As long as he receives the proper amount of stimulation, his synapses will form pathways using the brain tissue he possesses.

WE MAKE IT through the first week by the skin of our teeth. I still have no help during the day. Daily calls to the nursing agency are getting no results. Friday morning I reach for the diuretic bottle. It feels light. I check the volume and realize it's almost empty. I call the pharmacy close to my house to transfer the prescription from the hospital pharmacy that filled the prescription at Ryan's discharge. I estimate I have enough for a day and a half of doses so I need to arrange somehow to get it in the morning.

"According to the prescription that bottle should've lasted you all month," the pharmacist says.

"All month? My son's only been home a week," I say confused.

"You're only supposed to give him 1 ml four times a day. Are you giving him the right dose?" he asks.

"I'm giving him the right dose. I know how to draw up meds," I say dryly.

He apologizes for questioning my competency and I apologize for snapping. "I'm just trying to figure out why I don't have enough. I'll have to call the pharmacy downtown in the morning and see if they gave me the full amount," I say.

The next morning as the night nurse is giving me report I start to tell her I'm going to get more diuretic. "The Lasix . . ." I only get those two words out when she says, "Oh yeah, I meant to tell you, it's all gone."

"All gone?" I say astonished. The light bulb goes on in my head. I'm not the one drawing up the medication incorrectly. "There were at least 6 mls left last night. You're giving him the wrong amount." I hit my forehead with the palm of my hand. I really can't believe I'm having this conversation. I have no idea what damage the extra diuretic has done to Ryan's system, if anything. I take the calm route.

"I'm giving him 10 mls," she says defensively.

"The dosing is 1 ml, not 10," I exhale slowly. "I'll figure it out." I can't think of anything else to say. I feel like saying, "get out of my house." But I don't. Instead I let her finish her report and then email Dr. Donofrio to see if she has concerns.

I call the nursing company as soon as the nurse leaves. "Maria, it's Leighann. I need to speak with Becky," I say. Becky's the manager and the person I'm supposed to call with any issues.

"Hello, this is Becky," she says.

"Hey there, this is Leighann, Ryan's mom. I figured out this morning the night nurse is giving Ryan ten times the amount of diuretic prescription written ON THE SIDE OF THE BOTTLE! I can't believe it."

"You're kidding me," Becky says flabbergasted.

We talk through the situation at length. It's clearly a problem. My hesitation in firing her is that I'm barely getting through the days already on my own. Without a night nurse, I'm afraid I won't be able to properly take care of any of my children, let alone my medically fragile one. Becky and I agree she'll reprimand the nurse and let her know this can't happen again.

That night the nurse arrives visibly upset. Her eyes are puffy and she has a tissue in her hand. Becky called me earlier in the day to inform me she'd spoken with the nurse so I'm confused as to why she's crying. It annoys me. I ignore her drama. We go over all of Ryan's meds again including the change to his narcotic from that day's pediatrician appointment. She says she understands everything and she's so sorry about the Lasix mix-up. I head to bed.

"HOW'D RYAN DO last night?" I ask.

"He did great," she says. "He slept really well. He woke up once but fell back to sleep quickly. " She gives me the rest of the report and I see her out the door. At 8 A.M. I pull Ryan's narcotics from the refrigerator door. The nurse draws up the morning dose for me each night until I gain more confidence in weaning the narcotics. As I take the syringe of Ativan from the Ziploc bag, I notice there's way too much medicine in it. I double-check my list and the syringe. It's definitely wrong. In fact it's *double* what it should be. Seriously? I want to cry. No wonder my son slept so peacefully . . . he was drugged.

"Becky, this is Leighann. Get her out of my house. She's never allowed to step foot on my property again. She doubled Ryan's dose of Ativan last night. It's inexcusable and unacceptable." Thinking about the events of the week I recall the nurse saying to me after Ryan had a fitful night that perhaps the doctor could give him something to relax him. I brushed it off at the time. Now I ponder it. I have no way of knowing if she purposefully gave Ryan a double dose of sedative (you'd think she wouldn't draw it up incorrectly for me if she was covering her tracks), but after recalling her statement, I'm glad she's no longer caring for Ryan.

Completely overwhelmed with the idea I'm without a night nurse and on my own I threaten to take my business elsewhere if the nursing company can't staff the open shifts in a reasonable amount of time. They've known about Ryan's case for almost three weeks now and the two nurses they did staff either quit or got fired for incompetency. We're getting nowhere fast.

I make some calls to other mothers I know with medically fragile children to see what nursing agencies they use. I call the two nurses who came out to the house for Ryan's pre-Glenn visits to see if they know anyone who does homecare. I post on Facebook that I need a nurse in case any of my friends know anyone that would fit the bill. And I call two friends who are nurses and may be looking for additional work. I do anything I can think of to get help.

Becky quickly finds me a weekend nurse. I love Billie immediately. First, she's seems very nice. Secondly, she's my savior from doing every night and day by myself.

Along with doctors and nursing agencies, I'm also in contact with the insurance company. The second Monday Ryan's home I have the following conversation:

"Hi, is this the parent of Henry Marquiss?" the caller asks.

"This is his mom," I say.

"Hi, my name's Andrea. I'm calling from your insurance company to see how Henry's doing. How was his first week at home?"

"A little hectic, but we're hanging in there," I say. "I think the biggest concern I have right now is getting the nursing shifts staffed. Our agency's having some issues with it."

"How much nursing are you looking for? Aren't you doing most of it yourself?" she asks.

"I'm supposed to have seven nights and I requested they also staff three days," I say.

"I have in the file that Henry's on a feeding tube with feeds every two hours and 100 percent supplemental oxygen. Is that right?"

"Yes, plus twenty-eight doses of meds a day," I add.

"Believe it or not, medication doses aren't taken into consideration when we approve nursing. Eating overnight by tube and being on oxygen *is* considered. With the feeds he's at high risk for aspirating. He's on an NG tube, right?"

"Yes, and it does sometimes get pulled although he's pretty good at leaving it alone. It often becomes caught on things," I explain.

"That would have more of an affect on his case," she says. "Now why the three days? What makes you need nursing care on three days, but not all of them?"

"I'm thinking I don't need help every day. I can probably make it work the rest of the week. I really just need help. Ryan—we call him Ryan—takes a lot of time to care for so if I could have the three days help, I think I can get most my housework and administrative work done on those days and ignore everything the other four."

"I hate to tell you, but this isn't a babysitting service. You either need us or you don't. We're not here to make it easier on you. We don't provide nursing so you can get things done. We only provide nursing if the patient has care needs. We don't take into consideration how many other children are in the house or how much housework you have," she says.

I feel my blood pressure start to rise as panic sets in. I don't know what I'll do if the insurance company doesn't approve day shifts. It scares me to think I might be on my own. "What I'm trying to say is that Ryan takes so much care I don't have any life outside of that. He gets meds every two hours, which I'm working to consolidate, he eats all the time. . . . I know it says every two hours, but because of his reflux I have to pause the feeds every so often. By the time his feeds stop it's time to start them again. I can't keep this schedule up for sixteen hours a day. Right now I'm doing it twenty-four hours a day on some days. It's getting to the point where I push Ryan's meds and then wonder if I pushed the right dose, but they're in his system already. My brain is mush. There's no way I can be expected to keep up this pace. There are laws limiting how many hours in a row a nurse can work. There's a reason for that. I'm basically doing the work of a nurse and it's getting dangerous for me to be 'on' 24/7. It's not that I want a babysitter, it's that it isn't safe for my child to have me doing this alone."

"I understand," she says. "But we have to go by his medical needs. I'll present what you said to the medical director and try to make a case, but it's very rare to get day shifts unless the patient is seriously ill."

If I was a cat the fur on the back of my neck would be standing on end and my back would be arched. I might even hiss. I hang up the phone and say a quick prayer. I can't dwell on the negative and must push on. The girls are at school. Ryan's sleeping. I take a moment to collect my thoughts. What absolutely has to get done today?

Taking The Man in the Yellow Hat's advice from Curious George when he says, "Most people only talk about the future, not me, I put it in a binder!" I decide to make a few charts. I make a calendar-page format for daily care, like baths, NG replacement, daily temperatures, etc. It seems silly to keep track of these things, but I've noticed I can't remember from one day to the next. I make another one for feeding therapy. I'd like to set up speech therapy, but for now I'll keep track of how many ccs of water he accepts from a spoon. It gives me some sort of baseline to work off of. At this point Ryan only takes 5–10 ccs in a sitting so we have a long way to go. The most important chart is for his med dosages. I tried keeping track in a notebook of every dose, but the system isn't working for me. I decide to write each dose needed on each day of yet another calendar template and then make a check mark next to it when it's complete. I three-hole-punch each calendar page and place them in the front of Ryan's medical notebook.

By the time I finish the charts, Ryan is awake and it's time to pump again. I head to my favorite spot—the couch—with my pump, my calendar, my computer, and my phone. There is no time for rest. I have to keep going to get caught up on all the calls that need to be made. I work methodically down the list while the pump manipulates life-giving nourishment from my body for my son. Now that he's home, I find it more difficult to stay on a regular schedule. With Natalie and Ainsley my milk dried up at six and ten months. I prayed God would keep my milk flowing until Ryan is a year old. I only have a month to go.

Ryan watches me out of big hazel eyes as I work. "Now we'll call the physical therapist. Maybe she can come and see you this week or next. Your neck is so stiff I bet it'll feel good to have it stretched again. Let's see if we can get her on the phone."

He *helps* me call the physical therapist, County Services (who also will send therapists), the medical supply company, and the nursing agency for advice on getting the nursing shifts covered by insurance.

When I'm through with my phone calls and pumping, I take Ryan from his chair and offer him some of the milk still warm from my body. He takes one taste and decides it's not his cup of tea. I try water. He takes a few ccs before turning his nose up to the spoon altogether. Ten ccs of liquid is all I get into him. I write the time and amount on my newly made chart. I put down the food chart and pick up the meds chart. It's time for his noon doses. I draw up his potassium and sodium supplements, double-check their amounts with the labels on each bottle, then push them down his NG tube followed by a flush of 30 ccs water. I push his potassium very slowly. He gets 16 ccs—the most of any of his medication and a lot to push while he's also getting food. I've noticed if I push a cc at a time, a few seconds apart, he vomits less often. There's something about the potassium—either the amount or content—that makes Ryan sick to his stomach. In fact, since I've started this new technique, his vomiting has greatly decreased. Thinking of his vomiting, I remember Dr. Donofrio sent me the name of the GI doctor that saw Ryan on rounds when he was in-house. I look up her email for the contact info and give Dr. Bader a call to see if I can get Ryan in to see him while he's at the Fairfax cardiology clinic later this week. Luckily his office is right down the street from the heart clinic. I want to see if there's anything more we can do for Ryan's vomiting and reflux.

At 1:30 P.M., Ainsley comes bouncing through the door. Heather offered to bring her home the next few weeks until I get my sea-legs. She runs over to Ryan and gives him a big kiss not caring that he's almost asleep.

"Ainsley! Don't wake him up. Come over here instead and give your mama a kiss. How was your day?"

"Good. I didn't cry all day and my teacher gave me goldfish," she says in her squeaky little-girl voice. I pull her onto the couch. We lay nestled like two spoons in a drawer. She sticks her thumb in her mouth and lays her head on my shoulder. She loves to cuddle and would probably stay like this all afternoon if she could. I close my eyes and breath in the smell of her shampoo. I'd love to stay like this, too. "Okay, time to take Ry-Ry to get his bloodwork done," I say. "Let's hurry so we're done in time to pick up Natalie."

I decided after the long wait last week to try the lab in the afternoon. I grab Ryan's diaper bag and feeding pump, taking them to the car before coming back to grab him and his oxygen tank. I have an extra tank in the car as a backup. He doesn't get any meds until 4 P.M. so I don't have to worry about taking any doses with me.

TUESDAY IS JUST as busy as Monday with more phone calls and another doctor appointment. This time the appointment was to the pediatrician for a general checkup to make sure Ryan's sats and general vitals are baseline. Wednesday we get a full day at home and a night nurse! Having done Monday and Tuesday nights on my own, I'm about to fall over from exhaustion. It couldn't come at a better time. Ryan has two appointments on Thursday. First in the morning with Dr. Donofrio in the Fairfax clinic and then down the street with the GI doctor. Dr. Bader happened to be in the office and said he'd fit Ryan in if we came over directly after our cardiology clinic. Unfortunately since we're being fit in, the appointment takes three hours. Certainly not the way I wanted to spend the afternoon. The good news is Dr. Bader put Ryan on reflux medication to see if it'll help with his spitting up. By Friday, I'm on the phone again with the nursing company.

"Maria? This is Leighann, Ryan's mom," I say. "I think I have it all worked out. I talked to Heidi and she's able to do the three day shifts. I also talked to Jessica and she wants the weeknight shifts, which is perfect. I was afraid they might both want the day shifts. So that leaves us with Billie on the weekends and I'm totally covered."

"Wow, do you want a job? You made that really easy for me!" she jokes. "I'll give Heidi and Jessica a call and get them here to fill out an application and go through orientation. We can probably have them out to you in the next week to two weeks. It depends on when they can make it in."

The agency informs me Ryan is approved for three days of coverage. Knowing this is huge for me. It means I might actually be able to get the laundry put away *and* take the girls on a playdate or to ballet without lugging around a baby and several pieces of equipment.

On Friday night as I hand the reins over to my new BFF, Billie, I take a deep cleansing breath, happy at the thought of two whole nights of sleep. I walk to my dark bedroom, flip on the bathroom fan for white noise and slip into bed next to Henry. I'm asleep within two seconds of my head hitting the pillow.

TWO NIGHTS LATER, I stare wide-eyed at the orange puddle on my kitchen floor in disbelief trying to figure out the best way to get it back in the bottle . . . syringe it up? Dab it up with a napkin and squeeze it out over the bottle? Spoon it up? Then I thought of how long it's been since I mopped. (Don't even try to guess. You don't want to know.) I've managed to spill almost the entire bottle of Ryan's methadone.

Narcotics are tricky. If you stop cold turkey, your body goes through withdrawal—think coming off heroine. Ryan was on too fast a wean while in-house. He was so squirmy it looked like he was running in place, and he was extremely irritable. It was so painful to watch I almost didn't want to visit him.

I squint into the bottle. It seems like I have enough to get through mid-day tomorrow. I write myself a note to call the doctor in the morning for another prescription. It's 10 o'clock. I have no nurse tonight so I'm on my own. I have to pump at 11 and give Ryan meds at midnight. Do I pump early and try to sleep for an hour and a half, or do I just stay up and go to bed at midnight? I decide to try and get some sleep. Since Ryan's feeds are going and he's still having trouble spitting up, I grab a pillow and blanket to camp out on his floor. His feeds will beep when they're finished around 11:30 P.M. I grab the alarm clock from the guest bedroom and set it for midnight to give Ryan's meds. I lie down to sleep around 10:30.

I sleep until the high-pitched beeping of the feeding pump wakes me. Sitting up, I turn the machine toward me a little and hit the OFF button. I'm unconscious again within seconds.

Midnight comes quickly after. I groggily hit the alarm hoping it didn't wake anyone else in the house. Ryan doesn't stir at the noise. Alarms and loud beeping while he's sleeping aren't new to him. I move cautiously in the dark down to the kitchen to get the meds I drew up earlier. When I'm doing the nightshift, I always pre-draw the meds so I don't make a dosing mistake. It also allows me to stay in my semi-conscious state. I grab the sandwich baggie marked "midnight" from the fridge door and fill three 10-cc syringes with water to flush the meds. I also grab a pre-measured bottle of breastmilk and mix two scoops of formula into it. I shake it as I stumble back upstairs to Ryan's room. I push the meds and start the pump . . . most of it muscle memory. I reset the alarm for 4 A.M. for the next round of meds. Ryan's food will only take an hour and a half, but I decide he'll live if he skips his 2:30 feeding and starts back up at 4. I plan to silence the feeding pump at 5:30 and start his food back up with the 6 A.M. meds.

Ryan sleeps soundly until just before 4 A.M. at which point he becomes increasingly fussy and agitated. I pat his back to see if I can coax him back to sleep. When that doesn't work, I pick him up . . . I rock him . . . I change his diaper. None of it works. Willing to try anything, I go to the living room and get his swing. I put him in it and realize the batteries are out of juice. Agh!!

By now, I'm wide awake. I go down two flights of stairs to the office in the basement for a new pack of batteries. I grab a quarter from the kitchen on the way back through to open the battery cage on the swing and a pair of surgical scissors to cut open the battery pack. I get the swing in motion, but Ryan doesn't care. He's still going between whimpering and crying.

I pick him back up. I sway with him, bounce him and walk the room as much as his oxygen leash allows.

Nothing. Nada. Zip.

I can't figure out what the problem is. Is it the Ativan wean from a few days ago? Is he teething? In case he's in pain, I give him Tylenol. I put Lidocain on his gums, gently massaging them with my finger, hoping it does the job.

Still crying!

I pat his rear. I rub his head. I hug him tight. I unzip his outfit and put a cold rag on his head to ward off a fever from all his crying.

After three hours *I* want to cry. Instead, I lay him gently in his bed, turn on his music and shut his door behind me. It's time for a sanity break. I go to my bed and lie down while Henry's in the shower. Between the shut door and the shower, I can't hear Ryan crying. I doze for a few minutes.

The girls trickle into my room. "Mommy, Ryan's crying," Natalie says as she climbs into bed beside me. "Are you going to get him?"

"Yeah, sweetie, I'll get him in just a sec. Can you get your clothes on for school?" I say. I squeeze her to me and kiss her lightly on the hair. Ainsley's climbing in behind me to take Henry's vacant spot. This is one of my favorite times of the day . . . when the girls gather close and we cuddle before facing the day individually. "Okay, let's go," I say. "Up-and-at-'em."

All while we're getting ready for school, Ryan's still fussing. When we get home from taking Ainsley to school at 9:30 he finally falls into a deep sleep in his swing. Relieved I get on the phone with the pediatrician to track down a new prescription for the methadone I spilled last night.

Because methadone is a controlled substance, it's easier said than done. "Can you tell me again why you can't call the doctor who prescribed it to begin with?" she asks. "Because I didn't prescribe it first, I have a hard time justifying writing a new prescription."

"The doctor that prescribed it was part of a pain management team I don't have contact with. I don't even know their names. I'm not sure I ever met them. The CICU doctors don't play with the pain meds. The pain management team sets up the dosing and the in-house pharmacist helps with a wean schedule. I don't know any of these people. Maybe you could just write a prescription for the amount I need starting from today? I have a wean schedule in front of me so I can add up the amounts for you."

The pediatrician sighs, "If you fax me the wean schedule, I'll give you what you need from today forward, but that's it. And you'll have to get the hard copy. A pharmacy won't take a called or faxed in prescription for a narcotic."

"Okay," I say. "When can I come for it?"

"I'll have it ready in the next hour if you can fax me the wean schedule right away," she says.

"Thanks," I say. I hang up and wrack my brain for someone who might be able to pick it up for me. Meanwhile, I call my local pharmacy. They inform me that not every pharmacy carries narcotics. I decide to go to the specialty pharmacy thirty minutes from my house where most of Ryan's meds come from. They seem to have everything. After a few phone calls, I get a hold of my friend Jae.

"I have to take Audrey to preschool at 11, but I can go after that," she says. I'm so grateful she can run the errand for me. Ryan has physical therapy this morning and I need the medicine for Ryan's 4 P.M. dose.

"That'll work," I say. "If you swing by here, I'll give you my insurance card and some money. You'll have to present your license when you pick it up."

"Not a problem. I'll see you soon," she says.

Katie, the physical therapist, knocks on the door promptly at 10:30 A.M. I answer, still in my pajamas, a little embarrassed. I think of how pre-children I vowed not to be one of those moms who doesn't shower every morning and put on "real" clothes and makeup. *How can you just not get dressed?* I used to think.

Now I get it. I'm surviving on less sleep than I thought possible, have gotten two kids to school and done the care for one medically fragile child. Now, I'm standing at my door looking at an almost-stranger letting her come into my house that looks like a volcano erupted spewing forth clothes, dishes, toys, and other odds and ends to land where they may.

"Come on in," I say.

"How's Ryan doing this morning?" she says.

"Actually he was up a lot in the night fussing and I'm trying to figure out what's going on. He doesn't have a fever. We weaned his Ativan a few days ago so I'm wondering if he's having some withdrawal."

"Do you think he's okay to have therapy? We can always push it 'til next week," she says.

"No, I think he's okay. He's so tight that I hate to wait until next week to stretch him. I try, but I know I don't do as well as a professional."

"Okay, we'll see what he tolerates," she says.

I run upstairs to get Ryan from his room. I ordered an extra concentrator on his last return from the hospital so we'd have the flexibility of having Ryan in more than one room without having to lug a heavy machine around. He's still sleeping in his swing so I gently lift him up, careful not to get his feeding line or oxygen line caught. He looks at me through blurry eyes and faintly smiles. Yes, of course, now that I'm too busy to rest he's content enough to sleep!

While Katie stretches Ryan in the living room, I take the time to pump in the privacy of my bedroom and send some emails. One is to Dr. Donofrio to see if she thinks Ryan might be showing signs of withdrawal. I explain his symptoms from the night plus the fact that he doesn't seem to have any fever, more sweating than usual, or diarrhea . . . all signs of withdrawal. She emails me back before I'm done pumping to say to call the pharmacist at the hospital to get a new wean schedule just in case and to take him to the pediatrician to make sure there isn't anything else going on. Two more calls to add to the list.

I take advantage of having Katie here to take a shower. With Ryan's weird behavior I'd rather be on the phone where I can see and hear him than in the shower and him alone. I try to relax in the shower, but there's way too much to do and so little time to do it. I hurriedly apply makeup and halfway dry my hair before heading downstairs.

"How's he doing?" I ask Katie.

"He's doing okay," she says. "He's not overly fussy for me. You're right though. He's pretty tight. Do you know when you'll start services with the county? He could really use therapy more than twice a week."

"I have an appointment for them to come in early February for an evaluation. I think it'll take about a month after that to have a therapist in the home. So you're it until March. Speaking of which, do you know a good speech therapist? I don't want him to digress at all so I'm afraid to wait until March to start his feeding therapy."

"Yeah, a colleague named Kathryn. I'll give you her number before I leave," she says.

By the time Katie leaves at 11:30, I've spoken with the pharmacist for a new wean schedule for Ryan's Ativan and have a sick appointment at the pediatrician for 1:30 this afternoon . . . the same time Ainsley's supposed to come home from school. I arrange for a playdate at Heather's house with her daughter, Savannah. I have no idea what I'd do without the help of my friends. They make this life I'm living doable.

Ryan and I arrive at the doctor's office promptly at 1:30 P.M. A nurse holds open the door between the waiting room and back office for me. "Don't even sign in," she says. "We have a room waiting."

I push Ryan in his stroller laden down with the feeding pump and oxygen tank. Tubes are curled in piles like strings of spaghetti. It's not long before Dr. Shepherd's checking Ryan's eyes, ears, and nose.

"I think I found the culprit," she says. "This ear is pretty inflamed. I have no doubt he has an ear infection." She straightens up to look at me. "NG tube fed kids are particularly susceptible for ear infections, especially if they eat at night. They're lying down for over eight hours with fluid running. Many times it makes its way into the ears. For the typical kid I wouldn't prescribe antibiotics, but Ryan's not the typical kid. I think with all his issues we should put him on a standard antibiotic for good measure."

"That's fine," I say. It's funny how life changes you. With the girls I always questioned antibiotics, making the doctor justify their need. Now, I'm so used to hospital protocol of three days of antibiotics for any raised white-blood-cell count that I don't think twice.

An ear infection. To think I was all over the place thinking he was possibly having withdrawal from too quick a narcotics wean and all it is, is an ear infection. I email Dr. Donofrio the news when I get home to close the loop. Her response: "Congratulations on having normal kid stuff. It's about time!"

FRIDAY COMES. RYAN and I just got home from the heart clinic and he's taking his afternoon nap. I made it through the whole week . . . two of the nights without a nurse. I'm barely keeping my head up. I look around the house at the growing pile of things that needs to be done. I don't know where to start. One thing I'm learning is that when you're out of the house like we were when Ryan was in the hospital, it stays cleaner. Now we're home and the house is a wreck. I can't keep up with the girls . . . many times they're playing unsupervised, and as long as they're quiet, it helps me finish whatever I'm doing for Ryan. The result is a mess in every room of the house, from draped sheets made into forts to crafts scattered all over the basement table. It's easy to think it's a matter of telling them to clean up after themselves, but at five and three, they're still too young to do it on their own. I have to be in the room directing each thing for them to do. I don't have time to do it myself and I certainly don't have time to do it more slowly with them.

Henry's at the end of himself, too. He basically spends each weekend cleaning up the house while I maintain the girls and Ryan. He doesn't have the energy during the week. Most days he leaves the house early and doesn't return until eight at night. During his busy weeks when his team's getting the financials ready for the end-of-month reports, he may not come home until after midnight. By the time he walks in the door, he's fried and all he wants to do is space out in front of the television.

Although I know I've been doing the work of a full-time nurse along with trying to care for my family, I'm disappointed I can't keep on top of things. I was an executive-assistant-by-day and student-by-night before I had kids. I managed to organize Henry's and my life, a busy executive's life, and complete college reading and writing assignments while maintaining a high GPA. Those were the days when things stayed where I put them and I went potty in private. Now our third child has been home a total of three weeks (this go around) and I can't seem to manage running a household.

While I'm staring at my house wondering where to start, my phone rings. "Hi, Mrs. Marquiss, this is Dr. Shepherd. How are you?"

"Fine," I say. "What's up?"

"The girls in the office said you made an appointment for this Monday to have Ryan's blood pressure checked. Is this something the cardiologist wants done?"

"In clinic today she increased Ryan's Enalapril dose. She said there's a slim chance it would lower his blood pressure but that with the minute amount she increased it, there's really no concern. However, it's protocol to monitor blood pressure with this medication change so she asked we come see you on Monday, have Ryan's blood pressure taken, administer the new amount, then have you take his blood pressure again an hour after the dose just to make sure his baseline doesn't change dramatically."

"Since she's doing the dosing change is it possible for you to have her staff monitor Ryan's blood pressure?" she asks.

"Dr. Donofrio's willing to monitor Ryan, but gave me the option of seeing you since you're ten minutes from my house and she'll be in D.C. on Monday . . . an hour from here. Is there a problem bringing him in there?"

"I just think with her doing the med change, it should be her office doing the monitoring," Dr. Shepherd says.

"I see. So just to be clear, you think it would be better for us to drive an hour one way to get Ryan's blood pressure checked?" I say flatly.

She pauses. "Mrs. Marquiss, I'm going to be really honest with you. My staff is afraid of Ryan. They're afraid he's going to die in our office."

I take a deep breath. "Dr. Shepherd, that's ridiculous. Ryan is the most stable he's ever been. Yes, he's on oxygen and an NG tube and more medicines than I can keep track of, but he's stable. He's only expected to get better from here. He was closer to dying when you guys were watching him in April and May of last year.

Besides, Dr. Donforio wouldn't send Ryan home if she thought he was so unstable he might die suddenly. And if she thought there was *any* danger in making this med change, she'd admit him and watch him overnight. She's extremely cautious with Ryan's care."

"I understand," Dr. Shepherd says, "but it doesn't change the fact that the girls are afraid of him."

"Okay," I say. "I get it. I'll take him to Dr. Donofrio for the med change. Do you think your staff can give him his RSV shot? It's RSV season and since Ryan's breathing is compromised he qualifies for the monthly vaccine. Your nurse already ordered it. It's supposed to be delivered to your office on Monday."

"Why don't you swing by here on Monday and pick it up on your way downtown. I'm sure Donofrio's nurse can administer the shot at the same time they monitor the blood pressure."

I can't believe what I'm hearing. My pediatrician's office is unwilling to administer a vaccine or take my son's blood pressure. What are they going to do if Ryan gets sick? I dial the number for the pediatrician's office who gave the girls the H1N1 shot. "Is Ellen there?" I ask the receptionist. I'm put on hold.

"This is Ellen, how may I help you?" a voice says.

"Hi, Ellen. This is Leighann Marquiss. You gave my girls, Natalie and Ainsley, the H1N1 shots back in the fall so we could take them to the hospital to see my son who was there. I'd like to throw something out and see what you think."

"Sure, go ahead," she says.

"I need to find a new pediatrician, but this time it's for Ryan. As you know he has a heart defect. He was released almost a month ago from Children's and is pretty stable. But, he's high maintenance. He's getting weaned from narcotics, which is no easy task, and he's having Enalapril increased this Monday so he needs his blood pressure monitored. We're seeing the pediatrician weekly right now and the cardiologist every other. His cardiologist mentioned this won't be his only Enalapril increase so we'll have to do this again sometime in the near future. I'm calling to see if the doctors there are willing to take him on. I totally understand if they don't want to. He's intimidating and will take a lot of time for the next few months. Our current pediatrician's staff is afraid of him and I need a practice that's confident in me and in Ryan's cardiologist. Someone who'll work *with* me and be part of our team."

"Let me talk to the doctors here and I'll call you back," she says.

Ellen calls me back within the hour. "Mrs. Marquiss, I spoke with the doctors and we're happy to have your family in our practice. We're thinking to give you a team of three doctors instead of one for Ryan's primary physicians. We have hours from 8:30 in the morning until 8 in the evening six days a week and a sister-practice in Falls Church with hours on Sunday. By giving you a team of three doctors, we can pretty much guarantee they'll be someone here six days a week that knows Ryan well. Additionally, we'll have him listed as a VIP so the girls at the front desk will know he's top priority when you call. We'd also like to have a meet-and-greet where you can come and meet the team all at one time and show them Ryan when he's feeling good. This way, they'll know his baseline coloring and behavior to compare it to when he's sick. You said something about needing to have his blood pressure monitored at the beginning of next week so we're wondering if you can come in on Monday for the meeting and we can do it all at one time."

Ellen has just joined the ranks with Billie as one of my new BFFs. She's a Godsend. I feel incredibly blessed to have come across such a great group of doctors.

By the first week in February I'm fully staffed with nurses. I feel like a new woman! I'm sleeping all night, every night, and have three days when the nurse, Heidi, comes to help out. The best part of this scenario is that she's Henry's cousin. The girls love her and look forward to spending time with her after school. I love her because . . . well, she's sweet and part of my family. And she loves Ryan because he's her second cousin. It's a win-win situation.

It's also finally time for Ryan's evaluation with the county. Ryan qualifies for county services in the state of Virginia because his gross motor skills are delayed. The day the county caseworker, Debbie, and two therapists arrive for the assessment it's snowing.

"Thanks for coming in such terrible weather," I say as I hold the door open for them. They come in and remove their heavy coats and winter boots. "Can I offer you some hot tea or water?" I ask. They decline politely. I lead them to the living room where Ryan is stationed with his oxygen tank. They ooh and ahh over him for a minute before getting down to business.

"Where are his sisters?" Debbie asks.

"I put a movie on for them in the basement. I figured it'd be easier than trying to keep them quiet," I answer.

"Ah-ha. Well, today we're really just going to ask you a bunch of questions about Ryan, get to know him a little bit, and find out what services he needs. He definitely qualifies for anything he needs given his extensive medical situation. Today is our opportunity to assess him and write a goal for the next year. You'll tell us what you want him to be doing a year from now," She explains. Debbie is a middle-aged woman with dark hair cut into a fashionable pixie cut. Her face, build, and southern accent remind me of my friend, Melissa, so I'm comfortable with her instantly. "We'll start with Vicki. She's a physical therapist and will go over his motor skills."

Vicki, an older woman with graying hair, says, "Can you tell me what Ryan can do physically? Is he rolling over or sitting up at all?"

"No. He's basically a newborn. He lies prone most the day. About the only movement he does is to lift his legs into a 90-degree angle. He either stares at them or uses them to point at things."

"Point at things?" she clarifies.

"Yes," I say. "His arms were tethered to the bed pretty often when he was vented so in the last month in the hospital he started using his legs to play with his hanging crib toys or point at things."

"Oh wow, that's interesting," she says and makes a note.

"I've tried sitting him up in a Bumbo (a product that supports the child's waist and legs so they can sit up without having to support themselves), but his head is so heavy and his neck so bent that he doesn't like it that much. He does play with his toys, though. He'll spin his letter wheel and push the buttons on his frog mobile. He likes to watch the lights. But I'd like to get him some stuff that will have him progress past the infant stage."

"Can you give him one of his favorite toys so I can see how he uses his hands?" she asks.

"Sure," I say. I hand Ryan a little rattle shaped like a phone receiver—the kind of phone receiver my children will probably never see in their lifetime unless we're in an antique store. He shakes it a little bit before opening his hand, rolling it down to his fingertips and then closing his palm and fingers back over it in a fist.

"Did you just see what he did there?" she says. "His fine motor skills are great. He just manipulated that toy at an age-appropriate level even though his gross motor skills are twelve months behind. I'd say he knows exactly what to do with those hands of his."

She continues to assess him for a few minutes longer before indicating that she's done. "And now Dana will ask some questions regarding his speech and language reception," Debbie says.

"Does Ryan make very much noise?" Dana asks.

"No, he cries when he's upset or hungry. And he might coo here or there. Most of the time he's silent. He doesn't laugh yet. He smiles so big you know he'd be belly laughing if he could. It's almost as if because he was vented so long he doesn't know he can make noise," I say.

"How about with his sisters. Does he respond to them?"

"He responds by silently laughing at them . . . all the time. He loves them. But no noise," I say.

"Do you think he understands anything you're saying?" she asks.

"He understands his name. Recently he was reaching for a toy with his feet and I said, 'No, no. Not with your feet, with your hands.' He put his feet down and reached with his hand. I've been trying to teach him to high-five. The other day Natalie did something and I went to high-five her. She didn't realize it and left my hand hanging in the air. I said, 'Come on, Nat, high-five, high-five.' Ryan was sitting next to me and reached up and slapped my hand a few times. So I know there are things he definitely understands. They're just few and far between.

"He doesn't know the names of any articles of clothing or parts of his body or animals really. Not things my girls knew at this age. When Natalie was ten months I asked her to shut the door and she crawled over and shut the door. He can't crawl let alone understand a command like that."

"How about eating. What's his oral intake like?"

"It's pretty non-existent. When he first came home I worked with him to take a bottle, but he stopped opening his mouth for it after the first two weeks. I resorted to using a baby spoon with a little water on it and now a medicine dropper that instead of squeezing, I make him suck a little to get the water out. It's easier to measure how much he's taking that way and it makes him work a little. He probably accepts anywhere from 15 to 30 ccs that way. Thirty being very good. It depends on the day. He receives all this nutrition through his tube."

"Did he ever eat anything orally?" she asks.

"He nursed one time and accepted about the same amount as he does now of breast milk combined with formula back in July, but nothing really much since then. A spoonful of applesauce here and there with the therapist in the hospital, but they had trouble with him, too."

"Okay," she says. "Definitely something to work on."

Debbie takes the cue and says, "Okay, now we're going to ask you for some goals. These aren't set in stone and can be revisited at any point. We simply like to have something on paper to work toward and a metric at the end of the year to make sure we're on the right track. As far as moving, what would you like to see Ryan doing by this time next year? He'll basically be two."

"I'd love to see him walking. . . . Maybe that's too much to ask. But at least halting steps or pushing a push-toy," I say. Vicki jots down what I'm saying.

"Okay," Debbie says. "So he needs to learn to roll over, sit up, crawl, and walk this year. Is that reasonable, Vicki?"

"I think so. He may not be walking independently, but I think we can get him to at least cruising." She says.

"Great," Debbie says. "And as far as talking, what would you like to see?"

I'm in the hot seat again. "I'd love it if he could say fifteen or more words and understand most of what we're saying. Maybe follow directions if I asked him to get his shoes or come upstairs."

"Dana, is that reasonable to expect?" Debbie says. "I think so," she says making some notes of her own.

"And feeding," Debbie says. "What would you like to see Ryan eating next year?"

"Food!" I laugh. "I'd like him to be eating table food."

"Okay, I think we can work toward that," Debbie says. She pauses. "Now we'll wait a few minutes for Vicki and Dana to write up their notes and we'll review them to make sure we're all on the same page."

I take the chance to check on the girls. Their movie is almost over. I know I only have a few more minutes of their being distracted. I go back up to the living room. The ladies are finishing up.

"Vicki and Dana are going to read their assessment and then you can add anything you'd like," Debbie says. "Vicki, would you like to go first?"

"Sure," Vicki says. "I wrote: 'Ryan's an eleven-month-old male with ectopia cordis, tricuspid atresia and pulmonary stenosis, hypoplastic right heart syndrome, and a cor triatriatum membrane. Ryan's extremely sociable—smiling and flirting with his family and strangers. He's aware of his social surroundings and interacts well with people. He has two loving sisters and parents who are involved in his care. Ryan spent most of his life in the hospital and has only been home for one month after a six-month admission. Due to being tied to the bed, Ryan's gross motor skills are significantly delayed. He's unable to sit up or hold his head up for long periods of time. By the end of this year, Mom would like to see him walking behind a push toy and perhaps taking up to five steps between family members. It's recommended that he receive physical therapy appointments once a month to help him attain this goal. He should also receive soft-muscle massage to relieve any tightness from prior surgeries and stretching to correct significant tortecollis.'"

"Good," Debbie says to Vicki. Turning to me she says, "How does that sound?"

"Sounds good to me," I say.

"Okay, Dana?"

Dana begins with the same pattern. She begins listing Ryan's diagnosis and length of hospital stay. As she reads, I'm restless. Everything we're talking about today are the very things I've tried to ignore for the past year. Living them moment-by-moment is doable because there's so much being thrown at you it's impossible to process it all. When something bad happens, you go into shock and then slowly start to process and grieve as things let up. For us, things never let up. We've been going non-stop since Ryan's birth with little time to address our grief at our son's diagnosis. There's no time to think about year-long goals when you're wondering if there will be a tomorrow. I once told my sister, Amy, I was afraid to start crying because I wasn't sure I'd be able to stop.

Listening to a laundry list of Ryan's diagnoses and the amount of surgery and hospital time he's been through is hard. What's harder is listening to how delayed he is. Knowing this and accepting it are two different things. I haven't wanted to believe Ryan would be that delayed. Now it's staring me in the face. I feel the disappointment burn in my throat and sting at my eyes as Dana continues reading her assessment. I push it to the side as I have for the last year and focus on maintaining my composure through the rest of the meeting.

". . . By this time next year, mom would like to see Ryan eating table food with his family at the table," she concludes.

"Is there anything you want to add to either of these assessments?" Debbie asks.

"No, I think that's good for now. I would like to see if we can get physical therapy more often than once-a-month though. And speech. Ryan's so far behind I'm not sure once-a-month is enough."

"We can probably do PT twice a month, but speech will have to be just once," Debbie says haltingly. She looks toward the therapists who are nodding in agreement. "Have you had a swallow study yet?"

"I don't remember one," I say. "There were a lot of things that happened in-house so I don't always remember them, but I think I'd remember if they'd mentioned a swallow study."

"You'll need to schedule one as soon as you can," Debbie says. "The speech therapist will need that to know where to start."

"All right. That about does it for us. Thanks for letting us come by."

The ladies have been here quite awhile, so by the time they leave, it's lunchtime. After all our bellies are full and Ryan's noon meds are given, I take out the name Katie gave me for the private speech therapist. I keep meaning to call her and can't put it off any longer.

"Hello, this is Kathryn," the voice on the other end of the line says.

I give her Ryan's history and our current dilemma of his refusing anything but tiny medicine droppers of water.

"I'd be happy to come out and take a look at him and let you know what I think," she says.

"I appreciate that. Can you tell me if you accept our insurance?" I ask.

"I'm not sure. I don't think the company I bill under is a provider. We can work that out later, at least let me come look at him on my way home tonight for a free consultation. I'll be out your way anyway. I have a hard time sleeping at night knowing there's an infant feeder who may be aspirating and at risk for pneumonia," she says.

"I'll be happy to pay you. I don't want you to feel like you need to come for free," I say.

"Don't worry. It'll all come out in the wash. Is 4 o'clock okay with you?" she asks.

The rest of the day goes quickly. Before I know it Kathryn is standing at my door. I lead her to the living room where Ryan lies happily on his activity blanket playing with a dangling bird. "Do you want me to move him into his Bumbo? It's typically where I stick him to eat. He doesn't really sit in a high chair yet, and I can't hold him and feed him at the same time," I say.

"That'd be great. It's important he sits up straight during the feeding trials because he's not going to have good oral coordination yet and will most likely choke if he's lying back at all. When did he eat last?"

"He just finished a feed, but he pretty much eats around the clock. I'm trying to get the rate faster little by little," I say.

"Okay, why don't you show me what you've been doing and we'll go from there," she says.

I go to the kitchen and grab a medicine dropper and a small bowl. Bringing it back, I fill the medicine dropper and lift it to Ryan's mouth. I show her the technique I developed over the last month.

"I like this idea," she says. "I like that you know what your son can handle and you have a safe system. See how he coughed a little right there? He's not able to control the water so it ends up in his airway. Anytime you hear him cough, stop right away. He may cough on the first try and that's okay, try again in a few hours if you want, but don't make him try again right now. I'm going to do an assessment on his tongue to see what we're dealing with." She snaps on purple disposable plastic gloves that smell like Purple Pie Man. "Hey, little man," she coos. "What's your tongue doing in there?"

She strokes his tongue with her gloved finger and moves it all around his mouth cavity. "His tongue's pretty weak. He's not lateralizing or pushing back at my finger or curling it around my finger at all. These are all natural reactions we have when something is put in our mouth, like when you're at the dentist and you keep licking the little mirror. Unfortunately he's had so many tubes down his throat that he's desensitized. He figures something's *supposed* to be in there. Our job is to stimulate the tongue and get it active again. Here, watch. I want you to stroke his tongue like this ten times and then the insides of his cheeks. I also want you to rub his lips and around his mouth with your finger to show him that you're not going to hurt him." She writes all this down on a piece of paper for me. "He's not really ready to be drinking anything, but he isn't afraid of the medicine dropper so keep doing what you're doing, but stop as soon as there's coughing or sneezing."

"He sneezes a lot. What's that mean?" I ask.

"It means he's taking the liquid up into his nasal passages instead of down his throat. His tongue just needs to figure out which way to push. He'll get it. Don't worry. The most important thing is not to push him with it. And only use water. Nothing acidic. If he's coughing, he's probably aspirating . . . which means liquid is going into his lungs. The last thing we want to do is cause an infection or pneumonia. Do you know how to listen to his lungs?" she asks.

"We have a night nurse who listens to his lungs at the beginning and end of every shift. I'll make sure to ask her if they're clear or not, especially if I think he aspirated that day."

"Perfect," she says. "Okay, this is a start. I'm going to work out the insurance details with the company I bill through, and I'll get back to you."

"I appreciate that," I say. "I want to be able to start having someone come on a regular basis to help us speed things along. I feel like we've been at a standstill for months and I really want to be rid of this feeding tube."

"We'll get there. It may take time, but it'll happen."

And like that my son is assessed by the county and a speech therapist all in one day. The influx of professional visitors to the house has its effects. The girls still play doctor and nurse and now . . . therapist. Natalie came to me recently with her pad of paper in her hand and said something like, "What's your baby's name?"

"Henry," I said.

"Does he have a nickname?" she asked.

"Ryan," I answered.

"Oh yes, I have him on my list to see today. I'll be your nurse and I'm going to help you today. Okay? And I'll tell you what you have to do with him. He'll need some stretching with his arms. Oh!" she pauses noticing I'm pushing Ryan's meds. "Go ahead and give him his *meds*. I don't want to uh-sturb you." More pausing, then, "This is my assistant. She can't talk. (She whispers to Ainsley, "pretend you can't talk and I talk for you." Ainsley whispers back, "okay.") Ainsley does some popping noises with her mouth. "Her name's Elizabeth. That's how she says her name." The game goes on like this for quite some time.

We're adjusting to this month's new normal. It's nice having Ryan home . . . more than nice . . . but it brings with it a lot more work. While he was in-house everything was very compartmentalized and structured. I pumped to and from the hospital every day, and with the girls old enough to keep each other occupied, the time I was home, I focused on getting things done.

Now time becomes a hot commodity. I find it hard to sit down for fifteen minutes to pump five times a day and finally decide it's time to give it up. I let myself off the hook knowing I have milk stocked away in the freezer that should last me the next two weeks until Ryan's first birthday.

Once I make the decision to wean myself from pumping, I'm relieved. It's so different than weaning a baby. There's no "what if I'm not ready?" or "what if he's not ready?" or "what if I change my mind?" or "I'm really going to miss snuggling several times a day." There's only "how fast can I get rid of this extra piece of equipment?" I suppose if I hadn't made it the full year there'd be regret, but at this point I'm beyond ready. After a few weeks of cutting out a feeding per week, I'm totally pump-free. It's liberating!

Doctor visits are letting up a little, too. We now alternate the pediatrician and cardiologist every other week, which works well for me since there's always some question I have. This week we trek downtown to see the cardiologist. Thankfully, the girls stay with Katie to play with her boys.

Even though we've been gone for almost two months, everything is still familiar. "Hi, Jackson," I say to the security guard.

"Hi, Mrs. Marquiss," he says typing my name into the system. He stopped asking me for my ID and if I'd been there within the last three months about a year ago. "Are you headed to the clinic today?"

"Yep, just visiting this time."

"Your son looks good. How long has he been home now?"

"About six weeks. He came home the beginning of January."

"Congratulations," Jackson says handing me my visitor badge.

The clinic is busy today. I sign in at the counter and find a seat out of the way. That usually means right in the middle so my stroller doesn't block any of the smaller seating areas. Although I'm lighter without my breast pump, I'm still lugging Ryan's feeding pump, oxygen tank, and a large diaper bag. I look around at the other families. Most have small children under the age of five. There are a few with elementary-school age kids and only one boy who looks like he's over ten, probably in junior high.

There's a husband and wife sitting off to the side by themselves. She's obviously pregnant, her large round stomach a testament to the life growing inside her. I want to reach out and tell them it'll be okay, but quite honestly, I'm not sure that's the case. I remember being them. I remember when Henry and I sat in this same waiting room wondering what the cardiologist would tell us about our baby.

Now a year and a half later, I sit here with my son still waiting to hear what the cardiologist has to say, but this time there's no fear. This time I understand how to measure oxygen saturations, the practical side of giving meds, and the reality of a feeding tube. I know that all these things sound scary at first, but you get used to them. They become part of your world, part of your every day routine. Everything becomes normal if you do it enough times.

FEBRUARY 22, 2010: RYAN plays with the icing on his first birthday cake. I fantasized about a huge fanfare for our little miracle, but due to flu season it's a quiet family affair, quite anticlimactic actually.

Even when I knew it would be just family, I thought we'd be excited. I thought we'd feel like we'd accomplished something big. Instead we waited two days to eat his cake so Henry could celebrate with us. His year-end financials were due for the SEC. It's an extremely stressful time for him—working until almost midnight every night. I'm disappointed, but there's nothing Henry can do about it. We move the party to Saturday evening so he can go to the office in the morning. Our siblings and parents come down to help us celebrate.

Ryan looks pensively at the icing he's squishing between his fingers. It's a new sensation for him. He's never really had the chance to play with his food since at this point it's really just water. He's more caught up in the feel than the taste. It's almost as if he doesn't know he's supposed to put it in his mouth.

"Lick your fingers," I say. "See if you like it. It's sweet."

Ryan ignores my advice and continues squeezing his fingers closed and then opening them wide again. "Come on, try it," I say.

"Here, Grandma will help you," my mom says. She takes his fingers and puts them to his lips. He squints with dissatisfaction as the icing hits his taste buds. "He's not sure about that, is he?" my mom says. Ryan reaches his fingers up himself this time and takes another taste of icing. This time he doesn't pucker as much. He works the icing around in his mouth and I watch like a hawk to make sure he doesn't choke. He's not cleared for anything other than small sips of water but it seems dreadful not to have a least a little bit of cake on your first birthday.

After all the guests are gone and the kids put to bed, Henry and I clean the kitchen side by side. We've always worked together after hosting big events. "Our son turned one this week," I say quietly.

"Yeah, he did," Henry says.

"Did you think it would happen?" I ask.

Henry stops mid-drying and says, "No. I didn't. Do you think he'll ever be normal? That he'll be able to run around and climb trees? Little boys need to climb trees."

"All the therapists are telling me he'll catch up, but that it'll take some time. He's almost sitting up by himself and he's only been home two months. That's something," I say.

"I guess. He's still not eating anything. He's not interested in food at all."

"No, he's not." The silence hangs in the air, both of us lost in our own frustration and sadness. Our conversations about Ryan typically revolve around high-level planning like when he'll have procedures or get medicine changes. Friends ask me how I get everything done. The answer's simple. I put one foot in front of the other and work my way down the list of things to do for the day. Ryan's and the girls' care comes first followed by anything logistical. I've learned that most things can wait until tomorrow or the day after that or the day after that. The nursing care we receive helps tremendously. And the things I can't get to, get handled. They just do.

Once, when Ryan was in the hospital, my car was acting funny. It had to go into the shop to get fixed. It was an easy fix . . . I can't remember what it was now, but when I picked the car up the mechanic said, "I noticed your inspection expires in three days so I went ahead and did the new one for you. I hope you don't mind." Mind? I was extremely grateful. "*Thank you, Lord, for taking care of things I didn't even know needed to be done.*" I whispered.

There was a day when early on when we were still staying at the Ronald McDonald House. We came home to spend the night, get clean clothes, check the mail . . . things like that. Because we spent most our time downtown, the fridge was empty. I had a choice. I could go to the grocery store and make a great meal for dinner, or I could go visit Ryan. I couldn't stand to be away from him. "*You're going to have to cook dinner,*" I said to God. I was somewhat serious although I wasn't used to asking him for such hands-on matters. Within twenty minutes two calls came in offering a meal for that evening. I accepted both and thanked the One who had provided them.

Another time I was torn between cleaning the kitchen and heading down to the hospital for a visit. I'm not that great with clutter and it was starting to affect my spirits. "*I just need my kitchen cleaned.*" This time I said it into the air. Of course it was a prayer, but it was said with much frustration. That evening when I returned from the hospital, my kitchen was sparkling. I'm not making this up. The friend who dropped off that night's dinner saw the state of my kitchen and immediately took action! God bless her!

Even now I have friends who call when they're on their way to the drugstore or grocery store to see if I need anything. A year into our journey and our community hasn't forgotten us. Friends rearrange their schedules and spend their hard-earned cash to meet our needs in ways we'll never be able to repay. Pre-Ryan, friends and I would trade off child-care or errand running. Helping each other in reciprocal ways. Since diagnosis reciprocity has gone out the window. For this season of life our friends are giving without expectation of anything in return. It's a humbling place to be. We are truly grateful.

It's been a long week. Henry and I crash on the couch after the kids go to bed. The curve of his body is familiar . . . comfortable. It's cradled me for thirteen years and somehow, when I'm lying nestled into my husband's chest, I feel like everything will be okay. It's always been this way. When I found out my parents were starting down the road to divorce during my senior year of high school, Henry would hold me against his chest and sing our favorite songs.

In the early years of our marriage when we were young and immature—learning the ropes of clear communication and realistic expectations—he'd fall asleep quickly after disagreements while I'd cry myself to sleep softly beside him. Even in my anger, leaning into him would ease my tension and allow me to settle. There's just something about aligning my body with his that centers me.

"Want a drink?" he says.

"Sure. I'll cue up the movie while you're gone," I say.

He gets up and lopes off to the kitchen returning a few minutes later. We cuddle on the couch in the dark like we did as teenagers, sipping our drinks, and watching the movie. It turns out to be a dud. Henry's hand slips from my shoulder and down into my shirt. "Take your shirt off," he says.

"I can't. The nurse will be here in a little bit and I don't want to get caught naked," I say laughing.

"Well at least play around with me a little before she gets here," he says. I lean into him and give him a kiss in response. Within a few minutes we're full on making out. Suddenly I hear a, "Hello?" Billie's standing at the door to the family room. Seriously, like 20 feet away.

Henry and I quickly separate. I hoist the top of my shirt up not sure if *my girls* are in or out, if you know what I mean. "Hey there," I say. "Come on in. Sorry. We didn't hear the door."

"I knocked as I came in, but I think the movie drowned it out," she says acting as if she's used to walking in on two grown, semi-exposed people groping and kissing each other. I can feel the heat rise to my face as my cheeks flush grateful the lights are off. She makes her way to the phone, located beside the television, and calls in to start her shift. After updating Billie on Ryan's day, Henry and I get ready for bed. "So how much do you think she saw?" he asks.

"I have no idea. Was my boob in or out of my shirt?" I say, still mortified.

"Not sure. Either way, I'm pretty sure my hand was covering it so you don't have to worry that she saw it!" he says laughing. "This is why I don't like having people in the house at night," he says. "We can't relax and be ourselves." What he really means is he can't have sex on the couch at 11 P.M.

"Yes, but you aren't the one who has to get up with Ryan's feeds. I *love* having someone here. It means I can function the next day," I say.

"I know. I tolerate it for you," he says climbing into bed beside me. He reaches over and pulls me to him. "But forget about that. I want to talk about something else. . . ."

Juggling family life with nurses around *can* be a little harrowing, but it's totally worth it. Some moms have a hard time giving up control of the care for their kids. Not me! I learned early on I can't control the outcome of Ryan's health and that I couldn't be a good mom or nurse with everything he requires. I *need* someone to help me with this.

The daytime isn't a problem at all. We're already comfortable with Heidi so it's like having a friend over three times a week. And she's so incredibly sweet. When Ryan's napping she feels bad just sitting around so she does my dishes or cleans up the girls' playroom.

Jessica cleans my kitchen at night if I haven't gotten to it that day. I try to have it clean so as not to take advantage of her, but some days are busier than others and it ends up messy still when she starts her shift. These girls are the best.

I think the hardest thing for me is the steady stream of therapists coming through the door. The county started sending their therapists out at the beginning of March. Most weeks Ryan has at least three different therapists and four appointments. They're here so often there's absolutely no way I can have a company-ready house and be perfectly coifed for their visits. It makes me feel vulnerable to have these people I hardly know see the overworked and overwhelmed side of my life on such a regular basis. However the alternative is me lugging an oxygen tank and feeding pump all around town so in that regard I'm thankful.

The other day Katie brought Ryan a large piece of foam shaped like a piece of pie on its side. We call it "the wedge." Ryan's too weak to try lying on his stomach and lifting his head and shoulders off the ground. His muscles are atrophied and his head's enormous. With his tortecollis it's even harder. The wedge is supposed to make it easier for him. Ryan lies on it belly-down with his head on the 45-degree incline and his heart in the little nook Katie cut out to accommodate his anatomy. Supposedly it's easier for him to start at this angle and work his way to flat on the floor.

The problem is he hates the wedge. Hates it a lot. When Katie put him on it for the first time yesterday, he cried until his little face was the color of an eggplant. It must be a strange feeling to be on your stomach after almost a year on your back. I wonder sometimes if his back is stiff and hurts him. Or maybe his neck is so tight on the side with torticollis that he's in pain. Either way we have to keep at it to make his neck and back stronger.

I'm on my own today. I'm a "suck-it-up" type of person so I'm surprised how much I can't stand watching Ryan cry. Working your way through pain and making your compromised child do it are two totally different things. "Hey, baby," I coo. Ryan lies on his activity mat watching the blinking star. I pull him gently from the mat and lay him face-up on the wedge. I lay my head down beside his. "Hi there, sweet pea. Mommy loves you. Do you know? You're the sweetest boy I've ever met." Ryan gives me a big smile. He's tolerating the wedge on his back so I pull him up onto his side. We lay facing each other as I continue talking in a sing-songy voice. So far so good.

I decide to press my luck. I slowly roll Ryan to his stomach while maintaining eye contact. He turns his neck to keep his head stationary. "You're doing it, big boy! See, I knew you could do it. I'm so proud of you. Can you lift your head up?" I ask. He looks at me blankly. "Come on, Ryan. Up!" I say. I pick up my head, "Up. Come on. Up." Ryan picks his head up off the wedge. "You did it! Now can you put it back down?" He looks at me again still hovering over the wedge. I apply gentle pressure to the back of his head. "Down, Ryan. Down." I lay my head back on the floor still putting the pressure on his. He lays his head down. "Awesome! You did it." Several repetitions later, Ryan gets the idea and raises or lowers his head on command. All too soon the honeymoon is over. Ryan's little lip quivers and he lets out a wail. I pull him from the wedge and cradle him in my arms. "You did a great job," I say bouncing a little and patting his back. "You sure did. Miss Katie will be so proud."

We see Ryan hit small milestones like this every week in physical therapy. I wish I could say the same for speech. Kathryn still comes once a week. Ryan's tongue shows improvement, but we're still not getting much down him. He's just not interested. I had hoped the county therapist would help speed things along but because Ryan hasn't had a swallow study, she's unable to help him try eating. The county doesn't want to be liable if he comes down with pneumonia. She doesn't even check his tongue lateralization or strength. Instead she asks me what sounds he makes and tells me she'll have to focus on his language until he gets a swallow study. There's a lot of *ma-ma-ma*-ing and *ba-ba-ba*-ing during her sessions.

I thank God on several occasions for sending us Kathyrn. She knows he hasn't had a swallow study—in fact agrees he isn't ready for one. He's pre-swallowing. She continues giving me exercises to perform on his mouth several times a day to get him used to things near and in his mouth. I stroke the outside of each cheek ten times. Then trace his lips ten times. I teach him that when my hand comes up to his mouth I'm not shoving a tube down his throat.

I reach my index finger inside his mouth and stroke his tongue starting in the approximate middle. I notice as the days pass that his tongue now curls over my finger as I slide it forward. I reach my finger to each side of his mouth coaxing his tongue to follow it. After some time, it does. These movements are important for working the food around in his mouth. I offer him water with the medicine dropper. I keep details on my homemade care charts of how many ccs he accepts before he either coughs or chokes, and I note what it is that stops each session.

His lack of progress is extremely frustrating. I tend to take an opposing wall down one brick at a time, but this wall is heavier than any I've moved. In the past the walls have been my own. This is the first wall I've moved for someone else. And there is only so much I can do to help Ryan with these bricks. When I nag Henry to hurry up . . . off the couch, to the car, out of bed on a Saturday he'll say, "I'm moving so slow you can't see it." I guess in this instance the apple doesn't fall far from the tree.

"Moving so slow you can't see it" becomes the theme of the next twelve months. Then one day we turn around and see the long road we've traveled toward normalcy. We go through several changes in our nursing staff and in the therapists contracted by the county. Our private therapists, Kathryn and Katie, are the only ones who've been with us since the beginning. With their guidance I work with Ryan daily trying to get him to accept pureed foods, thin liquids, and finally solids; to get him rolling over, sitting up, getting up off the floor unassisted (that took forever!), cruising and finally walking. Ryan takes his first unassisted steps the week of his second birthday to Natalie.

By his second birthday, our heart baby is off oxygen and satting between seventy-seven and eighty-one most the time. He's only getting water at night in his feeding tube, but otherwise eats all his meals and drinks his daytime liquids by mouth. He's walking and saying a couple dozen words.

His doctor appointments are few and far between. He's supposed to see his cardiologist every six months and get an annual heart catheterization to look at his pulmonary arteries, although the most spread out we've gone is four months. His most frequent doctor appointments are to the pediatrician to get caught up on all his vaccinations. He's finally stable enough to finish off the regular stuff.

When our family moves to a new state in June 2011, a few months after Ryan's second birthday, we're equipment free and there are no strings attached. Ryan's feeding tube is removed two weeks before our move. There's no reason for durable medical equipment companies or a nursing agency in our new hometown. And when the county does his assessment, he no longer qualifies for speech therapy . . . he's talking like any average boy his age with lots of grunts and one-word sentences. The physical therapist assesses him at three months younger than he is. I think that's generous, but it tells me he's catching up.

We don't have any nurses in our home. It's just us. A normal family except for a shirt that moves with each beat of our son's heart. Ryan's doing remarkably well.

The rest of us seem relatively intact, too. The girls love their brother and play with him any chance they get. Whenever I see a little dip in behavior I show them extra love and attention in case it's because they feel left out or overlooked. Henry and I went through a few rough patches but have worked through the weaknesses the stress over the last three years brought to the forefront. We have a long way to go . . . but we know that we love each other and are committed to fighting for our marriage and family. We're coming to realize this isn't just another bump in the road. *It is the road.*

My worry for Ryan decreases with each milestone he meets. People continue to wonder how we ever managed to get through Ryan's diagnosis, birth, and time in the hospital, and now his time as a delayed toddler catching up to his peers. The answer remains the same: one day at a time. Although we now think in terms broader than today, we still don't approach the "what ifs" that could so easily distract us. The culture of the CICU is hard to shake.

When I was a child I had a skin tag on my ear. It wasn't overly large, but bigger than a mole and noticeable. My mother told me it was something God put there to make me special. It was so special the kids teased me about it at school. Apparently I came home every day from kindergarten crying about it. I don't remember that part.

My mother scheduled an appointment to have the skin tag removed. I only remember a few things about the appointment. The first is the hallway in the building where the doctor's office was located. I remember this because it was the same building our pediatrician was in and he was my pediatrician for twelve straight years.

I also remember the doctor telling me that for the medicine to work I had to push very hard on a metal plate with a gelled hand. I wasn't strong enough so my mother was going to help me.

I remember lying on my side (skin tag ear raised to the sky) and my mom wrapping her body around mine, legs hugging mine, her arms around mine with her hand pushing down hard on mine. I pushed on that metal plate as hard as I could willing the medicine to work. I felt the needle prick my ear. It felt like getting stung by a bee, startling at first, but not hurting much after that. The pain of getting my ears pierced when I was six was way worse.

In hindsight, I'm guessing I really didn't have to push on that metal plate and I'm guessing my mother really didn't have to help me make the medicine work. I'm just going out on a limb here, but I'm guessing they were afraid I'd kick and scream and it was their way of having my mother hold me down on the table while they performed the procedure.

I think of Ryan and all the procedures he'll go through to fix his heart; of what he's already been through in his short life. I wonder how many times I'll hold him down, or give him shots, or force him to endure pain. I wonder what he'll remember about me. I wonder if he'll look at me as the enemy and come to resent all we've put him through.

I wonder, too, about my girls. I wonder if they'll look at how much time and attention Ryan gets and imagine they aren't worth as much or loved as much. I wonder if they'll feel invisible or unworthy or unimportant.

I hope they remember me as I remember my mom when I got my skin tag removed. That we worked as a team. That we were in this together. That our family isn't complete without each one of them in it. And while Ryan's heart may be the center of many people's focus, it isn't the most important thing. The most important thing is how, by the grace of God, our family bonded in ways carefree families may never do. How our girls' laughter and love became our son's best form of treatment. How their parents look over the dinner table at one another in awe that we're in the place we are. . . . Still holding on, still going strong: a family united.

Epilogue – February 2013

It's been almost two years since we moved to Western Pennsylvania. Our first year brought some unexpected turns. Ryan was hospitalized for low oxygen levels in December. He continued to struggle into February when an echo showed his cor triatrium membrane was closing again. He underwent a major open-heart surgery in D.C. at the end of April to remove the membrane for good. I think I let out the biggest sigh that day knowing I wouldn't have to worry about the rigidity of that membrane anymore.

What should have been a five to seven day stay turned into three weeks when Ryan developed a virus post-surgery and required vent support for two weeks. He was so very weak when we left the hospital. He could hardly stand on his own, let alone walk. However, over the next month, he regained his strength and was better than ever.

He felt so good that he started preschool in the fall a few days a week. He absolutely loves school! He was excited to take a backpack and kept asking to ride with Natalie and Ainsley on their bus. He also asked for homework and piano lessons. I'm serious. The kid knows what's going on!

He already knew his ABCs and his numbers to ten before he started preschool, but he loves the activities and socializing with the other kids. And he's learning how to play. Starting out sickly didn't give him much time to learn the art of playing.

Ryan's pretty healthy for having such a compromised heart. He isn't sicker than the girls, sometimes not even getting their ailments quite as badly. He's working hard to catch up to his peers physically and, at four, is almost there. He's finally getting both feet off the floor when he jumps. Yeah!

We've talked to the team about giving Ryan a permanent replacement for his missing chest bone, perhaps in the form of a bone graft or titanium plate. However, because he still hasn't had the final surgery typically needed for a missing ventricle, the team doesn't feel the timing is right. For now, Ryan wears a plastic shield much like the one the occupational therapist made for him in his first few months of life. I should say he wears his shield to school and to play outside. When we're chilling at the house we let him go commando.

The surgery he would need, called the Fontan, usually happens between the ages of eighteen months and four years old depending on the status of the patient. Ryan's oxygen sats are stable—in the mid-to-high-seventies, a good baseline for him. Some hypoplast patients never get a Fontan so for now we'll wait.

His hydrocephalus is also stable. In fact, his latest exam showed the ventricles had shrunk a little, something that puzzled his neurosurgeon. We'll continue to watch him for signs of pressure, but honestly, I'm not all that worried.

Many people want to know what the doctors are telling us for the long-term. I tend to forget about this part because the CICU has trained me not to ask about the future. It wasn't until earlier this year I could admit that for the first time I thought about Ryan in something further than kindergarten. . . . I got all the way to the third grade while labeling file folders in the kids' memory boxes. When I finished labeling Ryan's folders absent-mindedly after doing the girls', tears sprang into my eyes when I saw what I had done.

Dr. Donofrio has told us on several occasions that single ventricle kids are living into adulthood though some need a heart transplant in their twenties or thirties. It seems the three-pronged approach of the shunt, Glenn, and Fontan allows the heart to work more proficiently on one ventricle, but may wear it out something fierce. That is Ryan's generic prognosis. He'll endure heart catheterizations and heart clinic visits annually (we haven't quite made it that far yet!), and hopefully his only other interventions will be the Fontan and, perhaps a heart transplant at some point in the future. After reading the last twenty-one chapters, though, you should know that twenty-five years is too far out to start planning for. So for now, we plan for the next few months. And for us, that means a clinic visit in June and a heart catheterization somewhere around there, too.

Since his surgery last spring, and for the year before that, Ryan's only been on three medications: a blood thinner, a blood vessel relaxer, and a diuretic. He takes his medicine like a champ and even likes giving it to himself most mornings and evenings. He doesn't rely on any medical equipment; although after last winter, we've been storing an oxygen concentrator so we don't get stuck at the hospital solely for O_2 support.

Some people want to know how the girls are doing with their kid brother. How this experience has changed them or shaped their outlook. Honestly, I'm not quite sure since I don't know what they would've been without Ryan's diagnosis. I know that Natalie sometimes worries about Ryan, but overall I can't see that it bothers her much. She's typically anxious when he goes in for a procedure, which is to be expected. Ainsley doesn't seem to have a care in the world. Her biggest concern is how long mommy will be gone.

I can say that their particular style of playing doctor differs from most kids I know. The other day they called Henry and me into their veterinarian clinic to show us their latest patient. It was our big carnival-sized stuffed bear complete with a nasal cannula (real) and a feeding tube (rigged with a funnel and string system). Ainsley told us he'd been shot by a hunter and they were nursing him back to health. They've also been known to ask me if they can borrow a syringe to give their patients medicine. I'm guessing most households don't have medical supplies in their laundry room cupboard.

Henry's and Ryan's relationship continues to grow. The latest is that Henry has been trying to teach Ryan chess, and Ryan would rather throw the football back and forth. I don't expect this to change much.

Henry and I are faring well. We continue to have our weekly date nights as much as possible, fight every once in awhile, and mostly love each other more and more each day. We did a lot of exploring the first year in our new town since we didn't know very many people. We joined the local museum system, took the kids hiking in the area state parks, and cheered on the local sports teams. We're really just a normal family living a pretty normal, active life.

As for me personally, I'm good. I live in the details of this life, rarely glimpsing the big picture—you know the one that includes things like prognoses, the future, and how this has all affected my heart. Someone recently asked me if "it was worth all the suffering." The hands-down, emphatic answer is YES! If you ever have the chance to meet my precious boy you'll understand. He's absolutely the sweetest thing you've ever encountered, with a smile that captivates all who meet him. He lives life to the fullest and has taught us that every day is a gift.

For all of the hardship his little heart has given us, he has also brought us much joy, and such dependence on God. A dependence I never knew before and rarely since. Some people will never experience God the way I have. There are no regrets on our part. People think there are easy answers—if something's broken—throw it out. The problem is you can't undo something that's done. So yes, the struggle was worth it all. I'm not necessarily overwhelmed with Ryan's care, especially now when there's only medicine and a weekly physical therapy appointment. I just know that my heart is changed in ways I'm unwilling to investigate yet. And that's okay.

Every once in a while I'm caught off-guard. It always surprises me when grief strikes. Tears flood my eyes and my heart aches as I hold a tiny baby in my arms. Not my tiny baby, someone else's. Yet it's my baby I grieve for. For all the times I wasn't able to hold his snuggly body and have him sigh contentedly against the steady rhythm of my chest. For the weeks I watched him sleep from the effects of narcotics not from the sweetness of warm milk. These moments aren't processed with words . . . they come in without great fanfare, creeping across the recesses of my mind until they are front and center without my being aware they were coming. They go just as quietly . . . usually pretty quickly, too. In these brief moments I catch a glimpse of things my heart yearns to say if I would take the time to listen.

For the most part, I'm rocking my babies, and teaching them math facts, spelling words, and how to play independently. I'm enjoying watching them bloom into little people right before my eyes. To outsiders our life isn't much different than theirs, other than having a little boy who shows a lot of heart.

ACKNOWLEDGEMENTS

Showing Heart is a personal account starting from Ryan's diagnosis through his second year of life. It's written as I remember it. I journaled and blogged throughout the process so have many things written out that I wouldn't be able to remember today. In fact, when I read some of the passages I still get anxious, cry, or start having a panic attack. That's how raw most of those days still are to me.

However, I'm certain I've misquoted several people in the writing of this manuscript. Additionally, to compress time and information, I took the liberty of merging different consultations, conversations, and appointments. Therefore, I apologize in advance to any doctors, social workers, therapists, friends, and family members that notice inaccuracies. It isn't my intent to misrepresent anyone. Some names have been change to protect the individual's privacy.

The poet, John Donne said, "No man is an island," and I've found that true throughout Ryan's illness *and* the writing of this book. I have many people I'd like to thank and many more that I'll inadvertently forget. Some of them are the fabulous doctors who worked day in and day out to make sure nothing fell through the cracks with Ryan's care.

Henry and I would like to extend a special thanks to our champion and hope-giver, Dr. Mary Donofrio and also to her colleagues on Ryan's team: Dr. Richard Jonas, Dr. Joshua Kanter, Dr. Richard Levy, Dr. Michael Boyajian, Dr. John Berger, Dr. David Wessel, and Dr. Anthony Sandler.

We would also like to thank the many doctors, nurses, and therapists who cared for Ryan during his nine-month stay in the Cardiac ICU and Heart and Kidney Unit and then again on multiple occasions for subsequent surgeries and heart catheterizations at Children's National Medical Center in Washington, DC.

We'd like to thank our friends in Northern Virginia who took care of us for a year while we focused on our children. They cooked us meals, cleaned our house, ran errands, did our grocery shopping, and prayed without ceasing. Thank you to

Bridget Goetz, Heather Baker, Elisa Palmer, Katie Marshall and the women who wish to remain anonymous to keep me from writing them thank you notes.

Thank you to my wonderful mother-in-law, Willa, who tirelessly drove an hour an half day or night to help with childcare for the girls; and to my sister, Katie, who drove the same hour and half to clean my house and do my laundry once a week over several months.

There are others who stepped forward at different times to fill in gaps and answer our prayers. For that we are extremely grateful.

Thank you to editor Richard Peabody for putting this manuscript on the right track. Thank you to Lori Wick, Pam Lewis, Margaret Foody, Kevin Foody, Hope Metzger, Molly Wetmore, Emily Dammeyer, Rosemary McLaughlin, Michelle Haseltine, and Nicki Saini who all gave me the invaluable feedback of an insatiable reader.

Finally, I'd like to thank my husband for not only being my rock, but also being my partner. There's no one I'd rather live this life with.

Made in the USA
San Bernardino, CA
04 September 2013